CAMBRIDGE SOUTH ASIAN STUDIES

PROVINCIAL POLITICS AND INDIAN
NATIONALISM

CAMBRIDGE SOUTH ASIAN STUDIES

These monographs are published by the Syndics of the Cambridge University Press in association with the Cambridge University Centre for South Asian Studies. The following books have been published in this series:

1. S. GOPAL: *British Policy in India, 1858–1905*
2. J. A. B. PALMER: *The Mutiny Outbreak at Meerut in 1857*
3. A. DAS GUPTA: *Malabar in Asian Trade, 1740–1800*
4. G. OBEYESEKERE: *Land Tenure in Village Ceylon*
5. H. L. ERDMAN: *The Swatantra Party and Indian Conservatism*
6. S. N. MUKHERJEE: *Sir William Jones: A Study in Eighteenth-Century British Attitudes to India*
7. ABDUL MAJED KHAN: *The Transition in Bengal, 1756–1775: A Study of Saiyid Muhammad Reza Khan*
8. RADHE SHYAM RUNGTA: *The Rise of Business Corporations in India, 1851–1900*
9. PAMELA NIGHTINGALE: *Trade and Empire in Western India, 1784–1806*
10. AMIYA KUMAR BAGCHI: *Private Investment in India 1900–1939*
11. JUDITH M. BROWN: *Gandhi's Rise to Power: Indian Politics 1915–1922*
12. MARY C. CARRAS: *The Dynamics of Indian Political Factions*
13. P. HARDY: *The Muslims of British India*

PROVINCIAL POLITICS AND INDIAN NATIONALISM

Bombay and the Indian National Congress 1880 to 1915

BY

GORDON JOHNSON

Fellow of Trinity College, Cambridge

CAMBRIDGE
AT THE UNIVERSITY PRESS
1973

Published by the Syndics of the Cambridge University Press
Bentley House, 200 Euston Road, London NW1 2DB
American Branch: 32 East 57th Street, New York, N.Y. 10022

© Cambridge University Press 1973

Library of Congress Catalogue Card Number: 73-79307

ISBN: 0 521 20259 0

Printed in Great Britain by
Alden & Mowbray Ltd
at the Alden Press, Oxford

CONTENTS

List of plates	*page* vi
Acknowledgements	vii
Abbreviations	x
Introduction	1
1 The Indian National Congress	5
2 The politics of western India in the later nineteenth century	53
3 Tilak, Gokhale and the Indian National Congress, 1895 to 1906	118
4 Tilak, Gokhale and the Indian National Congress, 1907 to 1915	157
A perspective	193
Note on sources	199
Index	203

PLATES

between pp. 54 and 55

1 Gopal Krishna Gokhale, 1908
2 Bal Gangadhar Tilak, 1900 (*Kesari-Mahratta Trust*)
3a Pherozeshah M. Mehta, 1911
3b Dadabhai Naoroji, *circa* 1906
3c Lajpat Rai, B. G. Tilak, Bipin Chandra Pal, 1907 (*Kesari-Mahratta Trust*)
4 G. S. Khaparde (*Kesari-Mahratta Trust*)

ACKNOWLEDGEMENTS

This book is based on part of my doctoral thesis (*Indian politics, 1888–1908*, Cambridge, 1967) and on an essay (*Maharashtrian politics and Indian nationalism, 1880–1920*) which was awarded the Thirlwall Prize and Seeley Medal in 1969. The present work has taken a long time to write and over the years I have incurred many obligations.

I am grateful to the Department of Education and Science for a Hayter Research Studentship that enabled me to work in India during 1965 and 1966. Since then, the University of Cambridge, the Master and Fellows of Trinity College, the Faculty Board of Oriental Studies, the Managers of the Smuts Memorial Fund, and the Social Science Research Council's Modern Indian History Project, have all contributed generously towards the costs of my research. In particular, I was able to make a second visit to India in 1970.

I wish to record the kind assistance of the librarians and staff at the India Office Library, the British Museum, the National Archives of India, the Nehru Memorial Museum and Library, the Gokhale Institute of Politics and Economics, the Office of the Maharashtra State Committee for a History of the Freedom Movement in India, and Cambridge University Library.

I am grateful to the Government of India, the Government of Maharashtra, the Servants of India Society, Shri M. G. Chitnavis, Shri V. R. Karandikar, the Trustees of the Dadabhai Naoroji Memorial Trust, Professor R. P. Patwardhan, the Kesari-Mahratta Trust and Shri J. S. Tilak, Dr V. R. Karandikar of the Deccan Education Society, Shri S. R. Venkataraman of the Servants of India Society at Madras, and the President of the Theosophical Society, Shri N. Sri Ram, for permission to consult records and private papers in their possession.

While in India I was grateful for the advice and kindness of many people, particularly Shri D. V. Ambekar, Shri V. C. Joshi, Miss D. G. Keswani, Professor N. R. Phatak, Shri B. N. Phatak, Shri Sourin Roy, Shri B. Shiva Rao and Shri M. V. Sovani.

Acknowledgements

I should like to thank those who examined my Ph.D. thesis, and those who invited me to read seminar papers at the universities of Chicago, Oxford and Sussex, for their helpful comments on earlier formulations of the arguments put forward in this book; and I am especially grateful to Miss L. Breglia who has laboured to save me from both infelicities of style and inexactitude of expression.

My greatest debt, however, is to Anil Seal and to my other colleagues in Cambridge. But for their researches and their stimulating criticisms this book might have been published much earlier, although it would have been the poorer for that; but for their friendship and their insistence it might never have been published at all.

Gordon Johnson

Trinity College, Cambridge
September 1972

For
Kenneth and Janet Easton
and
Robert and Delphine Baynes

ABBREVIATIONS

The following abbreviations have been used:

BM	British Museum
BPA	Bombay Presidency Association
DCI	Director of Criminal Intelligence
HFM	Office of the Maharashtra State Committee for a History of the Freedom Movement in India, Bombay
INC	*Report of the Indian National Congress* (followed by the year to which it refers)
IOL	India Office Library, London
IOR	India Office Records
NAI	National Archives of India, New Delhi
NMM	Nehru Memorial Museum and Library, New Delhi
PP	*Parliamentary Papers*
RNP (Bombay)	*Reports on the Native Press* (Bombay Presidency) (followed by the year to which the volume refers)
SB	Special Branch
SIS	Servants of India Society

Note: in 1902 the North-western Provinces and Oudh became known as the United Provinces.

INTRODUCTION

National politics in India were the creation of the later nineteenth century. Not until then did the government begin to function effectively at an all-India level, nor did Indians themselves organise nation-wide political associations. The roving commissions of enquiry in the 1880s, and the prodigious development of governmental institutions in the last quarter of the nineteenth century, introduced a new style of politics. Under pressure from the government in England to become more efficient for imperial purposes, and forced to assume wider responsibilities by change in India itself, the government ushered in a host of new legislative, consultative and administrative procedures. As the government impinged more on Indian society so it brought more Indians into the business of making and implementing policies. Increasingly, as the years went by, general principles were formulated on a national basis before being adapted to, and imposed on, the various provinces and regions of the subcontinent. Indians not only seized the opportunities afforded by constitutional change to influence government decisions, but they had also to devise new methods of making themselves heard from outside the framework of the raj.

The development of political responses to the growing effectiveness of imperial rule in India was an extremely complicated affair. The sheer size of the country and the intricacy of its government meant that there was no uniform progress. The different regions and the many local social, economic, and political structures were not affected in the same way or at the same time. Recent research has concentrated on much needed regional and parochial studies. Scholars have been concerned to track specific changes within limited contexts, and the result of their work has been to unsettle many cherished beliefs about the nature of Indian political change. But as the pattern has become more complicated, it has also become clear that all-India politics have an importance quite independent of those in the districts, and that all-India movements, while coupled to regional and local organisations, constituted separate and

Introduction

distinct political phenomena which were governed by their own rules. However, it is necessary to define carefully the area occupied by such national organisations within the political system before we can explore the relationship between them and other types of political activity.

The following pages do not pretend to give a full account of political change in India between 1880 and 1915. They are confined to what might be termed the internal, or domestic, history of the Indian National Congress. The Congress has been chosen for study because it was the first political association that attempted to approach the government at an all-India level. Moreover it became, and remained, the most important national party in twentieth-century India. The whole history of the freedom movement, and of mass political mobilisation in India, is intimately connected with the Congress and would be unthinkable without it. Although there are many other elements in the story, a discussion of the Congress is central to any understanding of recent Indian political history. The first chapter of this book is devoted to an analytical description of the early Congress. It attempts to delineate the main features of the movement so that the importance of the Congress can be assessed and, by indicating the limits within which the Congress worked, it suggests how all-India politics can be put into a more general perspective. The chapter shows the Congress emerging alongside the changing constitution of the raj, and it suggests that the Congress itself contributed to the transformation of Indian politics.

Although the Congress was an all-India body, it had to have a base from which to operate, a stronghold from which it could advance its national claims, and into which it could retreat when vital all-India issues were few, and when national politics were overshadowed by nearer concerns. Throughout this period (and in fact beyond it) the Indian National Congress was particularly associated with Bombay Presidency. That province was one of the most prominent in the early Congress, and for the first forty years of the organisation's history many of its most important leaders, and its most constant supporters, came from Bombay city and from nearby Poona.

The Congress derived many benefits from its close connections with Bombay Presidency, and it is doubtful whether any

Introduction

other place in India could have so successfully nurtured the all-India movement. But it was inevitable that through this connection the concerns of the provincial politicians should have come to play a prominent part in the affairs of the nation. When dealing with the activities of the first generation of nationalist leaders, or when considering how Congressmen worked with and reacted to each other, we have to remember that many of them came from western India and that their regional alignments affected their national strategies. From the early twentieth century a major factional crisis developed within the Congress hierarchy, the origins of which are to be found in the political history of Bombay Presidency in the last two decades of the nineteenth century. Consequently, before taking up the main narrative, the second chapter deals with those circumstances of politicians in the Presidency that alone make the later sequence of events comprehensible.

The arguments put forward in the first two chapters come together in the third and fourth, which describe what happened to the Congress during the late nineteenth and early twentieth centuries. Throughout these years, and particularly between 1904 and 1908, the movement was threatened by dissension and disaffection. The factionalism that almost wrecked the Congress is explained by reference both to national affairs and to events taking place in provinces other than Bombay; but because Bombay politicians provided the core of the national leadership, the divisions among them in western India ultimately determined the outcome of the general quarrel. No doubt the picture of all-India politics presented here would be different if seen through Bengali or Punjabi eyes, or viewed from Madras or the United Provinces, but similar themes would underlie all the narratives: a pattern of nationalism would emerge, of conflict, often bitter, and of resolution, often incomplete, which is only explicable when some account is taken of the local and provincial concerns of the politicians involved.

A great deal of emphasis is placed in the following account on personal antipathy as the driving force behind the fierce factionalism of Indian politics, but it is also argued that the stands politicians made were often determined by the needs of the constituencies which they represented or by the fears and

Introduction

ambitions of the followers which they mustered up. Like the politicians of all ages, those of nineteenth- and twentieth-century India exhibit a certain opportunism and ruthlessness in their quests for power. Inevitably it has happened that in the narration of the sharp controversies and stormy disputes that rocked the early Congress, some of those concerned do not always appear in the most favourable colours. Yet this does not necessarily bring into question their integrity or their idealism, and, when the dust is allowed to settle on their battles, no one can deny that the creation of the Indian National Congress was an outstanding political achievement.

I

THE INDIAN NATIONAL CONGRESS

On 28 December 1885 a gathering of 'certain well-known men'[1] assembled in Bombay with the object of enabling all 'the most earnest labourers in the cause of national progress to become personally known to each other'.[2] Close on one hundred gentlemen attended the meeting, but the number of active participants was seventy-two.[3] At this assembly, the Indian National Congress, the first all-India political association, came into being. A second meeting was held in Calcutta in 1886, and a third, held in Madras, followed in 1887. Thereafter meetings of the Congress became regular annual events. The organisers of the third session claimed with reason that 'What in 1885 was little more than an experiment, in 1887 bore every appearance of becoming a permanent National Institution.'[4]

The founding of the Congress was one of the most important political events in India in the later nineteenth century. The Congress soon became recognised as the main vehicle of nationalism in India, and it was to prove particularly good at adapting itself to political change in the twentieth century. As more and more Indians began to participate in the struggles for political power, the Congress continually reshaped itself and held on to its central dominating role. When India became independent in 1947 the Congress naturally assumed office, and with the coming of the mass franchise it showed once again its capacity for meeting new challenges. Few other nationalist organisations in Africa and Asia can match the long history of the Indian National Congress or rival its political sophistication, and even fewer have survived so successfully the ending of imperial rule. Almost everything about the Congress is remarkable, and yet it did not spring into existence by chance. It

[1] B. P. Sitaramayya, *The history of the Indian National Congress 1885–1935* (Madras, 1935), p. 86.
[2] *INC 1885*, p. 5.
[3] Most of the other people were government servants who attended as '*amici curiae*, to listen and advise'. *Ibid.* p. 8.
[4] *INC 1887*, p. 2.

emerged within a particular constitutional context and it was this that determined the form the Congress took and ensured its ultimate pre-eminence in Indian politics.

The Congress developed within the context of British rule in India, and it was around the centres of imperial power that political forces played. The structure of the Indian government in the later nineteenth century was exceedingly complex and the response to it accordingly assumed many forms. This was partly because of the anomalies inherent in imperial rule, and partly because of the political geography of India itself. Like all imperial regimes, that of the British in India depended for its success on the participation by the ruled in their government This meant accommodating vested interests in Indian society, compromising policies and methods of government to suit the needs of the localities, and governing lightly in order to maintain the systems of collaboration intact. However despotic the government of India might have seemed, it had to rely on Indian intermediaries for information about Indian society on which to base its policies and for the agency through which to promote them. It could not, therefore, fail to take account of Indian political demands. However, the country was so vast, the population so numerous, and the diversities of race, religion, language and economy were so great, that it was impossible to build up a single unitary state, just as it was impossible for Indian interests to formulate simple straightforward demands. Thus government in India, and the reaction to it, took many forms, and between them there was a clear distribution of powers and functions.

Imperial rule in India was flexible and pragmatic. In the lower reaches of government in particular, it allowed the continuation of old administrative habits and of long-established political practices. In many areas of government, and in many districts and localities, the fact that the East India Company had succeeded some other overlord went almost unnoticed. Yet British rule did bring several major changes. During the course of the nineteenth century the consequences of the establishment of one government over the whole of India began to make themselves felt. The early rule of the East India Company, built piece-meal on the wreckage of several eighteenth-century states, was a hotch-potch affair. The original settlements on the coast had little in common with each other, and the first Presidencies were allowed to develop very much in their own way. Yet increasingly the British, for reasons of strategy and economy, considered India as one country, and they began to develop new political and administrative institutions which overlaid the various provinces and districts.

At this level, the government of India was assuming quite new and distinct functions. Here it was not responsible for the routine tasks of government: those had to be done by its servants in the field and they had to be left large discretion if their work was not to be made impossible. But at the top the government would decide, with reference to wider imperial as much as to specifically Indian needs, the general principles and policies that were to be applied (however modified in practice) in the districts, it would determine the form (but not the detail) that the administrative machinery would take, and it would define the formal political constitution of the government.

The nineteenth century, then, saw the development of a new kind of superior government in India. Although at first it was rather weak and ineffective, the undoubted trend was for the provincial centres to interfere more with the districts under their charge, for the capital in India to devise policies that impinged more and more on the autonomy of the regions, and for the British government in London, as the sovereign of all, to lay down the purposes for which, and the limitations within which, India was to be governed. All this added up to an increasingly effective centralisation of government. The fact that political control from the centre was largely achieved by decentralising the administration and by involving more Indians in government should not obscure the fact that all-India governmental institutions came to be more powerful and more important as the years went by.

This precocious development of Indian government forced changes in the political response to it. As a new style of government emerged, forging connections across the districts and provinces, it was no longer enough for Indians to secure political benefits in the localities alone. The increasing power to be bargained for at the centres of government necessitated the creation of non-official provincial and all-India politics. While the vigour of village, district and small-town politics continued unabated in the undergrowth, political associations deploying new tactics and using a different grammar of politics came into being at regional headquarters, at Calcutta and in London. For the formal structure of the government provided the framework of politics, and it was only by operating within it that Indians could share and determine the distribution of power and patronage.

In order to influence the government at any level Indian demands had to be backed by credible support. This might be done in several ways, depending upon the issue involved and the appropriate level of government to be approached. Of course it would still be possible – and in many respects still most rewarding – to threaten or corrupt a tahsildar or to buy a district officer; but at constitutionally superior levels of government the tactics of the district would have to give way to the strategy of the nation. To be effective at the top, Indian politicians needed to generalise their demands. And, as the new centres of power became more imperious, Indians became more and more preoccupied with them. Politicians would be lured from the security of their localities into the uncertainties of the capital cities, and from there to the heart of the imperial government in London. Moreover, while the lathi or the rupee might be understood at home, at the new centres of power politicians would have to use techniques that were recognised as appropriate and legitimate there. The dialogue with the rulers about the share of spoils had to be conducted in the places of government and with due regard to the courtly manners practised there.

The later nineteenth century saw the beginning of a new political era in India and with it emerged a new type of politician. While wealth, property, or inherited ritual and social status might provide the indispensable foundations of power in the villages and towns, they were not assets greatly valued in the new political arenas. Here men had to know English and the way the organs of government functioned; they had to be familiar with the law codes and the administrative handbooks; and they had to be expert in the most recent theories of taxation and political economy. Above all, they had to be capable of mediating between several interests and of arranging broad alliances between them in order to formulate provincial and all-India demands. It follows that the most prominent politicians who appeared with increasing frequency from about 1870 were rarely the same men as the powerful zamindar, merchant prince or caste boss. Indeed, although nearly always respectable people, the new men did not usually possess, and never did depend upon, traditional political resources. They were hardly ever rich or socially dominant in their own right. Their success sprang from their capacity to seize the opportunities afforded to men of talent to learn a new political drill.

Typically the new politicians were men who lived in the capital cities and who were employed in literate occupations that brought them into contact with the day-to-day working of the government. For example, every effort was made to accommodate important regional interests on the legislative councils, yet it was discovered that in Bombay, of the thirty-nine non-official members of the legislature who held office between 1893 and 1899, twenty-two habitually lived in Bombay city itself. Many of them in fact represented mofussil interests on the council and were proposed by constituencies in the districts. Yet their political work led them inescapably to residence in the capital.[1] Moreover, when it came to suggesting names of provincial as opposed to purely local leaders, professional men, particularly lawyers, came to the fore. The Bombay government noted in 1899 that, with the sole exception of Bal Gangadhar Tilak, who was a journalist, all the electing district boards and municipalities in the Presidency had put up pleaders as their representatives.

That this should be so is not a matter for surprise [the government reported] for the reason that such persons as local merchants, bankers and landholders

---

[1] The rules for election laid down a minimum property qualification for members of the council. Thus many men who usually lived in Bombay were able to use the fact of holding some property outside as a circumstance qualifying them for election from that distict. The government saw that a flexible interpretation of the rule about property-ownership 'gives perhaps undue weight to residents of Bombay, [but] it is difficult to interpret the rule more strictly without excluding some most valuable candidates. While a stricter interpretation might ensure a more exact representation of local interests... it would certainly entail a lower standard of intelligence and education among the candidates for election by bodies outside the city of Bombay.' Govt. Bombay to Secretary of State, 12 April 1899, Bombay legislative proceedings, 1899, vol. 5772, IOR.

have, as a rule, only purely local influence which does not extend beyond their own town or district, whereas a pleader, notably a High Court Pleader, possesses influence in various districts, understands the art of canvassing and, what is of great importance, has the support and good will of his brother lawyers at the various centres of the Divisions. The only candidates likely to come forward with any chance of success are, therefore, members of the legal profession.[1]

The Bombay council was not unique in this respect, nor did the analysis apply only to government institutions. In Madras, Allahabad, Nagpur and Calcutta, both in the organs of government and in the informal associations growing parallel with them, the lawyer, the journalist and, to a lesser extent, the teacher and the doctor were making their mark.

Although as individuals the nationalist politicians were less powerful in their own domestic circles than many of the people they spoke for, their knowledge of how to deal with the government and their expertise as brokers between the government and Indian interests and between Indian and Indian, gave them considerable freedom of action. For the politicians usually found more in common with each other than they did with their several complex constituencies.[2] Possessing arcane skills which the rich and powerful could buy but need not learn, the new leaders tended to deal directly with each other, apparently without much reference to their supporters. This is what gives Indian politics their elite character and what at first sight makes plausible the arguments of Viceroys that Congressmen represented only themselves, and those of the later histories which suggest that provincial and all-India leaders stood for newly emerged social classes or the narrow concerns of fragmented literate groups. But this was not the case, for the Indian politicians retained close connections with their patrons and with their more general supporters. The most obvious characteristic of every Indian politician was that each acted for many interests at all levels of Indian society and in so doing cut across horizontal ties of class, caste, region and religion.

These generalisations about the nature of politics in late nineteenth-century India provide the background for further study of the Indian National Congress. The formal framework

---

[1] Govt. of Bombay to Secretary of State, 12 April 1899, *ibid.*
[2] This feature is, of course, characteristic of most political systems based on representative institutions.

The Indian National Congress

of government created national politics. After the abolition of the East India Company in 1858, when Parliament ceased by statute to review the activities of the government of India every twenty years, there was both need and opportunity for the representation of Indian interests to the government of India in Whitehall. This is what the provincial associations, and growing from them the Indian National Congress and the other all-India parties of the twentieth century, would try to do. They were specifically designed to appeal to the highest level of government and to the British electorate. They were most active when it appeared likely that there would be a change in government policy or, more significantly, when the administrative and constitutional structures of the government itself were brought into question. Thus Indian political activity, which had once been most apparent in the months preceding the renewal of the Company's charter, now coincided with the debates inspired by the government on financial devolution and local self-government, with the reform of the civil service and of state-aided education, and with the introduction and development of the legislative councils.

From the early nineteenth century, associations were founded, at first in Bengal, Bombay and Madras (where the new regime had been established longest), usually by those literate in English and closely associated with British rule, to press for reform in government that had, or seemed to have, general application. Both in their structure and in the way in which they presented their demands, associations like the British Indian Association and the Indian Association of Calcutta, the Bombay Association, the Bombay Presidency Association, the Poona Sarvajanik Sabha, and the Madras Mahajana Sabha, heralded a new development in Indian politics.[1] They grouped people together according to shared interests in public affairs, and their leaders, in rooms surrounded by portraits of eminences as Victorian as any to be found in the university debating chambers of Oxford and Cambridge, drafted in the phraseology of the Blue Books, resolutions, petitions and memorials for

[1] The best accounts of the early provincial associations are to be found in A. Seal, *The emergence of Indian nationalism: competition and collaboration in the later nineteenth century* (Cambridge, 1968) and S. R. Mehrotra, *The emergence of the Indian National Congress* (New Delhi, 1972).

presentation to the government. These associations exploited to the full the changing constitution of the government of India. In doing so they created new grounds for unity in Indian society. 'Since they were open groups, their members might belong to all castes and communities; since they commented on matters of concern to all, they claimed to stand for interests wider than those of their members.'[1] Such broad-based associations, formed for particular ends and built up out of compromise and alliance, were indispensable for dealing with the government at a provincial or national level. Moreover, within limits, these organisations were capable of maintaining continued co-operation among their members.

The newly founded political associations did not replace other forms of politics. The early associations, the Congress, and similar bodies did not supersede other associations and older methods of winning power and influence. Each particular political arena had its own appropriate style of politics. However, not only were the boundaries between them often blurred but the same man might participate in several kinds of political activity at once. Each politician might belong to several associations, very different from each other in aim, composition, size and scope. Thus, through their members, the secular, public alliances were linked to separate, and sometimes incompatible, religious, ethnic, caste, regional and economic groups. The stability of the grand alliance would depend on the extent to which the politician could reconcile conflicting loyalties, and upon the extent to which the larger association advanced the general purposes of the specific interests supporting it. However, the national associations were not entirely at the mercy of their separate parts, for aspects of their constitution and policies which particular interests might find disagreeable could be outweighed by long-term advantage. Each political association thus contained a host of ambiguities and contradictions, and the larger the organisation the greater they became. All provincial and national movements in India were constantly threatened by defection, yet because these organisations fulfilled certain vital functions within the political system, and because they offered protection to groups needing support from outside their own communities and regions, the all-India associations had an

[1] Seal, *The emergence of Indian nationalism*, p. 15.

importance greater than and different from the mere sum of their parts.

The Indian National Congress was a natural, but not an easy, development from the regional political associations. These latter had been adequate for framing and presenting demands in India, but finding the government there unreceptive, Indians realised that what was wanted was representation in England. Indian politicians argued that there they would be able to bring the weight of Parliament and of the British electorate to bear on the government in India. They rightly believed that so far as general policy decisions were concerned 'the centre of gravity, even in Indian politics, is in England, and ... the success of our political work depends in a considerable measure on the amount of public sympathy we create in that country'.[1] But, in order to influence English political parties it was essential to draw up a single all-India programme. There was no point in having several bodies at work in London all claiming to represent Indian interests. As an English sympathiser wrote to Pherozeshah Mehta, 'Nothing would more strengthen the hands of your friends in this country than to have an authoritative statement which should show to all the world what the people of India want ... To set the constituencies in motion will not be difficult as soon as we know for certain what the people of India wish for.'[2]

The organisation which finally produced the 'authoritative statement' was the Indian National Congress. Here, from a continental platform, Indians put forward the demands they had already been making through the provincial associations. Prominent among these were proposals for reform of the legislative councils in India (so that they would become more powerful and include more Indians), reform of the civil service (to allow Indians easier access to the highest ranks of the bureaucracy), reform of judicial administration and legal procedure (to bring them into line with the practices established in England), an end to discriminatory racial legislation (notably the acts which forbade Indians to carry fire-arms on the same terms as Europeans), proposals about how India might best be developed, and changes in the methods of levying taxes. In part these

[1] *INC 1898*, p. xxvi.
[2] Robert Osborne to P. M. Mehta, 18 April 1884, Mehta Papers, NAI.

demands, although general in tenor, represented the specific interests of the particular groups who provided the leadership of the Congress during its first forty years; but what is most remarkable about them is that they could genuinely be presented at an all-India level. Moreover, they were largely irrelevant to the detailed distribution of power in the localities. Congress propaganda was aimed primarily at England, and the demands put forward were made to seem moderate and reasonable within the context of English politics. While they might be frequently ignored, they were not easily opposed by the government to whom they were addressed.

In his introduction to the fourth annual *Report* of the Congress, W. C. Bonnerjee wrote:

the principle on which the Indian National Congress is based is that British Rule should be permanent and abiding in India and that, given this axiom, it is the duty of educated Indians to endeavour to the best of their power to help their rulers so to govern the country as to improve her material prosperity and make the people of all classes and communities happy and prosperous and contented as subjects of the British Empire.[1]

The resolutions passed annually by the Congress were intended to help the government bring about that universal contentment. Much of the debate in Congress centred on reform of government, and particularly on the question of securing for Indians a larger share in the making of decisions and in the top branches of the administration. 'Much has been done by Great Britain for the benefit of India', Bonnerjee had told the first Congress, 'but a great deal still remains to be done.'[2] The problems of India could be eased if the rigidity of the bureaucracy were softened.[3] The Congress did not want less rule, but more. 'The fact is', wrote A. O. Hume, a former district officer and *éminence grise* of the early Congress, 'our administration looks better on paper than it is in practice; it always reminds me of Porthos' belt, grandly gold-embroidered in front but very plain, some-

[1] *INC 1888*, pp. vi–vii.   [2] *INC 1885*, p. 17.
[3] A. O. Hume described the bureaucracy as a shoe that was too hard to adapt itself to the natural contours of the foot. A. O. Hume and A. Colvin, *Audi alteram partem: being two letters on certain aspects of the Indian National Congress movement with an appendix containing a letter to the 'Indian Mirror'* (Simla and London, 1888), p. 46. The rulers also were aware of the defects of the bureaucracy: 'I believe the main cause of the unpopularity which attaches to our Government in India is the angularity and rigidity of officialdom.' Hamilton to Curzon, 3 March 1899, Curzon Papers, Mss. Eur. F. 111/158, IOL.

what ragged leather behind.'[1] The way to gild the administration was to allow Indians a greater part of it.

The most Congress wanted was that more Indians be admitted to the legislative councils. At the 1885 meeting, K. T. Telang moved a resolution recommending reform of the legislative councils.[2] It was repeated in some form every year until 1894. The Congress drew up detailed proposals in 1886 and again in 1889. It demanded that one half of the members of the imperial and provincial legislative councils should be elected members, and that not more than one quarter of them should be government officers. The rest were to be nominated by the government.[3] The demand for elected members fitted in well with the traditions of English political theory, but the Congress had no illusion about mass votes: the right to elect members to the provincial councils was to be 'conferred only on those classes and members of the community, *prima facie*, capable of exercising it wisely and independently'.[4] The Congress considered suitable electoral colleges to be the members of municipalities and district boards, chambers of commerce, and the universities. It also stressed that the exact rules would have to be worked out separately for each province to meet the varying political needs of each.[5] The 1889 proposals were more radical in concept than those of 1886, perhaps because the

[1] Hume and Colvin, *Audi alteram partem*, p. 42.
[2] 'That this Congress considers the reform and expansion of the Supreme and existing Local Legislative Councils, by the admission of a considerable proportion of elected members (and the creation of similar Councils for the N.W. Provinces and Oudh, and also for the Punjab) essential; and holds that all Budgets should be referred to these Councils for consideration, their members being moreover empowered to interpellate the Executive in regard to all branches of the administration; and that a standing Committee of the House of Commons should be constituted to receive and consider any formal protests that may be recorded by the majorities of such Councils against the exercise by the Executive of the power, which would be invested in it, of over-ruling the decisions of such majorities.' Resolution III, *INC 1885*, p. 2.
[3] Resolution IV (i), *INC 1886*, pp. 41–2; Resolution II (i) *INC 1889*, p. xli.
[4] Resolution IV (ii), *INC 1886*, p. 42.
[5] In Bengal and Bombay the right to elect was to be conferred directly on the municipalities, district boards, chambers of commerce and the universities. In Madras an alternative to this scheme was that electoral colleges be formed, partly elected by these bodies and partly nominated by the government. In the North-western Provinces and Oudh, and in the Punjab, the government was to nominate up to a sixth of the members of electoral colleges. The overall aim was that 'care must be taken to see that all sections of the community, and all great interests, are adequately represented'. Resolution IV (ii), *INC 1885*, p. 42.

Englishman Charles Bradlaugh attended the session. He was later to move a reform Bill in the House of Commons.[1] The 1889 draft was also concerned with communal representation, and resolved that whenever Parsis, Christians, Muslims or Hindus were in a minority in a province, the total number of Parsis, Christians, Muslims or Hindus elected to the provincial legislature should not be proportionately less than the proportion each community bore to the total population.[2] Election to the imperial legislative council was to be made by the members of the provincial legislatures.[3]

The Congress plan for reform of the councils also involved the function of the councils. All legislative measures and all financial questions were to be discussed in the councils, and any member was to be allowed to ask questions of officials sitting in the council, and be entitled to an answer and the production of any papers 'requisite for the thorough comprehension of the subject'.[4] But the government was to retain the power of overruling the decisions arrived at by a majority of the councils, although it had to publish its reasons for doing so, and the matter had to be referred to a standing committee of the House of Commons.[5]

This kind of discussion was not confined to the Congress. In 1885 the Lieutenant-Governor of the North-western Provinces and Oudh had asked for a legislative council under the 1861 Council's Act,[6] and various other government officers thought that the time had come to develop further these provincial and

[1] Here it was resolved that revenue districts constitute territorial units for electoral purposes. All male British subjects over 21 were to have the vote, 'possessing certain qualifications, and not subject to certain disqualifications, both of which will be settled later'. The voters were to elect representatives to an electoral college at the rate of twelve per million of the total population of the district. The colleges were to elect members to the central legislative council at the rate of one member for five million people, and to the provincial councils at the rate of one member for each million of the population. Resolution II (ii–v), *INC 1889*, p. xli.
[2] Resolution II (v), *INC 1889*, p. xli.   [3] Resolution IV (iii), *INC 1886*, p. 42.
[4] Resolution IV (vi), *ibid*.   [5] Resolution IV (vii), *ibid*.
[6] Govt. North-western Provinces and Oudh to Govt. India, 14 September 1885, Home Judicial A, March 1886, 85, NAI. The Governor-General in Council sanctioned the establishment of a legislative council for the North-western Provinces and Oudh from 1 December 1886. The members were to be nominated by the Lieutenant-Governor. Notification No. 1704, 26 November 1886, Home Judicial A, November 1886, 258, NAI.

The Indian National Congress

all-India political bodies. Before he left India, Lord Dufferin recommended that an increase in the number of non-officials on the councils by election, the right of interpellation, and a full discussion of the budget, should be considered.[1] His successor as Viceroy, Lord Lansdowne, was most enthusiastic about the idea, and wrote to the Secretary of State as soon as he had arrived in India that 'A step in this direction would, I have little doubt do good:—by showing that our attitude is not one of obstinate and uncompromising resistance to the demands for moderate advance in the direction of institutions more representative in character than those at present enjoyed by the people of this country.'[2] It would also, of course, be a way of strengthening the top levels of the government, which were still very weak, and of devising formal means for making sure that the government kept in touch with, and contained, changes in Indian opinion. The Viceroy, however, ran into opposition in England, particularly over the introduction of the elective principle. Although Lansdowne realised that 'a considerable increase in the numerical strength of the Councils, and that the appointment of Members should to some extent depend upon election',[3] he also realised that opposition to the scheme in the cabinet, and concern about the possible embarrassment which a reform Bill would cause the government in a fractious House of Commons, meant that unless the idea of elected members was dropped altogether a Bill would never be introduced into Parliament.[4]

[1] Govt. India to Secretary of State, Despatch Home Public No. 67, 6 November 1888. Quoted in S. R. Mehrotra, *India and the Commonwealth 1885–1929* (London, 1965), p. 27.
[2] Lansdowne to Cross, 11 December 1888, Lansdowne Papers, I.S. 420/14, BM.
[3] Lansdowne to Sir S. C. Bayley, 1 May 1889, Lansdowne Papers, I.S. 420/16, BM.
[4] Lansdowne to Cross, 11 February 1890, Lansdowne Papers, I.S. 420/14, BM. The cabinet was reluctant to introduce the Bill because the Radicals would consider any reform too mild and the Conservatives would regard any Bill as too revolutionary. As Salisbury explained: 'during the last fifteen years no one has succeeded who has not had an overwhelming and homogeneous majority, and no majority, even much more homogeneous than ours ever was, has stood the disintegrating influence of four years' existence. Under these circumstances the block in Parliament is getting more and more hopeless, and a Bill like the Indian Councils Bill, which has some enemies and no ardent supporters, has little chance of forcing its way through.' Salisbury to Lansdowne, 27 June 1890. Quoted in Lord Newton, *Lord Lansdowne: a biography* (London, 1929), p. 73. Cross had earlier warned the Viceroy that the organised opposition to grants to the royal

As it was passed by Parliament, the 1892 Councils Act seemed a minor reform. Yet it contributed in an important way to the further development of provincial and all-India politics. The minimum number of additional councillors (that is non-official members) on the Governor-General's council was increased from six to ten, and the maximum raised from twelve to sixteen.[1] The Governors of Bombay and Madras were empowered to increase the number of their additional members from a minimum of four and a maximum of eight to a minimum of eight and a maximum of twenty.[2] The size of the legislative council of Bengal was not to exceed twenty, and that of the Northwestern Provinces and Oudh, fifteen.[3] The reformed councils were to be allowed the right to discuss the budget and to ask questions of the government, but 'under such conditions and restrictions, as to subject or otherwise',[4] as would be decided.

However, the Act was not totally illiberal, for it allowed the government of India to experiment. It contained a clause which enabled the Governor-General in Council to make regulations defining the conditions under which nominations to the councils should be made.[5] The actual working of this clause went some way towards meeting the demands of Indian politicians. While the Act did not concede any right of election, the provision relating to the drafting of regulations allowed the government to grant to various bodies of Indians the privilege of recommending councillors for nomination.[6] Thus indirectly

family, the obstructive attitude of the Irish members as to estimates, and the hostility to the government's Tithes Bill, made any legislation in the Commons quite impossible. Cross to Lansdowne, 9 August 1889, Lansdowne Papers, I.S. 420/14, BM.

[1] 24 and 25 Vic. c. 67, 10; 55 and 56 Vic. c. 14, 1 (1). The Governor-General and the Governors of Bombay and Madras had executive councils through which they ruled. The 1861 Act provided for the appointment of additional members to these councils for making laws. This constitutional form was continued in the new Act. Bengal and the North-western Provinces and Oudh did not have executive councils, so there the old councils existed solely for the purposes of making laws.

[2] 24 and 25 Vic. c. 67, 29; 55 and 56 Vic. c. 14, 1 (1).

[3] 55 and 56 Vic. c. 14, 1 (2). The additional members appointed to the councils of the Governor-General and to Bombay and Madras were to be nominated by the Governor-General and the Governors respectively, while in Bengal and the North-western Provinces and Oudh the councillors were to be nominated by the Governor-General in Council.

[4] 55 and 56 Vic. c. 14.   [5] 55 and 56 Vic. c. 14, 1 (4).

[6] The Secretary of State considered that the 'diffusion ... of education and en-

the legislative councils were opened to election and to a wider range of Indian opinion than they had been exposed to before, and, even though the government had the final say, Lansdowne considered that the Act would take the 'wind out of the sails of Congress'.[1] He was to be proved right for more than a decade.

The government framed the regulations to work the Act with the desire to find groups representing a 'substantial community of legitimate interests, professional, commercial, or territorial' to recommend legislative councillors.[2] The right to suggest members was vested in university senates, corporations, municipalities and district boards, chambers of commerce, and associations of landholders.[3] The arrangements were not unlike those discussed by the Congress when it planned to restrict the franchise to 'those classes and members of the community, *prima facie*, capable of exercising it wisely and independently'.[4] Inevitably, the government and the Congress would disagree on which particular interests were worth accommodating. The government was in no position to fill council seats with Congress politicians at the expense of ignoring other, and in some cases more important, interests.[5] But prominent Congressmen did not do too badly. In Bengal, Surendranath Banerjea, Lal Mohan

> lightened public spirit, and the recent organisation of Local Self Government may have provided in some instances ways and means of which the Governments may properly avail themselves in determining the character that shall be given to the representation of the views of different races, classes and localities'. Municipalities, district boards, and various non-official associations might with 'convenience and advantage' be asked for their views and recommendations with regard to appointments to the councils. Despatch, Secretary of State to Governor-General, Legislative, No. 15, 30 June 1892, Home Public A, August 1892, 239, NAI.

[1] Lansdowne to Cross, 1 January 1889, Lansdowne Papers, I.S. 420/14, BM.
[2] Despatch, Secretary of State to Governor-General, Legislative No. 15, 30 June 1892, Home Public A, August 1892, 239, NAI.
[3] The detailed distribution of seats was outlined in Govt. India to Secretary of State, 7 March 1894, Home Public A, March 1894, 101, NAI.
[4] Resolution IV (2), *INC 1886*, p. 42.
[5] The Lieutenant-Governor of the North-western Provinces and Oudh argued that 'changes in the Council here would gratify a few young graduates, a few pleaders, a Bengali judge or two, and their immediate followers, but would vex and disgust the whole of Oudh, the whole of the Muhammadan community whether in Oudh or the North West, and while proving a source of annoyance and discontent to the vast majority of the Hindu community in the North West would seem to them an innovation introduced at the demand of a small section whose inexplicable influence over Government must furnish growing ground for alarm'. Note by A. Colvin, 11 June 1889, Notes, Home Public A, August 1892, 237–52, NAI.

Ghose and W. C. Bonnerjee, active participants in the creation of an all-India movement from the 1870s, all found seats on the newly extended council, and so did the Maharajas of Darbhanga and Natore, who had provided much of the money to get the Congress going in that province.[1] In the North-western Provinces and Oudh, Charu Chundra Mittra, an expatriate Bengali, and Raja Rampal Singh, both active supporters of the Congress, found seats on the provincial legislative council.[2] The Raja was, however, also a great landowner, paying over 96,000 rupees revenue a year. Significantly the university at Allahabad returned a European member, as did the chamber of commerce. Seth Lachman Das, the head of 'the great banking firm of Muttra' was also proposed for nomination. The Lieutenant-Governor included in the council a large Muslim landholder from Aligarh, and the president of the British Indian Association of Oudh Talukdars, whose estates were spread over six districts.[3]

The people in the Bombay Presidency were less satisfied with the way in which the rules giving force to the Act were drawn up. Although the Bombay Presidency Association found two of its leading lights – Pherozeshah Mehta and R. M. Sayani – appointed to the provincial legislative council,[4] the voluble Marathi-speaking Central division had not been allowed to put forward a member, either through its district boards or municipalities. In order to contain what the government thought to be undesirable Maharashtrian influences, the Bombay government had decided that the Sardars of the

[1] Surendranath Banerjea was proposed by the Calcutta corporation, Lalmohan Ghose by the municipalities in the Presidency division, the Maharaja of Darbhanga by the district boards of Patna division, the Maharaja of Natore by the municipalities of Rajshahi division, and W. C. Bonnerjee by the senate of Calcutta university. Govt. India to Secretary of State, 7 March 1894, Home Public A, March 1894, 101, NAI.

[2] *Ibid.*; Govt. N.W.P. and Oudh to Govt. India, 25 January 1894, Home Public A, March 1894, 99, NAI. Charu Chundra Mittra was the son of Nilcolmal Mittra who had advised Surendranath Banerjea on the latter's tour of northern India in 1877 to raise support for a petition protesting against the lowering of age of entry into the Indian civil service. S. N. Banerjea, *A nation in making* (reprint, Calcutta, 1963), p. 41.

[3] Govt. N.W.P. and Oudh to Govt. India, 25 January 1894, Home Public A, March 1894, 99, NAI.

[4] Mehta was elected by Bombay corporation, and Sayani was nominated by the Governor. Govt. India to Secretary of State, 7 March 1894, Home Public A, March 1894, 101, NAI.

Deccan (a body of 190 landholders)[1] should be allowed to recommend one person to the Council, and, to counter the criticism that this left the urban communities unrepresented, the Governor nominated the president of Poona municipality to a seat, further claiming that the seats given to the municipalities of the Northern division and to the district boards of the Southern division would also represent the interests of local bodies in the Central division.[2] The Poona Sarvajanik Sabha claimed that the regulations drafted by the Bombay government 'gave small minorities an overwhelmingly preponderant share of representation' and that the rich and populous Central division was left unrepresented.[3] The Sabha argued:

> The Central Division has thrice the area of the Northern and over 50 per cent more area than the Southern Division. The area in Sind is considerable, but its population is only about 28 lakhs, while the population in the Northern, Central and Southern Divisions is respectively about 44, 61 and 44 lakhs. The number of villages and towns is again the largest in the Central Division, being twice those in Sind or those in the Northern Division. As regards land revenue, Sind shows a revenue of 92 lakhs, the Southern Division 100 lakhs, and the Central 133 lakhs. The gross revenue in the several Divisions is also nearly in the same proportion. The number of civil sub-divisions and of the police and magistracy have the same preponderance in the Central over those in the other Divisions. The Local Funds and Municipal revenues as given in the Administration Report for 1891-92 for the several Divisions are as follows:– The Northern Division: Local Funds 13 lakhs, Municipal revenue 15 lakhs; the Central Division: Local Funds 14¾ lakhs, Municipal revenue 12¼ lakhs; the Southern Division: Local Funds 11 lakhs, Municipal revenue 5¼ lakhs; and Sind: Local Funds 8 lakhs, and Municipal revenue 10 lakhs. It will be seen from these details that the Central Division is the largest of all in area, population and revenue, and is, besides, in point of education, the most advanced part of the Presidency outside the Town and Island of Bombay; and no arrangement, therefore, which ignores the claims of this Division can claim to be final or just.[4]

Public meetings were held at Poona, Satara, Sholapur, Ahmadnagar, Nasik and Dhulia, to endorse the complaint of the Sarvajanik Sabha.[5] There was little doubt that the govern-

---
[1] Poona Sarvajanik Sabha to Govt. India, 3 June 1893, Home Public A, July 1893, 137, NAI. Most of these held their largest estates in the Southern division.
[2] Resolution, 17 May 1893, Bombay legislative proceedings, 1893, vol. 4462, IOR.
[3] Sarvajanik Sabha to Govt. Bombay, 6 April 1893, ibid.; Sarvajanik Sabha to Govt. India, 3 June 1893, Home Public A, July 1893, 137, NAI.
[4] Sarvajanik Sabha to Govt. Bombay, 6 April 1893, Bombay legislative proceedings, 1893, vol. 4462, IOR.
[5] Sarvajanik Sabha to Govt. India, 3 June 1893, Home Public A, July 1893, 137, NAI.

ment of Bombay had deliberately attempted to cut down Poona's influence in the Presidency. The government of India, however, felt that the complaints of the Sarvajanik Sabha were justified, and the Viceroy decided to 'tell Lord Harris [the Governor of Bombay] privately that we think he might find a means of humouring the Central Division'.[1] In 1895 the rules were revised and the district boards of the Central division were given an opportunity to recommend a member. This seat was held successively by the two leading Poona politicians: Bal Gangadhar Tilak and Gopal Krishna Gokhale.[2]

In Madras, four seats were offered to municipalities and district boards; the corporation of Madras city returned a member, and a future president of the Congress, C. Sankaran Nair, was nominated by the Governor.[3] The Congress and government officials had always agreed that the best way to select members for the Governor-General's legislative council was for the non-official members of the provincial councils to elect one of their number to go to Calcutta.[4] This was duly done, and in the first instance Pherozeshah Mehta and the Maharaja of Darbhanga were among those chosen.[5]

That the Congress was not altogether unsatisfied with the 1892 Councils Act can be inferred from the fact that after 1894, when the delegates recorded their opinion that the rules introduced to work the Act could be framed in a more liberal spirit,[6] general demands about legislative councils were dropped from the Congress platform until the new century. The Congress

[1] Note by Lansdowne, 11 July 1893, Notes, Home Public A, July 1893, 136–140, NAI.
[2] Tilak was elected in 1895 and again in 1897; Gokhale was elected in 1899. The Poona politicians would really have preferred the right of recommendation to have been given to the municipalities, but the government seems to have been afraid that the Poona men would have had more influence in the towns 'and [would send] up to the Bombay Legislative Council an undesirably hot representative'. N. C. Kelkar, *Life and times of Lokhmanya Tilak* (translated by D. V. Divekar, Madras, 1928), p. 268. In the event the government's decision made no difference.
[3] Govt. India to Secretary of State, 7 March 1894, Home Public A, March 1894, 101, NAI. Sankaran Nair was president of the Congress in 1897.
[4] Resolution IV (iii), *INC 1886*, p. 42; Govt. India to Govts. Punjab, Central Provinces, Burma and Assam, 22 August 1892, Home Public A, August 1892, 249, NAI.
[5] Govt. India to Secretary of State, 7 March 1894, Home Public A, March 1894, 101, NAI.
[6] Resolution IX (b), *INC 1894*, pp. 3–4.

continued to press for a legislative council for the Punjab,[1] and, when it was granted, condemned the fact that all Punjab councillors were to be nominated, and that they did not have the right to ask questions of the provincial government.[2] Congressmen were also unhappy about the way in which the Central Provinces' representative was chosen to sit on the central legislature,[3] and urged that the laws and orders governing Berar should be passed through the Viceroy's legislative, and not his executive, council.[4] But these matters were mere details. The 1892 Councils Act not only widened the horizons of the central institutions of government, but it provided proper political arenas in which the ambitions of Indian politicians could be fulfilled. The councils may not have been very active, and their immediate power was negligible, but they did lay down the legal framework for the government. Councillors became 'honourable', and membership conferred great prestige. The accord between the government and the Congress about the need to reform the councils symbolised the growing importance and effectiveness of provincial and all-India government.

Reform of the legislative councils was the most spectacular demand of the Congress, but it necessarily affected only a few

[1] Resolution IX (a), *ibid.* p. 3.
[2] Resolution XV, *INC 1897*, p. 7. This resolution was also passed in 1898 and 1899.
[3] Resolution XV, *INC 1895*, p. 4. The resolution was also passed in 1896, 1897, 1898 and 1899. The interest in the case of the Central Provinces arose because several Maharashtrian Congressmen, who had links with Poona, lived in Nagpur. In choosing the first member to sit on the Viceroy's council the Chief Commissioner of the Provinces had divided the district boards into two groups, one from Jubblepore and Narbudda divisions, the other comprising Nagpur and Chhattisgarh divisions and five municipal councils. The Chief Commissioner had asked each group to select a person 'of influence and independent means', from which he chose one to go to Calcutta. (Govt. Central Provinces to Govt. India, 20 September 1892, Home Public A, February 1893, 82, NAI.) As a result, G. R. Chitnavis was nominated. In 1895, when his term of office came to an end, the Chief Commissioner appointed a man from the Narbudda division (and who was consequently not popular in the Marathi-speaking districts) to succeed without bothering to consult any of the district boards. The same happened in 1897, although then Chitnavis was re-appointed. However, Congressmen, although they approved of the choice, still considered that the local authorities should have been consulted. In fact the Chief Commissioner in 1893, Antony MacDonnell, had no authority under the Act to approach the district boards. Note by J. Woodburn, 6 October 1897, Notes, Home Public Deposit, October 1897, 215, NAI.
[4] Resolution XVI, *INC 1897*, p. 7. The resolution was repeated in 1898 and 1899.

people. More practical, and with wider application, was the demand for increasing the proportion of Indians employed in the civil service. Dababhai Naoroji told the first Congress that increased Indianisation of the administration was 'the most important key to our material and moral advancement. All our political reforms will benefit us but very little indeed if this reform of all reforms is not made.'[1] The administration had, of course, always been predominantly staffed by Indians,[2] but the Congress demanded that Indians should be more fully represented in the higher-paid posts, and in those which carried greater responsibility. Above all, this meant admitting more Indians to the covenanted civil service, a small body of less than a thousand men, which represented the 'only permanent English official element in India',[3] and which monopolised all the most powerful positions in the government.

Legally there were no barriers to Indians being employed in the highest offices,[4] but although a committee set up in 1853 had replaced patronage by competitive literary examinations,[5] the practical disadvantages facing Indians were many. The examination was held in London, and the papers were related to the syllabus taught in the English public schools. Apart from difficulties which might arise from caste and social taboos if a young man went to England to take the examinations, and apart from the difficulty of having to cope with Latin and Greek, the maximum age-limit for a competitor had been reduced to nineteen by Lord Salisbury in 1874.[6] Between 1864 and 1886

[1] *INC 1885*, p. 81.
[2] For example, almost all the posts where the salary was below Rs. 75 per month were held by Indians, and they even held 95% of the jobs in the executive and judicial department of the uncovenanted service. *Report of the India Public Service Commission 1886–87*, PP 1888, XLVIII, p. 38.
[3] *Ibid.*
[4] The 1833 Charter Act and the Queen's Proclamation of 1858 both stated that neither religion, place of birth, colour, nor race, disabled persons from holding any appointment in India.
[5] H. L. Singh, *Problems and policies of the British in India* (London, 1963), p. 14.
[6] *Ibid.* p. 26. The maximum age-limit had been twenty-one. Salisbury seems to have been influenced in his decision by the increase in the number of Indian competitors in 1873 and 1874. In 1873 there were eleven Indian competitors and there were twelve in 1874. In other years between 1862 and 1877 there had never been more than six. *Ibid.* p. 27. The reduction of the age-limit virtually excluded all Indian competitors. The Public Service Commission advised that the limit be raised to twenty-three, because that was the average age for completion of M.A. courses at Indian universities. *Report of the Public Service Commission*, p. 44.

only twelve Indians had managed to overcome the obstacles and enter the service. The government's policy was limited by the need to keep some part of the administration in English hands to ensure the stability and efficiency of its rule. Only a small proportion of those employed in the upper ranks of any department were Indians, although as the bureaucracy expanded so did the Indian share of top jobs.[1]

The Congress demanded that entry to the covenanted service be made easier for Indians by holding an examination in India simultaneously with the one in England, and then drawing up a single order of merit. A resolution proposing this was passed at the first meeting of the Congress[2] and it became a permanent fixture on the list of Congress policies. Although the opening of the civil service in this way was a logical development of the government's policies of increasing its control over the administration by making it open to the talents, the government was not able to meet the Congress demand. A competitive literary examination held dangers as well as advantages. The 1886 Public Service Commission was instructed to enquire into the claims for more extensive employment of Indians, but it had also to bear in mind 'the conditions to which such claims must be subject; and while they recognise the claims of one class, they do not ignore the claims of other classes to equal facilities of official advancement'.[3] The commissioners were unable to recommend the straightforward adoption of competitive examinations for entry into the civil service because they found a sharp division of Indian opinion on the matter. Contradictory evidence was given 'by witnesses belonging to those classes who have made the greatest progress in education; and others who feel that, in the present circumstances of the country, important classes of the community are practically debarred from success

---

[1] Between 1867 and 1903 the proportion of Indians employed in posts carrying a monthly salary of Rs. 200–300 rose from 51% to 60%; Rs. 300–400 from 23% to 43%; Rs. 400–500 from 21% to 40%; Rs. 500–600 from 9% to 25%; Rs. 600–700 from 15% to 27%; Rs. 700–800 from 5% to 13%. In 1867 four Indians drew a monthly salary of Rs. 800–1,000; in 1903 there were ninety-three. In 1867, 648 appointments carried a monthly pay of over Rs. 1,000. Only two were held by Indians. In 1903 the number of such appointments was 1,370 and Indians had 92 of them. Resolution No. 419–435, 24 May 1904, Home Establishments A, June 1904, 103, NAI.
[2] Resolution IV, *INC 1885*, pp. 2–3.
[3] *Report of the Public Service Commission*, p. 36.

in examinations designed mainly as tests of educational qualification'.[1]

Distribution of public employment among Indians was to remain one of the most controversial issues in Indian politics up to and beyond independence. The power which lay in the bureaucracy, and the patronage it controlled, meant that it was important for everyone to have friends in government service. The real question was not whether a few Englishmen should lose their jobs, but which Indians should take them over. The policy-makers found it impossible to apply any apparently objective criteria in making senior appointments because some Indians were – or what was just as important, appeared to be – better placed to succeed than others. In particular, the uneven spread of literacy in English gave certain groups an advantage in literary examinations. By the later nineteenth century, the traditional literate communities of Bombay (like the Brahmins, Parsis and Prabhus), Bengal (such as Brahmins, Baidyas and Kayasths) and Madras (mainly Brahmins) had established a formidable lead over the provinces of northern India in their knowledge of English, and the literary syllabus that went with it.[2] In the North-western Provinces and Oudh, and even more in the Punjab, although literate Muslims, Kayasths, Kashmiri Brahmins and Khatris were more than holding their own against fellow northerners, far fewer of them felt that they could compete effectively against the sheer numbers of English literates in the maritime provinces. They feared that they would lose all the most powerful positions in their own governments to outsiders, and they resented the threatened pre-eminence of Bengalis, Madrasis and Maharashtrians in the all-India services.[3]

The Punjab government considered that competitive examinations would bring the administration of that province largely under 'foreigners'.[4] The Chief Commissioner of the

[1] *Report of the Public Service Commission*, p. 39.
[2] Seal, *The emergence of Indian nationalism*, pp. 16–22, 25–130.
[3] On studying the topics debated at the third Congress, Syed Ahmad Khan, representing a literate service Muslim elite, wrote: 'Can any Bengali honestly say that the resolutions passed at the National Congress will be beneficial to any class of natives except Bengalis and Mahratta Brahmins ... The Congress is nothing more or less than a civil war without the use of arms.' *Aligarh Institute Gazette*, 4 February 1888.
[4] Quoted by Singh, *Problems and policies of the British in India*, p. 49. The Lieutenant-

Central Provinces argued that the system would flood his service with Mahratta Brahmins to the exclusion of all other classes.[1] Non-officials were equally emphatic about the need for policies of protection in public appointments. When the Public Service Commission toured the Gangetic plain, Dinshaw Wacha complained that the Congress campaign for opening the civil service 'has been spoiled by the people of Northern India – *Hindus and Muslims alike.* They have unanimously given *their* evidence against simultaneous examinations.'[2] Unequal development and the need to pursue a policy of equality of opportunity for all powerful and rising groups, forced the British to reject a system of competitive examinations alone for filling public appointments; and the need to compensate educationally backward groups has persisted to the present day. The Royal Commission of 1916 summed up the dilemma which must face any Indian government:

In the last generation English education has been greatly extended in India, but this extension has been made irregularly in the different provinces ... This consideration is of importance in the imperial Departments, which operate over the whole of India, as it is desirable that each portion of the country should obtain an adequate representation in the public services. English education has also been diffused unequally among the different communities. It has spread more rapidly in those which have had from early days an hereditary association with learning. Other classes ... are still backward in this respect. As long as these conditions prevail the result of recruiting by means of competitive examinations alone must be to exclude from the public services important sections of the Indian community.[3]

The Congress did not confine its attention to the higher ranks of the civil service, but, to begin with, it recommended that 'all other first appointments (excluding peonships, and the like) should be filled by competitive examinations held in India, under conditions calculated to secure such intellectual, moral and physical qualifications as may be decided by the Govern-

Governor wrote: 'Unless you exclude certain classes, such as Khatris, Kashmiri Pandits and Banias, which you cannot practically do, they almost invariably win.' Competition would result in the recruitment of the service 'not from among the classes who would naturally take the lead, but from amongst the men who obtain degrees in the universities'. Quoted *ibid.* p. 53.

[1] *Ibid.* p. 52.
[2] Wacha to Naoroji, 9 March 1888, Naoroji Papers, NAI. The words italicised are underlined in the original.
[3] *Report of the Royal Commission on the Public Services in India,* vol. I, pp. 29–30. PP 1916, VII.

ment to be necessary'.[1] This measure would ensure the dominance of local literate groups in the lower ranks of public service within their own regions. A system of competitive selection for the Provincial Civil Service was tried in Bengal. Between 1884 and 1893, sixty-six persons entered the service by that method. All but three were Bengali Hindus: one was a Hindu from Bihar, two were Eurasians. No Muslims were selected. The Lieutenant-Governor reported:

> At the present time, and probably for many years to come, the immediate effect of recruiting the Subordinate Executive on an exclusively competitive basis will be to debar Muhammadans, natives of Behar and Orissa, from any reasonable chance of obtaining appointments. Not only would this be unfair in itself and contrary to established policy, but it would tend to encourage feelings of race jealousy and antagonism, which have already begun to show themselves, and which might at any time give rise to serious difficulties.[2]

By persisting in its policy for recruitment to the public services, the early Congress was bound to alienate support. Moreover, as education spread to other social groups, and as it developed in regions which were behind the maritime provinces, the competition for employment became more fierce, and local inhabitants felt that they had a right to a certain proportion, at least, of the offices in their own provinces. The campaign for open competitive literary examinations would make rising literate groups wary of supporting the Congress. For example, Mysore state had been administered for many years by Sir K. Seshadri Iyer, who did much to improve the administration. But he had also imported many Tamil Brahmins, and they in turn had introduced their own *protégés* so that the civil list of Mysore had 'Iyers at the top, Iyers at the bottom, and Iyers everywhere'. Education had improved and there was a demand that Mysore should be the preserve of the Mysoreans. A correspondent, styling himself 'Congress wallah', wrote to the *Hindu* to say that if delegates from Mysore were to continue to

---

[1] Resolution IV, *INC 1885*, p. 3.
[2] Memorandum, pp. 93-4, Enclosed in Govt. India to Secretary of State, 1 November 1893, PP 1894, LX. From 1884 to 1889 appointments were made by competitive examination alone. Policy in Bengal after 1889 was to fill one third of the vacancies by pure competition; one third by selection from the rest of the people who took the examination and secured more than one third of the marks 'in such a way as to distribute the appointments fairly among the various divisions, races and creeds of the Province', and one third by nomination. *Ibid.* p. 94.

attend Congress, it ought to be agreed that the people of one province should not monopolise all the 'fat jobs' of another. 'Our aim should be as far as possible to increase the spirit of union in India, and the best way to do this is to leave everyone undisturbed in his own country.'[1] Adherence to a demand for competitive examinations meant that developing regions and communities were not attracted to Congress: the demand for simultaneous examinations united only those best able to take advantage of them.

A third major group of Congress resolutions sought to reform the methods of administration. The most important resolutions were those which concerned judicial administration. It would have been surprising if Congress, composed of and led by lawyers, had not directed its attention to this field. The system of law and the judiciary served as intermediaries between the government and the governed, providing institutions which, 'while independent of both, attracted the respect of both and influenced their attitudes'.[2] The courts in India were a positive and effective check on the executive power of the government. It was the intention of Congress that there should be a further extension to India of English jurisprudence, which would secure the independence, and enhance the importance, of the most important constitutional brake in the vehicle of state. This found expression in the annual demand for a separation of judicial and executive functions.[3]

Congress found plenty of legal and liberal thought in support of this reform, and both Kimberley and Cross pronounced in favour of it.[4] Financial expediency[5] and a reluctance to allow

[1] *Hindu*, 1 August 1906.
[2] W. H. Morris-Jones, *The government and politics of India* (London, 1964), p. 41.
[3] The Collector of a district was also District Magistrate. His immediate deputies also combined these functions. Thus in Bombay Presidency, below the Assistant and Deputy Collector level, the Mamlatdars had powers of first or second class magistrates, while the rank below them, the Aval Karkuns, whose salaries ranged from Rs. 40 to Rs. 60 p.m. were third class magistrates, as well as being local revenue officers. C. H. Setalvad, *Recollections and reflections* (Bombay, 1946), p. 163.
[4] *Ibid.* p. 165. A former Chief Justice of Bengal, the Rt Hon. Sir Richard Garth wrote 'to be tried by a man, who is at once the judge and prosecutor, is too glaring an injustice; and it is only wonderful, that a system so indefensible should have been allowed to prevail thus long under an English Government.' *A few plain truths about India* (London, 1888), ch. IV.
[5] Congress urged the separation 'even though this should, in some provinces, involve some extra expenditure'. Resolution XI, *INC 1886*, p. 45.

pleaders any further extension of their influence, led the government to ignore the proposal.[1] In 1908 the government of India decided to 'advance cautiously and tentatively towards the separation of judicial and executive functions in those parts of India, where local conditions render the change possible and appropriate'.[2] But the movement was desperately slow. When in 1937 Congress governments came into power in some provinces, they too disappointed the jurists by refusing to carry out the reform.[3]

The Congress wished to extend the system of trial by jury, and was against any move which would increase the powers of magistrates or revenue officers. The Congress wanted to tie the executive firmly to a set of rules and procedures, which would ensure the complete independence of the courts. Despite the fact that many district and sessions judges tended to be recruited from the administrative service rather than from the legal profession,[4] Indians attained prominence in the upper ranks of the judiciary. In Bombay Presidency alone, Telang, Ranade, Tyabji and Chandavarkar all sat on the bench of the High Court, and were highly respected by Indians and English alike.

The demands for equality for Indians before the law[5] led the Congress to demand the end of other forms of discriminatory legislation. In particular it requested a repeal of the Arms Act, thus enabling Indians to carry fire-arms on the same terms as Europeans, and that Indians should be allowed to organise volunteers so that they could come to the aid of government in times of emergency. Sir A. Colvin pertinently pointed out that the races assembled in Congress had no warlike traditions, and

---

[1] For example, the 1900 Punjab Land Alienation Bill transferred cases of usury from the courts to the executive power of revenue officers, with the specific intention of lessening the role of lawyers. One effect of the act was that the Punjab law school declined by half between 1897 and 1902. J. R. McLane, 'Peasants, money lenders and nationalists at the end of the 19th Century', *Indian Economic and Social History Review*, vol. I, no. 1 (1963), 72.
[2] Speech by Sir H. Adamson. Quoted by Setalvad, *Recollections and reflections*, p. 165.
[3] C. Rajagopalachari argued in the Madras Legislative Council against separation: 'Now that Congress is in office, we will see that executive officers will not go wrong and we shall control them.' *Ibid.* p. 166.
[4] Congress only once passed a resolution urging that more judges at these levels be recruited from the legal profession. Resolution VII, *INC 1894*, p. 3.
[5] In particular that Indians should be tried by juries composed at least half of Indians.

that the demand for the right to organise militia was but part of their general strategy to 'level up' to their European rulers.[1]

Congress politicians were also deeply concerned about the poverty of the Indian masses. The most responsible of them devoted much of their time to the study of political economy. R. C. Dutt wrote a brilliant economic history of nineteenth-century India; Gokhale's writings on economics bulk far larger than his political works; while Naoroji's economic essays exercised an overwhelming influence on economic thought in India at the end of the nineteenth century.[2] Chandra, in his survey of the economic thought of Indians at the end of the nineteenth century, concludes that while Indian leaders did not espouse the class interests of peasant or worker, they nonetheless exhibited a high degree of altruism in their proposals.[3]

But while the Congress devoted much time to economic matters, the economic theories advanced were in many cases inadequate for solving India's needs. Congress resolutions about Indian poverty were dominated by the theory of the drain. This was most fully formulated by Dadabhai Naoroji.[4] It assumed that Indian poverty was principally due to a drain of Indian wealth to England. A majority of Congress economic

[1] Note by Sir A. Colvin, 11 June 1889, Notes, Home Public A, August 1892, 237–52, NAI.

[2] R. C. Dutt, *Economic history of India under early British rule* (London, 1901), and *Economic history of India in the Victorian age* (London, 1903); R. P. Patwardhan and D. V. Ambekar, *The speeches and writings of Gopal Krishna Gokhale*, vol. 1 (Poona, 1962); D. Naoroji, *Poverty and un-British rule in India* (London, 1901).

[3] '... they opposed the removal of cotton import duties though the "middle class" was the chief consumer of foreign cloth; they supported protection for industries even though its price would be ultimately borne by this class; many of them supported the countervailing duties on beet sugar even though beet sugar was consumed mostly by this class; they preached swadeshi though foreign goods were cheaper; they supported the falling rupee even though it meant that as buyers of imported goods the members of this class had to pay more and as earners of fixed income the educated employed stood to gain from any increase in the purchasing power of the rupee and to lose by a decrease in it; most of them supported the income tax and opposed the salt tax ... they were willing to advocate higher taxation; they criticised railway development which increased the comfort of the "middle class" and favoured irrigation and industrial development instead; many of the nationalists opposed the development of the country by foreign capital, even though such development opened out new avenues of employment for educated Indians.' Bipan Chandra, *The rise and growth of economic nationalism in India* (New Delhi, 1966), pp. 751–2.

[4] Naoroji, *Poverty and un-British rule in India*; Chandra, *The rise and growth of economic nationalism in India*, pp. 636–708.

resolutions were devoted to ways of preventing this drain. If more Indians were employed in the public services, they could be paid less and their salary would not leave the country; the exchange compensation for Europeans should be stopped; the cost of military expenditure beyond India's frontiers should be borne by the British Treasury, as should the cost of maintaining the Secretary of State's establishment in King Charles Street. In 1896, 1897 and 1899, Congress alleged that famine in India had been caused by excessive government expenditure.[1] The most practical of the Congress resolutions was that more money should be devoted to expansion of technical education.[2] But apart from this, and apart from a demand that the land revenue owing to government should be fixed for long periods, of, say, sixty years,[3] Congress considered that most of the ills could be cured by changes in the administration. Indianisation of the civil service would result in a *'complete material saving* to the country';[4] and 'the introduction of Representative Institutions will prove one of the most important practical steps towards the amelioration of the people'.[5]

The political programme of the Congress could be interpreted as representing the demands of particular social groups who sought for themselves greater power in the Indian administration. The perennial demands for more posts in the higher civil service and for reform of the law courts especially, give the early Congress its apparently class interest. For who would benefit more by the immediate implementation of its policies

[1] Resolution XII, *INC 1896*, Resolution IX, *INC 1897*; Resolution XIII, *INC 1899*.
[2] E.g. Resolution VII, *INC 1887* and subsequent years. See also Gokhale's presidential speech, *INC 1905*, p. 16.
[3] E.g. Resolution XIV, *INC 1888* and subsequent years. There is some doubt as to who would benefit most from a permanent settlement of land revenue in Bombay and Madras. J. R. McLane argues that the reform meant different things to different people, and that some were, like Surendranath Banerjea, really concerned about the lot of the peasantry. He also points out, however, that people with large landed interests – Pillai from Madras, Mudholkar from Berar and Boikunta Nath Sen – were the most frequent speakers on the Congress resolution. 'Peasants, Money Lenders and Nationalists at the end of the 19th Century', *Indian Economic and Social History Review*, vol. 1, no. 1 (1963), 69. It will not be possible to clear up this point until more work is done to discover which were the social groups that drew wealth from land and what their legal titles were in each of the different provinces.
[4] Speech by Naoroji, *INC 1885*, p. 100.
[5] Resolution II, *INC 1886*, p. 41.

The Indian National Congress

than the literate elites of the coastal presidencies? Yet it would be a mistake to see nothing more in the annual resolutions than the naked self-interest of babus, for they were also a response to a radically changing governmental situation. Nearly all the issues brought forward at the meetings of the Congress concerned the way in which the central institutions of the government were being made more effective and were becoming more important. They also concerned the general principles by which the rulers would frame detailed policies. Not unnaturally, since these changes would eventually make themselves felt at the lowest levels of government, and ultimately their consequences would become apparent in every village in India, it was essential for Indian politicians to play some part in the decision-making. The Indian National Congress was the formal and ordered way in which this could be done.

It is clear from studying the demands of the Congress that its function was highly specialised. Closely related to the most recent developments in Indian government, and addressing itself to the highest levels of the raj, its organisation and its activities in India were different from those of other political bodies. The Congress did not, until elections became a feature of Indian politics, have much permanent organisation in India. In its early years it was not concerned with the problems of constant control of a locality or constituency. The main sign of activity was that 'after the usual sleep of long eleven months'[1] politicians would assemble in a different town to debate topics which hardly changed from year to year. The arrangements were made by a local committee, often synonymous with a local political association, which raised money to hold the Congress, housed the delegates, and published the final report. The main effort was then devoted to work in England. For most of its history the principal vehicle of Indian nationalism devoted its time to raising money which financed activity in London. Lal Mohan Ghose stood as Parliamentary candidate for Deptford in 1885; Dadabhai Naoroji returned to England in 1886 determined to find a constituency so that he could advance the Congress cause in Parliament. A 'Political Agency', run by William Digby, was set up to represent Indian views in England. Dadabhai Naoroji offered to distribute copies of Congress

[1] *Mahratta*, 11 December 1898.

The Indian National Congress

Reports from London[1] and at the beginning of 1887 the first step towards the creation of a permanent Congress organisation in England was taken.[2] To maintain interest in Indian affairs the British Committee of the Congress was formed in July 1889,[3] and thereafter Congress voted annually a sum of money for its expenses. From 1890 the British Committee published a newspaper, *India*, to present Congress views to the English public.[4] As the difficulties of raising money show,[5] the impulse behind these politics was still weak in the 1880s and 1890s. Yet it was a significant indication of how all-India politics would develop.

Since it was the function of Congress to put demands to government at a high level of generality, unity was its most important goal. It was no good speaking to England with a babel of tongues. Congressmen were well aware of the differences between Indians and of the uneven development of the sub-continent. From the start they concentrated on those issues that could unite most of them and eschewed matters that were divisive. This meant that many crucial political, social and

[1] Naoroji to Hume, 20 February 1887, Naoroji Papers, NAI. Naoroji's offer was conditional on adequate funds being raised to cover his costs.

[2] 'Let us at once appoint 3 or 4 persons to form the Committee here in London...' Naoroji to Telang, 27 February 1887, Naoroji Papers, NAI. Dadabhai Naoroji wrote from London 'These Congresses whatever other good they may do or not, are really creating a good deal of interest in India here. If they continue actively and perseveringly, year after year, and take steps after a careful consideration to petition Parliament from time to time on the most important reforms... I have every hope that success will at last crown its efforts.' Naoroji to Hume, 30 December 1887, *ibid*.

[3] The first members were Sir W. Wedderburn, W. S. Caine, W. S. B. Maclaren, J. E. Ellis, Dadabhai Naoroji and George Yule. Resolution XIII (d), *INC 1889*, p. xliv. W. C. Bonnerjee and A. O. Hume joined the Committee later. The active members were Wedderburn, Caine, Naoroji, Bonnerjee and Hume. For Indian activity in England see M. Cumpston, 'Some early Indian Nationalists and their allies in the British Parliament, 1851–1906', *English Historical Review*, vol. LXXVI (April 1961), 279–97.

[4] Ironically, more copies of the newspaper were sent to India than were ever distributed in England. This was because each province guaranteed to subscribe to a certain number of copies in order to finance the British Committee. However, even here the publishers were over-optimistic. Madras, for example, was expected to buy 2,000 copies, but there were only 800 willing subscribers. M. Vijaraghavachari to Naoroji, 9 September 1896, Naoroji Papers, NAI.

[5] Remittances voted at Congress were often badly in arrears. The British Committee was in serious financial difficulties in 1896, 1903, and 1912. 'We are a very dilatory people', W. C. Bonnerjee wrote, 'and it is very difficult indeed to get us to put our hands into our pockets except for the purposes of holding on to the money that may be in them.' Bonnerjee to Naoroji, 10 January 1901, Naoroji Papers, NAI.

economic issues were never even considered by the Congress because their immediate relevance threatened the unanimity of the movement. Thus, for example, the Congress asserted that it was not competent to discuss social reform, since each caste and community had its own domestic arrangements and it was not the duty of Congress to interfere with them.[1] Hence also the resolution passed in 1888 that no subject could be discussed at Congress to which a majority of the Hindu or the Muslim delegates as a body objected.[2] The strategy for maintaining unity was simple. As Ananda Charlu told the delegates at Allahabad 'If we are all agreed on any matter, then we will submit the universal view to Government; but if we cannot come to a substantial agreement amongst ourselves, then we drop the subject until we can'.[3] Since anything that would divide was ruled out of court, it is not surprising that the progress of all-India organisations seems in some respects so unreal. It was easy for the civil servant, for Indian critics, and for the later historian to jibe at the quixotic nature of all-India politics. But these weaknesses do not destroy their importance. It is the existence of such bodies, not the content of their programme that matters, and their existence was a necessary corollary of the new forms of government.

Unlike the government, however, non-official all-India political organisations lacked a definite structure. During this period, for example, the Congress had no effective constitution, no influential central secretariat, no provincial or district organisation, and no funds. This meant that it was unable to do

[1] Dadabhai Naoroji told the 1886 Calcutta Congress 'We are met together as a political body to represent to our rulers our political aspirations, not to discuss social reforms, and if you blame us for ignoring these you should equally blame the House of Commons for not discussing the abstruser problems of mathematics or metaphysics.' The reason why it was not proper for Congress to discuss social reform was that 'there are here Hindus of every caste, amongst whom, even in the same provinces, customs and social arrangements differ widely, – there are Mahomedans and Christians of various denominations, Parsees, Sikhs, Brahmos and what not – men indeed of each and all of these numerous classes which constitute in aggregate the people of India ... How can this gathering of *all* classes discuss the social reforms needed in each individual class? ... Only the members of that class can effectively deal with the reforms therein needed. A National Congress must confine itself to questions in which the entire nation has a direct participation, and it must leave the adjustment of social reform and other class questions to class Congresses.' *INC 1886*, p. 54.
[2] Resolution XIII, *INC 1888*.
[3] *INC 1888*, p. 86.

very much at all; but paradoxically, this was essential for its survival. In its quest for unity the Congress found it necessary to work through a very loose and informal organisation. Just as its programme was one which offended most people least, so the lack of definition in the shape of Congress enabled it to modify its nature with the greatest ease. A very informal gathering, in which anyone could participate, also had the advantage of glossing over the inconvenient criticisms made of its unrepresentative nature. Its leaders – lawyers and constitutionalists almost to a man – thus remained reluctant to make hard and fast rules for the Congress. Flexibility was essential, not only to contain most people but to be able to make the most of the rapidly changing political situation in India during these years. The Congress leaders carefully balanced the need for some administration against the disputes that would be the result of a too definite one. Throughout this period they tacitly agreed that the best government for the national movement was one that governed least.

The first session of the Indian National Congress had no rules or constitution to guide its formation and deliberations. A circular had been sent round during March advertising the meeting, and associations were invited to send representatives.[1] The resolutions passed at the Congress were ordered to be 'communicated to the political Associations in each province, and that these Associations be requested with the help of similar bodies and other agencies within their respective provinces to adopt such measures as they may consider calculated to advance the settlement of the various questions dealt with in these resolutions'.[2]

The need for an independent organisation for the Congress was recognised, but so too were the difficulties. On the one hand, if only to convince the government and other Indians that it was a viable movement, the Congress needed organisation; but on the other, it was doubtful how much organisation the movement could stand without destroying its support. In particular, the relationship between the Congress and the provincial associations was complex and ambiguous. While it was decided in 1886 that 'Standing Congress Committees be constituted at all important centres',[3] this did not result in the

[1] *INC 1885*, pp. 4–5.   [2] *Ibid.* p. 4.   [3] Resolution XIII, *INC 1886*.

establishment of a Congress network divorced from the local political associations. Well-established provincial associations were unwilling to give up their position. They had formed plausible links with the government, and had become recognised as non-official spokesmen for their region. For example, the British Indian Association, commenting on rules framed at the Madras session in 1887, complained 'we have the constitution of a distinct political body perfectly independent of the existing political institutions, and nowhere and in no respect showing any subordination to them'.[1] On the other hand, some political associations might be prepared to work in with the Congress because their links with it would help to give them standing in their region. Thus in Bengal the Indian Association, which in the 1880s and 1890s still had to make its influence felt, was more enthusiastic about the Congress than its senior rival, the British Indian Association. Indeed, its close connection with the Congress would help its leaders to oust the British Indian Association from its dominating position.

Where there was no immediate rivalry between associations in a province, supporting the Congress presented fewer problems. In Bombay city, for example, the Bombay Presidency Association had effectively taken over from all earlier political clubs, and in the Deccan the Poona Sarvajanik Sabha held similar sway until its demise in 1897. Both these associations were established local voices and neither lost anything by being Congress spokesmen as well. In regions of India where political centres were less developed it was easier for a new society to claim far wider interests than its membership actually embraced. In Madras city, for example, the Mahajana Sabha became recognised as the main regional association for lack of any other. It also acted as the obvious focus for Congress activity. What usually happened was that political associations deemed themselves, or sub-committees of themselves, to be the Congress committees for their locality.[2] Even when district committees were established, their membership coincided with

[1] Secretary, British Indian Association to General Secretary, National Congress Committee, 6 December 1888, quoted in Seal, *The emergence of Indian nationalism*, p. 290.
[2] At its Council meeting on 4 March 1887 the Secretary of the Bombay Presidency Association 'requested the Council to nominate a Standing Committee in terms of the 13th Resolution passed at the Second Indian National Congress in Cal-

that of the parent association. Thus, to all intents and purposes, bodies like the Poona Sarvajanik Sabha, the Madras Mahajana Sabha, or the Indian Association were synonymous with the Standing Congress Committees of their area. Although this meant that there was hardly any control over the Congress committees from the centre, it had the advantage that Congress organisations could be established in any district whenever there was a local nucleus of support. More generally, it meant that the Congress could pull into its movement almost any organisation working at any level of society.

However, the purposes of the Congress made it necessary to claim a representative character for the random support it attracted. From the beginning, Congress leaders were sensitive about the representative nature of their movement if only because representative government was important in the English political tradition to which they belonged.[1] Here again there was a problem. It might not be possible to devise a representative system that would work for all parts of India. Worse, such organisation might take effective power away from the small groups who had obvious interests in maintaining an all-India organisation. When in 1886 A. O. Hume urged the adoption of a system whereby graduates, professional men, income-tax payers, and regional associations would form in each province an electoral college to send delegates to Congress,[2] the Bombay

cutta'. Five persons were so nominated and, together with the secretaries of the Association, were declared the Bombay Standing Congress Committee. Minutes of Council meeting, 4 March 1887, Bombay Presidency Association Papers. The Council reconstructed the Committee by the same method on 24 January 1888, *ibid*. The government noted in 1906 that the Bombay Presidency Association 'more or less answers the purpose of, if it has not actually usurped, the functions of a provincial [Congress] committee. The District Standing Committees at such centres as Poona, Dharwar, Ahmednagar, etc., which are self-constituted, appear to correspond on matters connected with the National Congress, either with the Presidency Association or direct with the joint General Secretaries Wacha and Gokhale. At the same time the District Standing Committees do not appear to be in any way subordinate to the Bombay Presidency Association.' Para. 586 (Bombay, 30 July 1906), Bombay Police Abstracts, vol. XIX, 1906, Bombay HFM.

[1] The British continually denied that educated Indians represented anyone other than themselves. See Lytton to Salisbury, 11 May 1876, in Lady Betty Balfour (ed.), *Personal and literary letters of Robert, First Earl of Lytton* (London, 1906), vol. II, p. 21; and Dufferin's Minute on the Congress, November 1888, in C. H. Philips (ed.), *The evolution of India and Pakistan 1858 to 1947: select documents* (London, 1962), pp. 143–5.

[2] Appendix I, *INC 1886*.

leaders quickly decided that it was unworkable because 'the backward provinces may fight shy of elective members for the Congress'.[1] A formal constitution would raise a host of quarrels about the fair proportion of representatives from each area. Some regions were more powerfully represented in the Congress than others at the annual sessions, and some areas sent no representative at all. The most constant support came from parts of Bengal, Bombay and Madras.[2] The best way of masking the predominance of these regions in the Congress was to avoid formal methods of election. The 1889 Congress resolved that the number of delegates allowed to attend the Congress from each Standing Congress Committee was to be limited to five per million of the total population of the area covered by each committee.[3] The consequence of this rule, as Wacha complained before the 1890 Congress, was that Bombay city 'can only send six delegates which is indeed a poor number for a city like ours. The rule of representation in the rates of population is not quite the thing for Presidency Cities, and will have to be replaced.'[4] Indeed, the resolution was never implemented.

Flexibility in the composition of the Congress was also extended to membership of the Subjects Committee, the only important committee the Congress had until the twentieth century. This body decided what issues were to be debated. To begin with it had been the practice of a few men to meet in A. O. Hume's bungalow to decide what resolutions should be put before Congress. In 1887 the rank and file from Bombay and Bengal objected to this and a procedure was worked out which held good for the coming years. After the President had finished his address, the Congress elected a Subjects Committee, and the general session was adjourned until the following day while this Committee drew up the agenda.[5] However, the size of this

[1] Wacha to Naoroji, 23 September 1887, Naoroji Papers, NAI.
[2] Thirteen of the first twenty-six Congress sessions, for example, were held in the cities of Bombay, Calcutta and Madras. A further three were held in other towns in the Bombay Presidency, and two more were held in Marathi-speaking districts of the Central Provinces and Berar. Five meetings were held in the United Provinces and three in Punjab.
[3] Resolution XIII (a), *INC 1889*.
[4] Wacha to Naoroji, 6 December 1890, Naoroji Papers, NAI.
[5] B. C. Pal, *Memories of my life and times* (Calcutta, 1951), vol. II, pp. 35–41.

Committee was not defined, and elections for membership on it were not contested. In practice what happened was that delegates from each of the various Congress circles handed in slips of paper bearing the names of the delegates chosen by them to represent their circle. These names were then read out and the people declared elected. This meant that anyone of importance gained a seat on the Subjects Committee. The number of Congress circles participating in any Congress varied, and so did the overall size of the Subjects Committee.[1] Not until 1903 was the Subjects Committee composed by province rather than by circle, and even then the number of delegates eligible to sit from each province was not specified.[2]

While this underlined the open nature of the Congress, the very informality of organisation also allowed a small group of people to direct the movement. These were the Bombay city leaders who made Congress politics their life's work. They considered that control of the Congress was of vital importance and they recognised that it could only be achieved by conceding a measure of participation and by avoiding any action that would provoke hostility from potential supporters. Thus everyone was welcomed and no one's credentials were scrutinised too closely. So also the local committees of the Congress were allowed to work or not without any directions being given them. Usually the only active committee was the one charged with the preparations for the forthcoming Congress.[3] Wacha reported to Naoroji

[1] For most purposes the early Congress was content to accept the arbitrary provincial boundaries drawn by the British; but not for all. To give some regions a larger say, and to give any locality a place, the provinces were subdivided into a variable number of Congress 'circles'. This stratagem, a convenience in a period when the Congress had little formal organisation, came to be a threat to the coherence of the movement once it began to achieve real power.

[2] *INC 1903*, p. 35. At this Congress the Subjects Committee was composed of eight ex-officio members, 51 delegates from Madras, where the Congress was held, 46 from Bengal, 28 from Bombay, 6 from the United Provinces, 4 from Punjab, 2 from the Central Provinces, 2 from Berar and 1 from Burma.

[3] In 1893 Dadabhai Naoroji expressed the hope that the local committees might help to gather information for him about the poverty of India. Wacha told him not to 'count upon *any* Congress Committee helping you in the matter. Almost all go to sleep during eleven and a half months of the year and wake up for half a month in view of the Congress session.' Wacha to Naoroji, 1 April 1893, Naoroji Papers, NAI. (The word italicised is underlined in the original.) *Mahratta* also complained 'The different Standing Congress Committees in India except the one when the Congress meets for the year, practically spend the year in doing nothing.' *Mahratta*, 15 December 1895.

'There is no *directing* spirit who could continually nag at these bodies, show them the way to work, and make them *really* helpful for our purposes on your side [i.e., in England].'[1]

The Congress several times debated the need for a formal constitution and for the establishment of a central co-ordinating committee. The 1887 Congress appointed a working party to lay proposals before the next Congress,[2] but the matter was dropped. The question of a constitution was debated in a desultory fashion throughout the eighteen-nineties, but it was not until 1898 that any further action was taken. A committee was then set up to prepare a report for the 1899 Congress.[3] Its most important recommendation was that an Indian Congress Committee be established. In laying the proposal before Congress, R. N. Mudholkar hinted at some of the difficulties the Congress leaders faced in attempting to appear representative and at the same time to make the organisation manageable.

At present we have no such body [an all-India Committee]. We have Circle Committees and Standing Congress Committees scattered all over the country. But the only officer who is the officer of the Congress is the General-Secretary who is in England, or the Joint-General Secretary who is in India. Every other person is a member of a District Committee and there is no body which can during the year carry on the work of the Congress and call upon District Committees and Provincial Committees to do their work. The necessity of such a general body was felt for a long time, but there were great difficulties experienced in finding out the way of creating such a body. For such a large country as India, it was considered that all the different parts of the country ought to be represented on the committee, that is to say, the interests and opinions not only of the chief parts of the Presidencies but also of the chief Provinces ought to be represented. But it was at the same time seen that to do that would be to create a committee, the number of members of which would be too large for any executive work, and that such a committee would have required at least one thousand members, and a committee of one thousand members can not act effectively.[4]

Eventually the Congress settled for an Indian Congress Com-

[1] Wacha to Naoroji, 1 April 1893, Naoroji Papers, NAI. (The words italicised are underlined in the original.) Wacha was full of complaints that local Committees often neglected to reply to his letters – especially when he was asking for money. See, for example, Wacha to Naoroji, 26 October 1895 and 18 November 1899, Naoroji Papers, NAI.
[2] Resolutions I and IX, *INC 1887*.
[3] Resolution XIX, *INC 1898*. For the discussion on the need for a constitution see *ibid*. pp. 126–32.
[4] *INC 1899*, p. 130.

mittee composed of forty-five members.¹ It was supposed to meet three times a year, and Provincial and District Congress Committees were to be organised under it.² Although the Congress session held at Lahore in 1900 re-elected the Indian Congress Committee, it sank into oblivion at the following year's meeting in Calcutta,³ and there is no evidence that it ever met.⁴

The question of a formal constitution for the Congress was not brought up again until the 1904 session when Lajpat Rai, at the prompting of the Punjabi delegation, protested against the disappearance of the committee set up at Lahore in 1900.⁵ After he had been reassured that the Indian Congress Committee had not been deliberately disbanded by the Calcutta Congress of 1901, he was prepared to support a proposal which referred the whole matter to a select committee.⁶ This committee duly prepared a report for further discussion at the next session of the Congress. However, its only recommendation, which the delegates assembled at Benares in December 1905 accepted unanimously, was that a 'Standing Congress Committee' composed of fifteen prominent Congressmen 'be appointed to promote the objects of the Congress and to take such steps during the year as may be necessary to give effect to the Resolutions of the Congress'.⁷ In fact this was no advance on

---

¹ Resolution X, *ibid.* Bengal and Assam had eight members, Bombay and Sind eight, Madras eight, North-western provinces and Oudh six, Punjab four, the Central Provinces three and Berar three. Five members were to be elected at the Congress session itself from any province.

² *Ibid.*

³ The Lahore Congress made a slight adjustment to the regional distribution of seats on the Indian Congress Committee. Bengal, Bombay and Madras each lost a representative while the United Provinces gained one and Punjab two. In addition all past Presidents of Congress and various other officials became ex-officio members of the committee. Resolution I, *INC 1900*. For the constitution of Congress see also N. V. Rajkumar, *Development of the Congress constitution* (New Delhi, 1949).

⁴ As R. C. Dutt explained, 'Our experience of the constitution of 1899 shows that a large body will not do for India. India is a country of vast distances, and men from different parts cannot meet and work together. To be a practical efficient body, the *Executive Committee* must be small.' Dutt to Gokhale, 12 November 1903. Gokhale Papers, Reel 4, NAI. Dutt went on to suggest that Pherozesha Mehta and himself be appointed executive officers, for 'To some extent Mehta represents Southern India, I represent Northern India.' *Ibid.*

⁵ *Panjabee*, 12 December 1904 and 19 December 1904.

⁶ *Ibid.* 6 February 1905.

⁷ Resolution XXI, *INC 1905*. The men appointed were: P. M. Mehta, D. A. Khare,

the position in 1900, and the new Committee was equally inactive.

Without a formal hierarchy of committees the main responsibility for organising Congress fell into the hands of a few men: its secretary and those leaders of political associations most interested in Congress work. To begin with, Hume, the General-Secretary, personally co-ordinated all the various committees and associations, supervised the work of the Congress session, and drew up the reports.[1] In 1889 a Joint-Secretary was appointed to assist him,[2] but Hume retired permanently to England in 1892 and the main burden fell on the Joint-Secretary. From 1895 until 1913 this post was held by Dinshaw Edulji Wacha. He, however, acted as clerk and office-boy to the movement on behalf of more powerful patrons in Bombay. Whenever it seemed that Congress activity was taking a new turn, Wacha's talents were supplemented by those of men with real political skill. Thus during the important years 1903-8 Gopal Krishna Gokhale was appointed an additional Joint-Secretary[3] and he played a crucial part in directing the policy of Congress. After 1908 such work again became less urgent. Gokhale resigned and he was succeeded by D. A. Khare, another political nonentity who helped Wacha with the paper-work.[4] However, all three of these men were members of the Bombay Presidency Association, and it is to this association that we must look for the hard core of Congress leadership during this period. When the leadership of Gokhale and Pherozeshah Mehta came under attack between 1904 and 1908, the Bombay Presidency Association's hold over such formal Congress organisation as existed was to prove a decisive advantage.

While the lack of a formal constitution rendered Congress flaccid and weak, it also had considerable advantages. Regional

---

G. Subramania Iyer, Nawab Sayyid, S. N. Banerjea, A. Chaudhuri, Maulvi Abdul Kasim, S. Sinha, M. M. Malaviya, Ganga Prasad Varma, Lajpat Rai, Harkishen Lal, R. N. Mudholkar, D. E. Wacha and G. K. Gokhale. The three latter were to act as secretaries of the committee.

[1] Hume exercised a 'loving and lovable despotism'. Ananda Charlu in *Hindustan Review*, July–August 1903, p. 21. No doubt his rule was tolerable because for most of the time he was so far from his kingdom.

[2] Resolution XIII, *INC 1889*. Five thousand rupees a year were also voted for office expenses.

[3] Resolution XV, *INC 1903*.   [4] Resolution XX, *INC 1908*.

antipathies could be ignored, even if they were not overcome; and personal vendettas could be neutralised since there was no Congress organisation to fight over. As the *Madras Mail* acutely commented in 1906, the most likely reason for the lack of Congress organisation was 'that the Congress leaders have feared that a regular Constitution would tend towards the creation of sectional intrigue and factional differences. With a more or less regular electorate, the leaders would certainly be less independent and unfettered than hitherto.'[1]

In the same way there were considerable advantages in letting Congress move about the sub-continent without insisting on a rigid form for its composition.[2] Inevitably the number of delegates to Congress from the host province far outstripped the number of those coming from outside.[3] Since Congress was peripatetic this meant that, while its programme and aims remained constant, it appeared that each region in turn supported the movement.

The early Congress was an amorphous body. Yet the creation of a centre for Indian politics, even one as fragile and uncertain as this, had the effect of involving the provinces and localities with it. And so the Congress began to acquire a larger significance in Indian political life. It began to add up to more than a simple alliance between certain provincial associations; and, travelling around the sub-continent, it came to wield an influence of its own. Significantly, groups with a claim against the government or involved in local contests would associate them-

[1] Quoted in *Panjabee*, 29 December 1906.
[2] The Congress held its meetings in towns in all the provinces:

1885 Bombay	1896 Calcutta	1907 Surat
1886 Calcutta	1897 Amraoti	1908 Madras
1887 Madras	1898 Madras	1909 Lahore
1888 Allahabad	1899 Lucknow	1910 Allahabad
1889 Bombay	1900 Lahore	1911 Calcutta
1890 Calcutta	1901 Calcutta	1912 Bankipur
1891 Nagpur	1902 Ahmadabad	1913 Karachi
1892 Allahabad	1903 Madras	1914 Madras
1893 Lahore	1904 Bombay	1915 Bombay
1894 Madras	1905 Benares	1916 Lucknow
1895 Poona	1906 Calcutta	

[3] Usually well over half the delegates belonged to the host province. Between 1885 and 1909 the proportion of local delegates was lowest at Benares in 1905 (26·8%) and highest at Ahmadabad in 1902 (88·6%). Calculated from attendance figures in P. C. Ghosh, *The development of the Indian National Congress 1892–1909* (Calcutta, 1960), pp. 25–6.

selves with the all-India movement. In 1899, for example, *Tribune*, an influential Lahore newspaper, argued

> It is especially necessary that the Punjab should be strongly represented in the National assembly this year. Considering that legislative measures fraught with most momentous and far reaching consequences are in contemplation, those who are entitled to speak on behalf of the people of this province should not miss their opportunity of making their voices heard through the Congress with regard to the changes proposed.[1]

Although it was always said that strictly provincial matters were the concern of provincial conferences, the chance of airing a local grievance on an all-India platform was a powerful incentive to participate in Congress. Thus a stream of resolutions were passed about legislative councils in Punjab and the Central Provinces, about framing laws for Berar, about the composition of the executive councils in Bombay and Madras, about the status of the Punjab chief court, about the Punjab Land Alienation Bill, and about the partition of Bengal.[2]

[1] *Tribune*, 5 December 1899. In a later article *Tribune* specified the issues: 'Coming to our own Province, we have had an instance of singular indifference to public opinion in the passing of the Punjab Courts Bill in the face of the unanimous opposition of *all* (literally all) sections of the community. Our Province should make itself heard on this matter through the Congress. The Land Alienation Bill again, has spread the greatest alarm among the non-agricultural classes in the country, and agriculturists themselves (though most of them are in a fools' paradise just now) are having a foretaste of what is in store for them if the proposed measure becomes law. In the direction of Criminal administration also there is need for public criticism. Then, we have our standing demands with regard to the raising of the status of the Chief Court, the extension of the right of interpellation to the local council, and so forth. The alteration recently made in connection with the Municipal election rules at Mooltan indicates an important departure from hitherto accepted policy. This matter too, though it may not be of imperial importance, is worthy of the attention of the Congress.' *Ibid.* 14 December 1899.

[2] This list is far from being comprehensive. While the details of the demand changed with time, for Punjab legislative councils see Resolution III, *INC 1885*, Resolution I, *INC 1889*, Resolution XII, *INC 1892*, Resolution I and II, *INC 1893*, Resolution IX (a), *INC 1894*, Resolution XV, *INC 1897*, Resolution XXI, *INC 1898*, Resolution XVIII, *INC 1899*; for the demand that the Central Provinces should have an elected representative in the Viceroy's Council see Resolution XV, *INC 1895*, Resolution XIX, *INC 1896*, Resolution IV part 2 (d), *INC 1897*, Resolution XX ii (c), *INC 1898*; for Berar see Resolution XVI, *INC 1897* [when the Congress was held in Berar], Resolution XXII, *INC 1898*, Resolution XVIII, *INC 1899*; for executive councils in Bombay and Madras see Resolution XVI, *INC 1896*, Resolution XI, *INC 1897*, Resolution XIV, *INC 1898*, Resolution XII, *INC 1899*; for the status of the Chief Court of Punjab see Resolution XVIII, *INC 1893*, Resolution XIII, *INC 1894*, Resolution XI (h), *INC 1896*, Resolution IV (g), *INC 1897*, Resolution XX i (g), *INC 1898*, Resolution XIV i (e), *INC 1899*; for the Punjab Land Alienation Bill see Resolution II, *INC 1899*; for the

The Indian National Congress

Besides providing a convenient forum for local grievances against the government, the Congress began to have some relevance for the power-struggles taking shape within each region. Local interests looked increasingly to the Congress for allies outside their own province. This meant, of course, that the Congress began to enlist supporters of a different kind. But it also meant that the movement acquired more critics. Local opponents of groups associated with Congress would also seek wider alliances and so combinations would be built up against the Congress. For example, much of the legislation which in the closing years of the nineteenth century Punjabis wished to attack through the Congress was in fact directed against certain Hindu social groups.[1] Consequently, once the Congress had taken up their cause, other Hindus, Muslims and Sikhs in the Punjab opposed it. In 1888 some of the Congress support in the North-western provinces and Oudh came from Kayasths, a mobile social group who looked to the all-India organisation as a vehicle for realising their expectations. Not unnaturally, combinations formed in opposition to them, and these in turn attacked the Congress.[2] Among the Muslims in northern India, Sir Syed Ahmed Khan and his friends at Aligarh fiercely denounced the Congress. This prodded the ulema of Deoband, who had long criticised the theology of the Aligarh school, to come out in support of the Congress.[3] When the Congress met in Lucknow in 1899, it was attacked by the successful taluqdars headed by the Raja of Mahmudabad, but it won the ardent support of a faction descended from the dispossessed Oudh royal family led by Nawab Ali Mahomed Khan Bahadur.[4] Brahmin participation in the Congress in Maharashtra led to

partition of Bengal see Resolution IX, *INC 1905*, Resolution XIV, *INC 1904*, Resolution XII, *INC 1905*, Resolution VI, *INC 1906*.

[1] For example, the Punjab Land Alienation Bill was an attempt to stop the transfer of land from agricultural castes to trading castes. Khatris, Aggarwals and Aroras had, during the eighteen-nineties, borne the brunt of a whole range of government legislation aimed at them in particular. See N. G. Barrier, *The Punjab Alienation of Land Bill of 1900* (Duke University Commonwealth-Studies Center, 1966).

[2] Seal, *The emergence of Indian nationalism*, pp. 328–9.

[3] *Ibid.* p. 337; Ziya-ul-Hasan Faruqi, *The Deoband School and the demand for Pakistan* (London, 1963), pp. 43–5.

[4] One consequence was that out of 789 delegates, 313 were Muslims, mostly from Lucknow. Appendix I, *INC 1899*. See also *Tribune*, 7 December 1899, 9 December 1899, 12 December 1899, and 19 December 1899. This faction, which later

The Indian National Congress

its being condemned by some early non-Brahmin leaders as an engine of Brahminical despotism.[1]

As Congress became more important so it came to be a forum for rivalries between regions, between social groups within them, and among politicians themselves. Congress had opened up new opportunities for political manoeuvring. Obviously, these alliances did not remain constant. As the local situation changed so did the attitude of local groups towards the all-India movement. And similarly, changes within the all-India movement could turn allies into enemies and critics into friends. The permutations and combinations of support were without number.

A clear example of the temporary nature of political loyalty comes from the Punjab. Those Punjabi Hindus who had been supporters of the Congress at the turn of the century came out against it in 1909. In that year the Congress leaders accepted the communal arrangement in the Morley-Minto legislative councils reform. This worked to the disadvantage of some Punjabi Hindus, and, although the previous year they had invited the Congress to Lahore, they campaigned against the 'chimerical and unpractical ideal' of a secular all-India organisation: in other words they attacked the very basis of Congress. Lal Chand wrote

> A person who believes in the Indian ideal would subordinate the Hindu interests as of secondary importance, and this has actually happened in the conduct of Congress leaders ... those who believe in the Hindu ideal must subordinate the Indian as of secondary significance and lend their support to it so far only as it does not militate against the real Hindu interests.[2]

By the end of the nineteenth century the all-India organisation had fought its first battle for survival and in varying degrees

organised the Shia College, continued to support the Congress during the first three decades of the twentieth century. I am indebted to Dr F. C. R. Robinson for this information.

[1] Seal, *The emergence of Indian nationalism*, p. 241, D. Keer, *Mahatma Jotirao Phooley: father of our social revolution* (Bombay, 1964), pp. 219–21; *Dinbandhu*, 30 January 1887, 11 December 1887, 14 October 1888, 20 October 1888, RNP (Bombay) 1887 and 1888. The Din Bandhu Sabha held a meeting in Poona on 19 December 1889 at which 'Objection was taken to the National Congress shortly to be held in Bombay, which, the meeting was of opinion, in no way represented the poorer classes but the interests of the Brahmins only.' Para. 6 (Poona, 23 December 1889), Bombay Police Abstracts, vol. III, 1890, Bombay HFM. See also Para. 14 (Poona, 29 December 1895) and Para. 56 (Poona, 8 January 1896) *ibid.* vol. IX, 1896.   [2] *Panjabee*, 22 July 1909.

it had become more involved with the regions and localities. Yet each accession of strength brought with it problems of reconciliation and control. The leadership had to campaign on the basis of drawing support not only widely, but deeply, from Indian society. Its claims to represent even the poorest ryot were often factitious, but through local power structures and through the overlaying of one interest upon another, people were associated with the Congress who did not attend its meetings and who would have found its resolutions incomprehensible. Aswini Kumar Dutt, a prominent figure in Bakarganj district in east Bengal, brought to the third Congress a bundle of over 45,000 signatures supporting legislative council reform. In a speech lauding the common sense of the common people, he pointed out that most of the names had been collected by touring among the Muslim and Chandal peasantry who were often bound by social, ritual and economic ties to the Bengali Congressmen.[1] In northern India the Congress was greatly strengthened by its ambiguous association with Hindu revivalism and with the cow-protection movements. The patrons and organisers of religious, cultural and caste associations sometimes in other capacities also supported the Congress. When they did, their publicists campaigned on all issues at once. Thus before the Allahabad Congress in 1888 'itinerant swamis alluded to the Congress, and ... in turn Congress stump-orators used the appeal to the cow'.[2] Throughout its history in northern India the Congress was able to attract such Hindu religious elements; yet at the same time it retained the support and active participation of many social groups in the area to whom Hindu orthodoxy in its several manifestations was an anathema. In Maharashtra, Tilak combined his agitation for the Congress programme with festivals in honour of Ganpati and Shivaji, and with a campaign against social reform. The relationship between them was again ambiguous, but in this way people without an interest in the Congress became momentarily attached to it.

While these connections did not bring regular mass support

[1] *INC 1887*, p. 102.
[2] C. A. Bayly, 'The development of political organisation in the Allahabad locality, 1880–1925" (D. Phil. thesis, Oxford, 1970), pp. 245–6, and *passim*. See also, *idem*, 'Patrons and politics in northern India', *Modern Asian Studies*, vol. 7, no. 3 (1973).

to the Congress, there could be at a particular place and at a particular time a temporary fusion of interests resulting in a widespread agitation. The significant fact is not that support of this kind was occasional in nature or that it rapidly broke down (for this is true of every supra-local agitation in Indian history from the mutiny to civil disobedience), but that the Congress could, and did, draw upon support from deep in Indian society, and that this was a feature of the movement from the earliest times. The followers it won at two or three stages removed, however, as the extremists' campaign in east Bengal or the non-cooperation movement were to show, were unpredictable and difficult to control.[1]

As a political organisation the early Congress was thus a curious amalgam of strengths and weaknesses. Every year it met to present demands to the government, yet it had no means of forcing the government to concede them. It remained closely tied to a few local political associations, it had no independent finance, and only rudimentary organisation. But the Congress had also displayed mercurial qualities. It had proved flexible and adaptable. It had a capacity for gliding over anomalies. Since the movement was continually being re-formed, even with the same participants, the mistakes it made were conveniently forgotten. Its successes, however, became enshrined in myth and gave substance to the Congress. By the end of the nineteenth century it was clear that the whole was greater than the sum of its parts. The Congress was beginning to exert an independent influence on Indian politics. By providing a centre for them where none existed before, the Congress had fundamentally altered the rules by which Indian politics were played. The way was open for the emergence of all-India leaders – politicians who were, perhaps, not in themselves powerful in an accepted sense – who could rise to influence through the Congress itself. If it was not possible to build up a power-base from the localities, it was now possible to transcend them and work outwards from the centre.

The men who composed this political elite at any time in the

[1] On this point see, for example, G. Johnson, 'Indian politics 1888–1908' (Ph.D. thesis, Cambridge, 1967), pp. 238 ff; W. F. Crawley, 'Kisan Sabhas and agrarian revolt in the United Provinces 1920 to 1921', *Modern Asian Studies*, vol. 5, no. 2 (1971), 95–109.

history of the Congress were few in number, and although they might represent powerful interests, or have been thrust forward by social upheaval, once they became involved in national politics it was the way in which they reacted to each other that mattered most. The patterns of all-India politics were made by a handful of men in constant tension with one another, and the continual struggle for recognition and for the maintenance of prestige and position in national affairs was conducted within a small arena. As in other societies, high politics were 'primarily a matter of rhetoric and manoeuvre'.[1] Each politician had to build up his own cause, to create his own catch-calls, and to stake his claims for leadership. While he would constantly appeal – by speeches, by pamphleteering, and by his actions – to supporters outside the closed circle in which he moved, it was recognition of his position within the political elite that was at once his most valuable and his most vulnerable political asset.

In the India of the later nineteenth and early twentieth centuries there were severe restraints placed on those who sought national leadership. There was very little scope within the system itself for fundamental change, for if once the rather precise functions of the Congress were called into question then the movement itself was doomed. It was a situation in which even the most radical critic or the most reckless intriguer would accept limitations on what he might do to win power. No one could afford to see the system, and with it the prizes, disappear. The rhetoric of nationalism in India thus seems often flat and hollow. There appears an excess of casuistry and a seemingly indiscriminate quality about the ideologies the politicians preached. Moreover, there was an anxious grasping of political cliché and a constant appeal to uncontroversial symbols to conceal the great gulfs opening between men and interests and threatening to destroy the ground on which they stood. The slogans and the symbols (such as 'boycott', 'swaraj', 'self-help', 'khadi' or the Gandhi cap) were often capable of many interpretations and were in themselves innocuous. Their function was to provide a point at which all could rally, no matter how fierce the internal wrangling or how strong the centrifugal forces.

There was a further difficulty facing Congress politicians. In

---

[1] M. Cowling, *The Impact of Labour 1920–1924: the beginning of modern British politics* (Cambridge, 1971), p. 4.

such a loosely organised body there were problems in establishing leadership, but even greater ones in discrediting or displacing it. Since the Congress existed to present unanimous demands to government, and since its purpose was to impose unity on the political society of India, it was virtually impossible to create a viable opposition group within the movement itself. No matter how strong the personal antipathies, or how hard the bargaining, the compromise and the reconciliation were everything. Hence, if the organisation was to survive, there was a need to ritualise, and so to neutralise, the rivalries within it. It was essential to make sure that the tensions between the politicians and what they stood for did not destroy the movement. Since the Congress existed for a particular purpose, and since the real differences between political interests could be considerable, the contestants would seize on apparently trivial issues to test their relative strengths. The precise wording of resolutions would become matters of major controversy; who should be president of the annual session would be decided not on the basis of personal qualities but as an indication of where the balance lay among the leaders themselves. There was, from the beginning, an accepted convention that in all-India politics the real battles were fought at one stage removed.

These general propositions are best considered by reference to political events themselves. The vicissitudes of the Congress during the first years of the twentieth century provide as clear an indication as possible of the validity of the arguments advanced so far. Between 1904 and 1908, the unanimity of the Congress was broken; Congressmen were divided into 'moderates' and 'extremists'; there were wordy disputes about the resolutions passed at the annual meetings, and a public divergence of opinion about their interpretation. The presidency and the place of meeting were hotly contested. The established leaders came under fire, and the Congress became more active and agitated than it had ever been before.

This confusion had several interesting consequences. The most important was that the Congress survived. Not only did it survive, but in the process it began to develop a more formal structure and a clearer identity that ultimately strengthened the all-India movement. It was obviously necessary to establish better means of controlling and disciplining Congress supporters.

But, by setting up a new constitution, the Congress leaders not only pointed towards more effective ways of organising their party, but they also provided more formal means for changing the leadership itself: with the establishment of new procedures it became possible, in a way in which it had not been possible earlier, for politicians to work their way to power in the Congress by capturing vital parts of it. A further important change was that some of the main participants in the struggle were temporarily driven out of the Congress. Congressmen had come to realise that, if the all-India movement was to have a proper life of its own, it might be necessary to give it a less amorphous character and that coherence might be achieved by exclusion as well as by compromise.

Now the divisions of 1904–8 would not have occurred in precisely the way in which they did, had the principal politicians involved not all come from the Bombay Presidency and had they not there been engaged in controversy for over twenty years. The figures around whom the action was played were two Poona men: Bal Gangadhar Tilak and Gopal Krishna Gokhale. Both had been involved in personal quarrels in the 1880s, and the 1890s had seen each develop his own style of politics and build up his own political reputation. By 1900 the two men, and the interests behind them, found no further room for manoeuvre within the context of provincial politics. The more fluid political situation that developed from 1904 allowed the Bombay politicians to resume their struggles, but within an all-India context. Gokhale then played from a position of strength: he and his friends constituted the accepted Congress leadership and they controlled its embryonic organisation. But Tilak found that, for a variety of reasons, he was able to win support for a campaign against Gokhale from discontented elements in nearly every province, and from almost all the politicians in Bengal. He attempted, therefore, to bring a grand alliance together within the Congress to challenge and oppose his provincial rivals. The division in the Congress turned upon Bombay, and it is to developments in that Presidency in the later nineteenth century that we must look for the background of the 'ignoble fratricidal strife'[1] that preoccupied Indian politicians in the first decade of the twentieth century.

[1] Mudholkar to Gokhale, 15 October 1906, Gokhale Papers, Reel 8, NAI.

2

THE POLITICS OF WESTERN INDIA IN THE LATER NINETEENTH CENTURY

In the later nineteenth century, Poona, the former capital of the Mahratta empire, established for itself a reputation for liveliness in public affairs. Men from that city exercised a disproportionate share of influence in the politics, education, social reform, journalism and literature of western India, and many Poona leaders achieved recognition throughout the subcontinent. Although reduced since the defeat of the Peshwa to being a mere divisional headquarters in the Bombay Presidency, Poona's influence continued to flow beyond the formal administrative boundaries of that Presidency into Berar and into parts of the Central Provinces and Hyderabad. To all those who spoke Marathi it remained 'the hub of Maharashtra'[1] and with the revival of Maharashtrian aspirations it was to Poona that the inhabitants of the Deccan looked for a lead.

Poona politicians were among the first to set themselves up as spokesmen for India, and like leaders in the other seaboard presidencies they were among the first to found modern political associations and to consider carrying their campaign to the all-India level. But from the time of the first embassies to the court of the Peshwa, the British realised that in Poona they were dealing with proud men, past masters at the art of intrigue, and puffed up with political ambition. The Bengali, even when he turned to throwing bombs, might be dismissed as a simple baboo 'full of inappropriate words and phrases'[2] but so harm-

---

[1] *Census of India 1921* (Bombay, 1922), vol. VIII, pt i, p. 75. For a concise description of the political configuration of western India in this period see Seal, *The emergence of Indian nationalism*, pp. 64–93 and G. Johnson, 'Chitpavan Brahmins and politics in western India in the late nineteenth and early twentieth centuries', in E. R. Leach and S. N. Mukherjee (eds.), *Elites in south Asia* (Cambridge, 1970), pp. 95–7, and the map facing p. 266.

[2] G. H. Aberigh-Mackay, *Twenty-one days in India* (8th edition, London, 1910), p. 41.

less an epithet was never applied to Maharashtrians. There was hardness about the men of the Deccan, and an apparent reluctance to accept the permanence of British government in India that always disquieted the rulers.[1] 'Never have I known in India a national and political ambition so continuous, so enduring, so far reaching, so utterly impossible for us to satisfy as that of the Brahmins of western India', Sir Richard Temple wrote when he was Governor of Bombay.[2] Maharashtrians appeared to believe that 'the Hindoo policy ... will one day reassert itself over the white conquest'.[3] Temple described the state of feeling in his province by asserting that:

> Throughout the whole of the Deccan, the mind of the people is ... affected by the past associations of Maratha rule, which, so far from being forgotten, are better remembered than would ordinarily be expected, and by the long-retained memory of the Maratha uprising against the Mahomedans ... This memory constantly suggests the analogy between the position of the British and that of the Moguls in the Deccan. There is a general tendency also to criticise to an extreme degree, not only the proceedings of Government and its officers, but also the national conduct and policy of the British in respect to India.[4]

Temple's observations came in the wake of a minor revolt in the Deccan led by a former government clerk, Wasudeo Bal-

---

[1] Lord Minto's private secretary, for example, wrote in 1906 'The Bengalis are a low-lying people in a low-lying land with the intellect of a Greek and the grit of a rabbit. It's the Mussulman with the green flag calling for blood and the Mahratta Brahmin – *not* the Mahratta but the [Mahratta] Brahmin – whom we have to watch.' Dunlop Smith's diary, 10 September 1906, quoted in M. Gilbert (ed.), *Servant of India: a study of imperial rule from 1905–1910 as told through the correspondence and diaries of Sir James Dunlop Smith private secretary to the Viceroy* (London, 1966), p. 56. The word in italics is underlined in the original. The word [Mahratta] does not appear in the published version of Dunlop Smith's diary although it exists in the original.

[2] Temple to Lytton, 9 July 1879, quoted in Seal, *The emergence of Indian nationalism*, p. 234.

[3] *Ibid.*

[4] Minute by Temple, 31 July 1879, quoted *ibid.* Independent testimony of this feeling is provided by the Russian, I. P. Minayeff, who visited Poona in 1880. He recorded that in that city there were 'numerous legends of Maratha rule. There is hardly a house worth the name where there is no legend or some sort of link with the recent past ... Strong, though not active disaffection with the British government ... Local Maratha patriotism is given expression to even in literary enterprises – songs about the grandeur of the times of the Peshwas and different family chronicles etc. are collected and published here.' I. P. Minayeff, *Travels in and diaries of India and Burma* (translated by H. Sanyal with S. Bhattacharya and S. C. Sen Gupta, Calcutta, no date), pp. 54, 92.

1 Gopal Krishna Gokhale 1908

2 Bal Gangadhar Tilak 1900

3a Pherozeshah M. Mehta 1911

3b Dadabhai Naoroji *circa* 1906

3c Lajpat Rai, B. G. Tilak, Bipin Chandra Pal 1907

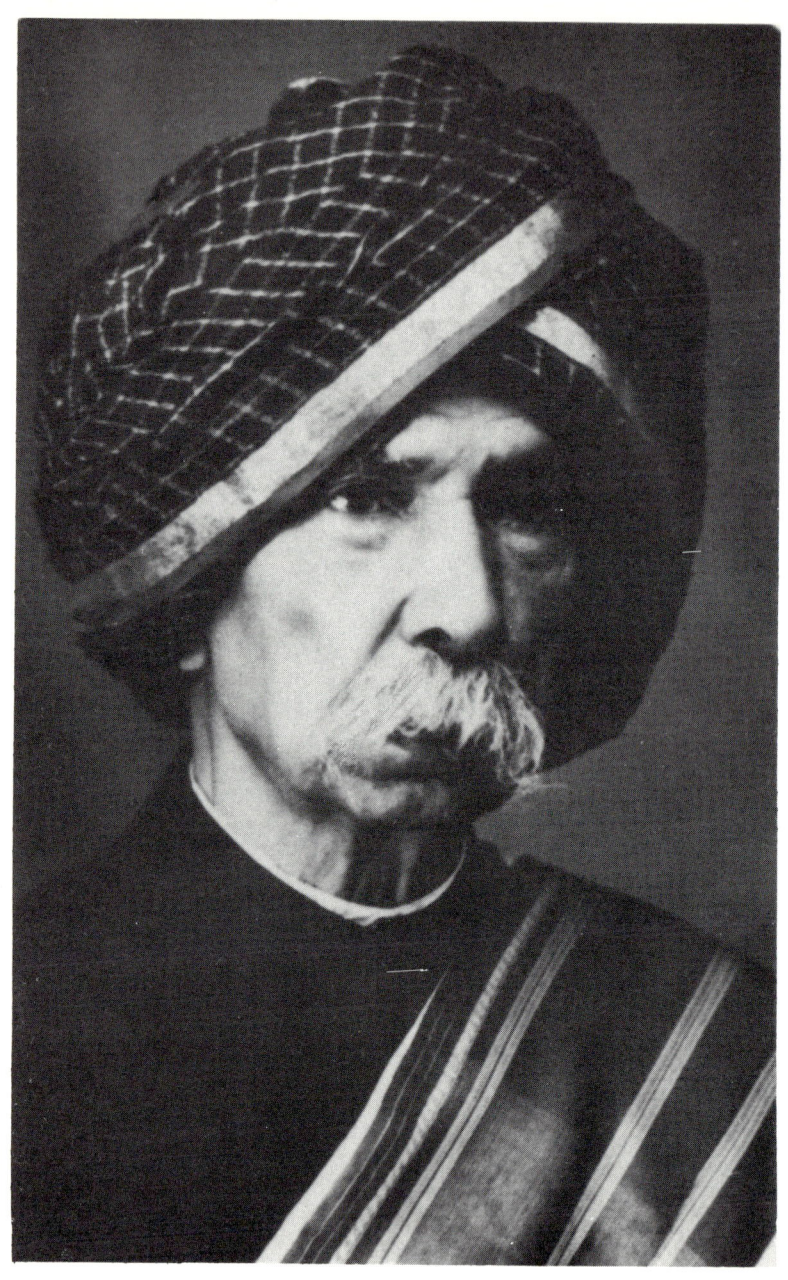

4 G. S. Khaparde

The politics of western India in the later nineteenth century

want Phadke.[1] Although it was easily contained, the sympathy expressed for Phadke and his cause by the Maharashtrian press served only to confirm the government's deepest suspicions about the rumblings against British rule in the Deccan.[2]

Nearly all the Poona leaders with whom we are concerned were Brahmins and, moreover, a particular kind of Brahmin: Tilak, Gokhale, and many of the prominent writers, educationalists, social reformers, civil servants, lawyers and journalists were Chitpavan Brahmins. In some respects this fact had important political consequences; in others it did not matter at all. But there can be no proper grasp of political development in western India in the later nineteenth century without some consideration of the social position of the men we are studying and some discussion of the way in which caste descriptions intruded into politics.

Despite Maharashtrian historical consciousness, hardly anything is known about Chitpavan Brahmins before the eighteenth century. Mythical accounts of their origin, their fair complexions, and their large settlements along the coast, particularly in Ratnagiri, suggest that the Chitpavans may have come to Maharashtra by sea, possibly from northern India.[3] They were much less numerous in Maharashtra than the Deshastha Brahmins who composed the traditional religious elite of the region,[4] returning only 113,605 people at the 1901

[1] For Phadke's revolt see *Source material for a history of the freedom movement in India (collected from Bombay government records)* (Bombay, 1957), vol. I, pp. 73–129; Seal, *The emergence of Indian nationalism*, pp. 234–5; V. S. Joshi, *Vasudeo Balvant Phadke: first Indian rebel against British rule* (Bombay, 1959).
[2] The Marathi press praised Phadke for his patriotism and for his ideals, but argued that his method of implementing them was unrealistic. See the extracts printed in *Source material for a history of the freedom movement*, vol. I, pp. 126–9 – especially those quoted from *Shivaji* and *Deccan Star*.
[3] V. N. Mandlik, 'Preliminary observations on a document giving an account of the establishment of a new village named Muruda, in Southern Konkana', *Journal of the Bombay Branch of the Royal Asiatic Society*, vol. VIII (1864–66), 3; J. Wilson, *Indian caste* (Bombay, Edinburgh & London, 1877), vol. II, pp. 20–1; I. Karve, 'The Parasurama myth', *Journal of the University of Bombay*, vol. I, i (July 1932), 115–39; *idem*, 'Ethnic affinities of the Chitpavans', *ibid.* vol. I, iv (January 1933), 383–400; *idem*, 'Ethnic affinities of the Chitpavans (II)', *ibid.* vol. II, i (July 1933), 132–58.
[4] As the original Brahmin inhabitants of Maharashtra the Deshasthas were held in greatest esteem and considered themselves superior to other Brahmins. J. Grant Duff, *History of the Mahrattas* (Indian reprint, Bombay, 1863), vol. I, p. 8; *Gazetteer of the Bombay Presidency: Poona* (Bombay, 1885), vol. XVIII, pt. i, p. 101; R. E. Enthoven, *The tribes and castes of Bombay* (Bombay, 1920), vol. I, pp. 244–5. From

census.¹ Almost half lived in the Konkan, the narrow coastal strip running from Bombay to Goa.² But the original families had settled the least fertile part of the coast and from the first, while preserving their connection with the Konkan, they migrated eastwards spreading 'sparsely perhaps but effectively over the best part of Western India'.³ Proverbially 'a very frugal, pushing, active, intelligent, well-taught, astute, self-confident, and overbearing class' Chitpavans followed 'almost all callings and generally with success'.⁴ In the Konkan, the Chitpavans were cultivators, priests and traders. Those who migrated to the Desh did so to become administrators, diplomats and soldiers. In contrast to their caste-fellows on the coast, and unlike the Deshastha throughout the region, Chitpavan Brahmins in the Deccan were concentrated in towns. Almost 80 per cent of those living in Poona district lived in the sub-division containing Poona city, and the same pattern of settlement occurs in other Deccan districts.⁵

Chitpavan Brahmins were conscious of a common bond. Partly this sprang from a recognition of their superior status in society, and partly from their peculiar ties of kinship. The caste was divided into fourteen exogamous patrilineal sibships called gotras. Thirteen of these gotras were grouped into six gatas or ganas, five of two gotras each and one with three gotras. Families belonging to gotras within the same gata were not permitted to intermarry, but families belonging to the fourteenth gotra were allowed to marry into any of the other gotras,

the thirteenth century many of the region's literary and religious leaders were Deshastha Brahmins. Most of the village priests and accountants, or *kulkarnis*, belonged to this caste. For an ethnographic account of Deshastha Brahmins, see *Gazetteer of the Bombay Presidency: Kolhapur* (Bombay, 1886), vol. XXIV, pp. 43–60.

[1] *Census of India 1901* (Bombay, 1902), vol. IX-B, table XIII. There were five times the number of Deshastha Brahmins in Maharashtra. *Ibid.*
[2] Particularly in Ratnagiri district, *Ibid.*
[3] Temple to Lytton, 9 July 1879. G. R. G. Hambly, 'Mahratta nationalism before Tilak: two unpublished letters of Sir Richard Temple on the state of the Bombay Deccan, 1879', *Journal of the Royal Central Asian Society*, vol. XLIX (1962), 154.
[4] *Gazetteer of the Bombay Presidency: Ratnagiri and Savantyadi* (Bombay, 1880), vol. X, p. 112.
[5] In Ahmadnagar 62% lived in the Nagar subdivision; in Nasik 60·5% lived in Nasik subdivision; 41% lived in Sholapur subdivision; 30% lived in Alibag in Kolaba district; in Satara district 27·5% lived in the Wai sub-division, 27% in Tasgaon, *Census of India 1901*, vol. IX-B, Table XIII.

The politics of western India in the later nineteenth century

thus knitting together the entire caste.[1] However, despite the close connections of blood – or perhaps because of them – individual Chitpavans did not scruple to struggle towards success in bitter competition with caste-fellows and kin. The quarrels between the Patwardhans during the early nineteenth century were notorious,[2] and a fierce independence of opinion and action was a characteristic Chitpavan attribute.[3] There was no recognised Chitpavan aristocracy to dictate the way in which the caste should behave. No family or group of families wielded either hereditary or elected power within the caste, and there were no caste organisations as such. Unlike the Gujarati trading castes, or some of the lower Maharashtrian castes, the Chitpavans had no caste panchayats or formal system of organised interference in domestic matters. Legitimate caste leadership was not fixed; there were no firm guidelines about how their social life was to be conducted, and so competition for leadership among themselves was a permanent feature of Chitpavan society. Their chief religious authority was the Shankaracharya of Sankeshwar, who deputed agents in each town to arbitrate in caste disputes. However, such cases were dealt with at public meetings which could be called by any adult Brahmin, and the decision was determined, subject to an appeal to the Shankaracharya, by a majority of the votes of those present.[4] In practice this usually meant that neither party accepted an authoritative decision in the end, and each faction, based on personal or family loyalties, barred social intercourse with the other as a matter of course. Such a caste organisation left a wide area of discretion open to individual members and the open dissension among Chitpavan Brahmins must be largely

[1] M. L. P. Patterson, 'Chitpavan Brahman family histories: source for a study of social structure and social change in Maharashtra', M. Singer & B. S. Cohn (eds.), *Structure and change in Indian society* (Chicago, 1968), pp. 407–9; I. Karve, 'What is caste?' (1), *Economic Weekly*, x (1958), 135.
[2] K. Ballhatchet, *Social policy and social change in Western India 1817–1830* (London, 1957), pp. 52, 56.
[3] I. Karve, *Journal of the University of Bombay*, I, i (July 1932), 118–19.
[4] *Census of India 1911* (Bombay 1912), vol. VII, pt i, p. 245; A. Steele, *The law and custom of Hindoo castes within the Dekhun provinces subject to the Presidency of Bombay, chiefly affecting civil suits* (new ed. London, 1868), pp. 82–3. For an account of the settlement of a caste dispute using this machinery see C. V. Vaidya, *On the history of Hindu social reform agitation and the proper method of carrying it on* (Poona, 1890), pp. 11–13.

ascribed to the very great degree of freedom from caste restraints and caste authority they enjoyed.

Chitpavan Brahmins became powerful in western India with the rise of the Mahratta empire. But they did so as individuals and not as members of a particular caste. Indian society has always provided plenty of opportunity to scale the ladders of success for people prepared to change their customary occupation or to move their habitual place of residence. Since successful men have sometimes helped their immediate kin or used new-found wealth and power for the advantage of relatives, such social change in India has often been interpreted as the rise and fall of whole castes or sub-castes. But this is to falsify the analysis and to give undue importance to the role of caste affiliation in social mobility.[1]

In the later seventeenth century some men, who were also Chitpavan Brahmins, were employed as clerks and messengers by the Mahratta chiefs;[2] from the appointment in 1713 of Balaji Vishvanath Bhat as Peshwa, Chitpavan Brahmins found their way into all departments of government. They settled in Poona and Satara; they followed Mahratta princes to Nagpur, Baroda and Indore. In the south, bordering on the Karnatak, the Patwardhans, a Chitpavan family, established themselves in Sangli, Miraj, Kurundvad and Jamkhandi.[3] As Poona under the Peshwa became the mainspring of the Mahratta confederacy, Chitpavan Brahmins used political influence to strengthen their position in the Deccan: the Peshwa rewarded his kin and dependents with tax reliefs and grants of land.[4] During the eighteenth century, individual Chitpavans emerged as Indian

---

[1] This important point has been greatly clarified by Christopher Bayly, 'The political development of the Allahabad locality', and by David Washbrook's review of R. L. Hardgrave, *The Nadars of Tamilnad: the political culture of a community in change* (Berkeley and Los Angeles, 1969), in *Modern Asian Studies*, vol. 5 (1971), 278–83; and *idem*, 'Politics in the Madras Presidency 1880–1920', (Trinity College, Fellowship dissertation, Cambridge, 1971).

[2] J. Grant Duff, *History of the Mahrattas*, vol. I, p. 8. The employment of Chitpavan Brahmins in these particular roles is itself significant: as men seeking their fortunes and willing to travel anywhere they made ideal brokers in the confused politicking of the Mahratta chiefs because they seemed to pose so little threat to the parties involved. However, as is often the case, the impartial go-between could use his position to become a powerful arbitrator.

[3] *Gazetteer of the Bombay Presidency: Kolhapur*, p. 324.

[4] M. L. P. Patterson, 'A preliminary study of the Brahman versus non-Brahman conflict in Maharashtra' (M.A. thesis, Pennsylvania, 1952), p. 82.

princes, as administrators and statesmen, as diplomats, as landholders, bankers and merchants, and as commanders of the Peshwa's army.

The defeat of the Peshwa by the British altered the situation in the Deccan. It destroyed the patronage of the old ruling families and it deprived the Chitpavans of any special advantage that membership of their caste might bring. The British also introduced new forms of government, established new rules for recruitment into its services and set up new norms of political behaviour. But Chitpavans had first made their mark in Maharashtra by their adaptability, particularly in employment, and by their willingness to learn new skills.[1] Literacy in particular, which had won them such a powerful place in the eighteenth-century governments, continued to be their most valuable asset. Albeit in open competition with other people, Chitpavans found that their command of reading and writing not only enabled them to hold their own, but enabled some of them to exploit to the full entirely new fields opened up by the new regime.

The most favourable opportunities came with the expansion of government in the nineteenth century and with the rapid development of the professions. As the administration became more complex it employed more civil servants; as it became more effective it employed more revenue and judicial officers. With the imposition of new legal procedures and the establishment of new law courts came the growth of the legal profession. The setting up of printing presses coupled with the increase of those able to read brought journalists and writers. Feeding into all these literate pursuits was a growing number of schools, colleges, and the university of Bombay, each requiring in turn teachers and administrators. Maharashtrian Brahmins were among those who moved with determination and speed to take advantage of the new openings. They not only dominated the schools and colleges in Poona, but those in Bombay city as well: Maharashtra could justly be proud of its high proportion of literate people.[2]

[1] Miss Patterson has given a very thorough account of the way in which Chitpavans diversified their occupations during both the Mahratta and British periods. M. L. P. Patterson, 'Changing patterns of occupation among Chitpavan Brahmans', *Indian Economic and Social History Review*, vol. VII (1970), 375–96.

[2] Seal, *The emergence of Indian nationalism*, pp. 84–93; Johnson, 'Chitpavan Brahmins', in E. R. Leach and S. N. Mukherjee (eds.), *Elites in south Asia*, pp. 101–3.

Brahmins were particularly prominent in government service in western India. Deshastha Brahmins, being more numerous, probably held a greater number of offices, particularly in the lower levels of the bureaucracy and in village administration, but the Chitpavans had, during the nineteenth century, made their preserve all the posts where knowledge of English was required.[1] The key position in the Bombay Service was that of mamlatdar. Brahmins, most of them Chitpavans, occupied over three-quarters of the places in this grade.[2] The Public Service Commission found that in Bombay Presidency 41·25 per cent of the deputy collectors were Brahmins.[3] Moreover, while the most senior administrative posts fell to the Englishmen in the nineteenth century, the superiority Chitpavans derived from their knowledge of English told in the higher ranks of the judicial service where Indians could reach the top: in 1886 thirty-three of the 104 subordinate judges in the Bombay presidency were Chitpavan Brahmins.[4]

English literacy gave the Chitpavans a strong position in the administration and professions, but literacy in the vernacular gave them a virtual monopoly of the new methods of communication in Maharashtra. The growth of Marathi literature as shown in Tables 1 and 2, and in particular the growth of Marathi journalism, had the effect of knitting together the centres of the Marathi-speaking country in a way which had not been possible when the spoken rather than the printed word was the main means of communication. It meant, moreover, that successful writers could play upon and give expression to widely held sentiments in quite a different way. By the later nineteenth century, 'access to the flow of information in the rural areas was no longer completely dependent upon participation in personal networks of relationships. New formal communicative institutions provided opportunities for new social,

[1] E. E. McDonald, 'The modernizing of communication: vernacular publishing in nineteenth century Maharashtra', *Asian Survey*, vol. VIII, no. 7 (July 1968), 596.
[2] For a list of mamlatdars serving in the Central division of Bombay see 'Return giving copies of, or extracts from, correspondence with the governments of India and Bombay as to the mamlatdars incriminated in the Crawford case', PP 1890, LIV, pp. 152–61. A clear majority of these officers were Brahmins. For the exact proportion serving as mamlatdars in the whole Presidency see *Report of the Public Service Commission. Proceedings relating to the Bombay Presidency (including Sind)* (Calcutta, 1887), vol. IV, pt i, section B, p. 91.
[3] *Ibid.* [4] *Ibid.*

intellectual and economic ties between literate groups in the regional centers and scattered throughout the hinterland.'[1] At first these structural changes in communication worked to the advantage of those already literate: the old literate castes

TABLE 1. *Growth in numbers of authors writing in Marathi, 1800–1918*

	1800–18	1818–36	1836–56	1856–66	1866–76	1876–96	1896–1912	1912–18
Poets	2	0	1	3	11	41	41	45
Dramatists	0	0	2	3	5	68	36	45
Novelists	0	0	0	0	18	50	19	74
Prose writers	3	6	7	17	25	88	167	162
Christian writers	2	0	3	2	9	13	2	2
Totals	7	6	13	25	68	260	265	328

SOURCE: Bhate, *A history of modern Marathi literature, 1800–1938* (Mahad, 1939), p. 512.

TABLE 2. *Growth of Marathi and English–Marathi newspapers in the Bombay Presidency*

Year	Marathi		English–Marathi	
	Number	Circulation	Number	Circulation
1887	58	19,696	10	7,775
1892	59	26,875	12	10,565
1897	82	48,960	14	16,250
1902	60	53,004	12	11,355
1907	67	63,937	13	15,610
1912	48	48,457	6	8,850
1917	34	58,293	8	9,050
1921	64	110,415	9	10,350

SOURCE: Calculated from lists of newspapers, RNP (Bombay), January 1887, 1892, 1897, 1902, 1907, 1912, 1917, October 1921.

manned the new printing presses. Out of 128 nineteenth-century Marathi authors listed by G. C. Bhate in his *History of Modern Marathi Literature*, 114 were Brahmins and 10 were Prabhus. Only four came from outside the traditionally literate groups.[2] Of the Brahmins, some 75 were Chitpavans.[3] The

[1] E. E. McDonald, 'The modernization of communication', *Asian Survey*, vol. VIII, no. 7 (July 1968), 606.
[2] *Ibid.* p. 604.   [3] *Ibid.* p. 604.

Bombay government's caste-analysis of newspaper editors reveals a similar picture. Brahmins account for about two-thirds of all editors listed between 1901 and 1921, and throughout these years, as Table 3 indicates, Chitpavan Brahmins never accounted for less than a quarter of vernacular editors and they usually made up a third or more.[1]

TABLE 3. *Caste of editors of Marathi newspapers in the Bombay Presidency*

(a) *Caste of editors of Marathi newspapers*

Caste	1902 No.	%	1907 No.	%	1912 No.	%	1917 No.	%	1921 No.	%
Chitpavans	23	38·3	29	41·4	16	32·7	12	35·2	19	29·7
Other Brahmins	26	43·3	30	42·9	19	38·8	14	41·2	22	34·4
Total Brahmins	49	81·6	59	84·3	35	71·5	26	76·4	41	64·1
Non-Brahmins	11	18·4	11	15·7	14	28·5	8	23·6	23	35·9
Total editors	60	100	70	100	49	100	34	100	64	100

(b) *Proportion of circulation of Marathi newspapers controlled by different castes*

	1902 Circulation	%	1912 Circulation	%	1921 Circulation	%
Chitpavans	32,900	62·1	25,807	53·3	57,685	52·2
Other Brahmins	17,779	33·5	8,500	17·5	28,655	26·0
Total Brahmins	50,679	95·6	34,307	70·8	86,340	78·2
Non-Brahmins	2,325	4·4	14,150	29·2	24,075	21·8
Total circulation	53,004	100	48,457	100	110,415	100

SOURCE: Calculated from lists of newspapers, RNP (Bombay), January 1902, 1907, 1912, 1917, October 1921.

In political terms these literate Maharashtrians possessed some tangible assets. They were spread throughout the region, yet linked by ties of kin and interest and holding common sentiments. They were a group very easily organised for certain kinds of political activity. Moreover, by the end of the nineteenth century, Poona had established an almost unchallengeable hold over the Maharashtrian press. The dynamic professionalism of Poona editors and publishers not only tended to

[1] *Ibid.* p. 604.

put the district broadsheets out of business, but their papers set a model which was simply copied in the remaining independent centres.¹ Consequently, a striking similarity of news and unanimity of opinion ran along the webs of literacy. The wide distribution of relatives and of service and professional colleagues meant that public meetings could be quickly and simultaneously held in several towns. Owing to the free-floating nature of the Chitpavan literate elite, its members could continue to act as brokers between a large number of other Indian interests, and as intermediaries between the Indian society and the government. Already by the 1870s and 1880s Poona Brahmins were building up a credible claim to be the representatives of public opinion in Maharashtra, and, as such, deserving of greater political benefits.

However, there were also constraints on the Poona politicians. Towards the end of the century opposition began to form to the influence of literate Maharashtrians. If rivals could make it appear that the leaders stood for no one other than a narrow group interest, the Chitpavans were very exposed, even though their success as individuals continued unabated. Their strengths also proved to be their weaknesses. Thinly spread and isolated in the towns and in offices, identifiable for the most part with a particular caste, enjoying near monopolies of education and public employment, they were particularly vulnerable to pressures from the government and from the rest of society.

Like the Bengali bhadralok, or the Kayasths and Muslims of north India, the Chitpavans of Bombay were extremely dependent upon government service for their livelihood. Therefore, whatever dreams of grandeur they might have had, there were limits to how far in practice they could alienate the government which was their greatest patron and benefactor. By the late nineteenth century the British were beginning to worry about becoming too dependent upon particular communities.

[1] Almost every district had its own newspaper, but few had a circulation of more than a hundred, and even fewer survived for very long. Among the Poona papers, *Kesari* was without doubt the most successful and the most widely read. S. M. Paranjpe's *Kal* also had its followers, but it was written in a much more Sanskritised Marathi and so had less popular appeal. The chief constable of a taluka in Satara district commented on the readers of *Kal* in his locality: 'it is chiefly Brahmans who read it, and only educated Brahmans, as men not well educated cannot understand its style'. Para. 424(b) (Satara, 24 May 1904), Bombay Police Abstracts, vol. XVII, 1904, Bombay HFM.

In Maharashtra, as elsewhere in India, the operations of the government itself had tended to make people more aware of the value of caste and communal links. The regime, riddled with sociologists, counted men by caste and distributed or withheld benefits according to its classification. Although the categories used in the census and in the administration reports were often the crudest approximations to the actual divisions of society as defined by ritual criteria or kinship terminology, men stepped forward to fill them in order to take advantage of public bounty.[1]

All over the continent, towards the end of the nineteenth century, the government attempted to break the hold of vested interests in the administration by changing the qualifications needed for office and the method of recruitment. Often these exercises were clearly intended to spread government patronage among more social groups. In Bengal, this policy meant employing more Muslims,[2] in the North-western Provinces and Oudh it meant employing fewer.[3] In the Punjab it meant discriminating against the literate trading groups,[4] in western India it meant being wary of the Chitpavans. For of all the service communities, they seemed the least pliable and the least dependable. As Temple had so forcibly put it 'They are inspired with national sentiment and with an ambition bounded only with the bounds of India itself. Nothing that we do now, by way of education, emolument, or advancement in the public service, at all *satisfies* the Chitpawuns.'[5] The moral was obvious for all to see: other people should be employed in preference to them.

Of course, as in other parts of India, the government's attempts to open up the administration meant little actual

[1] Again, this argument derives *inter alia* from the work of C. Bayly and D. Washbrook.
[2] See 'Memorandum by the Lieutenant-Governor of Bengal' in PP 1894, LX, pp. 93–4. See also the policy statements formulated for east Bengal in the papers included in the Home Establishments Deposit, December 1906, 6–9 and Home Establishments A, May 1907, 103, NAI.
[3] F. C. R. Robinson, 'Consultation and control: the United Provinces' government and its allies, 1860–1906', *Modern Asian Studies*, vol. 5 (1971), 321–4.
[4] N. G. Barrier, 'Punjab politics and the disturbances of 1907' (Ph.D. thesis, Duke University, 1966), *passim*.
[5] Temple to Lytton, 3 July 1879, quoted in G. R. G. Hambly, 'Mahratta nationalism before Tilak', *Journal of the Royal Central Asian Society*, vol. XLIX (1962), 154–5.

change in the social composition of the service (for literacy was still desirable in a civil servant and that restricted the government's choice to the educated), so in Bombay the government found that it could not do without the Brahmins.[1] Yet it became extremely sensitive to the potential threat they posed. Officers were frequently transferred from district to district so that they could not establish independent bases of local power; those regarded with suspicion might find themselves posted to remote parts of the Presidency with which they had no previous connection, and just promotion might be denied to them.[2] From the late 1870s, and particularly after an investigation into corrupt practices in the civil service in 1888,[3] the government of Bombay expressed openly hostility to Chitpavan Brahmins as a group.

Of course other interests in society were not slow to respond either to the changing structure of the government or to the

---

[1] Even those most hostile to Brahmins as a class saw that there were difficulties in doing without their services. The dilemma was that of reconciling the need to establish the public service 'on a basis of thorough efficiency' with a secondary aim of including in it 'the reasonable representation of important sections of the community'. Note by A. P. Macdonnell, 4 May 1894 (in a file considering the predominant share of government posts held by Brahmins in Bombay), Notes, Home Public A, June 1894, 245–51, NAI.

[2] As happened in the case of M. G. Ranade, see R. P. Tucker, 'The proper limits of agitation: the crisis of 1879–80 in Bombay Presidency', *Journal of Asian Studies*, vol. XXVIII, no. 2 (February 1969), 349–54.

[3] On 18 July 1888, Arthur Travers Crawford, the commissioner of the Central division, was arrested as he tried to leave Poona in disguise and later charged with bribery and corruption, indebtedness within his division, and disgraceful conduct in borrowing money from subordinates. The special commission of enquiry set up to investigate these charges cleared Crawford of bribery and corruption but found him guilty on the other counts. The government of Bombay held that the evidence showed that 'Mr Crawford did accept illegal gratifications for showing favours, or forbearing to show disfavour, in the exercise of his official functions'. Crawford was heavily in debt, and it was proved that between 12 February 1887 and 19 June 1888, his agents and immediate subordinates had managed to raise for him various sums amounting to Rs. 66,000. During the course of the enquiry, forty-two of the sixty-six mamlatdars serving under Crawford in the Central division were investigated. See 'Correspondence relating to the case of Mr Crawford C.M.G., of the Bombay Civil Service', PP 1889, LVIII, and 'Correspondence with the governments of India and Bombay as to the mamlatdars incriminated in the Crawford case', PP 1890, LIV. Crawford was dismissed from the service, and from an embittered retirement wrote an anti-Brahmin polemic entitled *Our troubles in Poona and the Deccan* (London, 1897). He was extravagant with public money as well as being reckless with his own: many of the grand building schemes in Bombay city were made possible by his lavish overspending of the corporation chest when he was commissioner there in the 1860s.

prejudices of its officers. Granted the known hostility in high government circles towards Brahmins, other groups would present themselves as deserving consideration because they were not Chitpavans. What could be simpler in Maharashtra then to mount a non-Brahmin campaign? Wrangles about ritual, and a persistent cultural anti-Brahminism were long-established features of Maharashtrian society.[1] The case for privileges for non-Brahmins on the make could be bolstered with emotive arguments about centuries of Brahmin oppression and religious intolerance. Perhaps a good way to get government money for your school, or a government post for your kin, would be to emphasise that you did not belong to superior social categories.

Jotirao Phule, the founder of the Satya Shodhak Samaj,[2] exhorted the Education Commission: 'Let there be schools for the Sudras in every village; but away with all Brahmin schoolmasters! The Sudras are the life and sinews of the country, and

[1] For example, the Satya Shodhak Samaj challenged Brahminical supremacy by preaching the fundamental equality of mankind, and it attempted to prove from Hindu scriptures themselves that there was no need for priestly mediation between man and god, and hence no need to employ Brahmins for the performance of religious rituals. Seal, *The emergence of Indian nationalism*, p. 241. Throughout the 1880s and 1890s reports came into police headquarters of lecturers touring Maharashtra urging that the services of Brahmins, particularly at marriage ceremonies, be given up. Although some of the speakers were members of the Satya Shodhak Samaj, the proposals met with approval from several caste-groups: Marathas, Kunbis, Malis, Kolis, and Sonars could all be found suggesting that members of their own castes be employed in ritual functions rather than Brahmins who had 'cheated them in many ways'. Para. 1375 (Thana, 4 October 1891), Bombay Police Abstracts, vol. IV, 1891, Bombay HFM. See also a report of a lecture advising Marathas not to use Brahmins for marriage ceremonies (no. 16 of 1888, para. 3 (Poona, 2 June 1888), *ibid.* vol. I); reports of marriage ceremonies in Savantvadi taking place without Brahmins (no. 18 of 1888, para. nil (Savantvadi, 16 June 1888), *ibid.*); lecturers touring Ahmadnagar and Sholapur advising kunbis not to employ Brahmins (no. 34 of 1888, para. 1 (Ahmadnagar, 6 October 1888), no. 35 of 1888, para. 2 (Sholapur, 13 October 1888), *ibid.*); for a meeting of Kolis, who discussed the question of reducing fees paid to Brahmins see para. 471 (Kolaba, 23 March 1892), *ibid.* vol. V, 1892; and also para. 1313 (Thana, 19 September 1892), para. 1487 (Thana, 16 October 1892), *ibid.*; para. 1164 (Kanara, 19 August 1895), *ibid.* vol. VIII; para. 1201 (Kanara, 2 September 1895), *ibid.*; para. 378 (Thana, 21 February 1897), *ibid.* vol. X, 1897; and para. 937 (SB Central Provinces, 6 December 1902), *ibid.* vol. XV, 1902.

[2] For Phule, and an account of the Satya Shodhak Samaj, one of western India's earliest and most active anti-Brahmin societies, see Seal, *The emergence of Indian nationalism*, pp. 240–2 and D. Keer, *Mahatma Jotirao Phooley: father of our social revolution* (Bombay, 1964).

it is to them alone, and not to the Brahmins, that the Government must ever look to tide them over their difficulties, financial as well as political.'[1] From demanding more places in schools it was a short step to demand more places in the administration and if the existing rules did not permit this then they would have to be changed. The editor of *Dinbandhu* told the Public Service Commission in 1887 that so far their control of English education had enabled Brahmins to monopolise all government offices:

Their chief object is to keep the masses in ignorance, and impart to their own people the fruits of Western liberality. In a large town like Bombay, it is not possible to know the oppression they exercise over the other castes, but I have no hesitation in saying that to their machinations is to be attributed solely the backwardness of the other people.[2]

The solution was simple: 'strict orders' should be passed 'directing that henceforth ... we non-Brahmans alone may be employed till the number of Brahman and non-Brahman employees becomes equal'.[3]

Although these threats to the Brahmins of Maharashtra proved not very serious – at least not until later in the twentieth century – they gave the politics of western India a dangerous undercurrent. For one result was to encourage the Chitpavans in their separate identity, to make them more inward looking, more prone to brood over past glories, and apparently more coherent as a political force than they would have been otherwise. They would increasingly consider themselves an embattled minority and they would pledge their support to leaders who both fed and offered to dispel their fears. Yet for the time being Poona Brahmins reigned supreme and their fiercest contests were with each other for leadership.

The nineteenth-century Maharashtrians noted for their political zeal could nearly all subscribe to the ideal of Vishnu Krishna Chiplonkar that the people 'should be educated and that they should come to know principles of politics and that they should once again inaugurate a golden era in this ill-fated

[1] *Education Commission: Report of the Bombay Provincial Committee* (Calcutta, 1884), vol. II, pp. 141–2.
[2] *Report of the Public Service Commission (Bombay)*, vol. IV, pt iii, B, p. 107.
[3] *Ibid.* pt iii, C, p. 200.

country'.[1] Of course when they attempted to deal with the problems of poverty and the other ills they associated with foreign rule, Maharashtrian leaders would have different remedies and different methods of dosing the patient. However, the controversies which so characterised Poona life from the eighteen-eighties sprang only in part from differences of opinion about the aims and means of modernising Maharashtra: they derived their peculiarly bitter edge from the personal antipathies of Maharashtrian leaders. Perhaps these fierce and often unseemly controversies were the inevitable product of idealistic and strong-willed individuals working within the narrow confines of one town and a few institutions. Once opened, the disagreements were quickened by the desire and need of each contestant to acquire and retain local respect and power. The dissensions between Tilak on the one hand and Ranade, Agarkar and Gokhale on the other can be traced to the Deccan Education Society in the eighteen-eighties. Although the rift was never complete, for each shared friends, kin and even supporters, it dominated Poona politics in the eighteen-nineties and Congress politics in the following decade.

In 1880 a group of young graduates, inspired by V. K. Chiplonkar, opened the New English School at Poona. The school was started 'with the object of cheapening and facilitating education, which is the most efficient and peaceful means of bringing about the intellectual, moral and physical regeneration of the country'.[2] To begin with, the venture was so uncertain financially that salaries had to be kept low. To help overcome the problem, M. B. Namjoshi suggested that his newspaper, the *Deccan Star*, be taken over by the school, and that a vernacular paper be started as well. Apart from the educative role the newspapers could play in society at large, it was intended to utilise the profits from the press to subsidise the school. The beginning of 1881 found Chiplonkar, Tilak, Agarkar, Namjoshi and V. S. Apte working together in the New English School and publishing the *Mahratta* (which was the new version of the *Deccan Star*) and the *Kesari*.[3]

[1] Obituary notice of V. K. Chiplonkar, *Kesari*, 21 March 1882, reprinted in *Kesari*, 19 March 1912, RNP (Bombay), 1912, 23 March, p. 17.
[2] Agarkar to Bhagwat, 8 September 1888, Agarkar Papers, SIS, Poona.
[3] B. G. Tilak, 'Statement of reasons for his resignation from the Deccan Education Society', p. 5. Tilak's statement has been printed in full as Appendix 1,

The politics of western India in the later nineteenth century

The success of the school led to the foundation of the Deccan Education Society in 1884 and the establishment of Fergusson College at the end of the same year. The registration of the school and college for government grants in 1885 necessitated the formal separation of the newspapers from the Society. The newspapers brought to a head the first serious disagreement among the friends. Although supposed to be the voice of all, the newspapers carried radically different editorials, depending upon who had written them. There was a clear division between Agarkar and Tilak on questions of social reform. Agarkar, for example, was in favour of educating women. In *Kesari* he wrote: 'What greater foolishness is there than to say that by good education and by acquiring learning, women will become immoral, imprudent and irresponsible? To suppose that education and learning will have such an effect upon women is to insist that they are not human beings, because we find that knowledge does not have such an effect upon us men.'[1] Tilak's view of the Hindu woman was that her place was in the home. Her foremost virtues should be 'obedience to her husband', 'affectionate devotion to her husband and children', and 'contentment with her lot in life'. Least important was 'knowledge of the three R's in the vernacular language', while 'All the education implied by a B.A. degree would not compensate a Hindu woman for the absence of the higher of the above enumerated qualities.'[2] Gradually, from 1884, Agarkar and Tilak were drawn into open polemic about social reform. *Kesari* would carry articles advocating social reform before political emancipation, and even contemplating the necessity of government legislation to regulate Hindu society, while *Mahratta* of the same week, under Tilak's pen, would urge the contrary.[3]

Agarkar thought that it was especially important to present an impression to the outside world of enlightenment and progress, since the society had drawn much upon the goodwill

P. M. Limaye, *The history of the Deccan Education Society (1880–1935)* (Poona, 1935). The pagination given here and subsequently refers to this appendix.

[1] *Kesari*, 5 August 1884. Quoted in S. A. Wolpert, *Tilak and Gokhale: revolution and reform in the making of modern India* (Berkeley and Los Angeles, 1962), p. 36. Agarkar, writing about a widowed relative maintained: 'she must be educated at any cost. Education alone will make her life tolerable.' Agarkar to his Uncle, 25 November 1890, Agarkar Papers, SIS, Poona.
[2] *Mahratta*, 7 April 1889. Quoted by Wolpert, *Tilak and Gokhale*, p. 36.
[3] Limaye, *Deccan Education Society*, p. 101.

of European and Indian reformers. Perhaps in order to coerce the more conservative members of the Society to present less orthodox statements of opinion in public, Agarkar, who was treasurer in 1886, refused to allow Tilak's request that the school, which was thriving, should make a loan to the press, which was in temporary difficulties.[1] This squabble over the press persuaded the members to separate the journals from common control and make one man financially responsible for running the newspapers. Accordingly, in October 1886, the press was made over to V. B. Kelkar, Agarkar having been given first refusal.[2] Tilak was ordained 'next hypothecated member for the Press', and from that time his views alone appeared in the newspapers.

In 1887, *Kesari* levelled a series of vehement personal attacks against Ranade and Bhandarkar for the liberal views they expressed on the Rakhambai marriage case.[3] Agarkar felt that Tilak's attacks on the reformers were rendering a disservice to the Deccan Education Society by breaking the happy relations between its members and influential Indians and Europeans outside it.[4] A correspondent of *Mahratta* denied that the two papers in any sense represented the official view of the Education Society. Not only was the Society no longer responsible for the papers financially, but it was 'absurd ... to charge such a body collectively with one set of opinions. There is as much difference of opinion on public questions among the members as there is a likelihood of finding among any ten men.'[5] Agarkar, angered by the way in which the two papers had become separated from the Society, and aware of the lost opportunities

[1] Tilak, 'Resignation', p. 11. As a majority of members voted for the loan, Agarkar consented to make it, but not without having managed to make all future loans from the Society's funds dependent on a unanimous vote of the life-members. This petty manoeuvre backfired on him, for in 1887 when Gokhale 'was in great need' the rule was applied rigidly, and Gokhale withdrew his request when he knew that Tilak would oppose it. Tilak, 'Resignation', p. 19; Agarkar, Minute on the internal situation, 21 May 1889, Deccan Education Society Papers, Poona.
[2] Tilak, 'Resignation', p. 11.
[3] Rakhambai, the daughter of a Bombay physician, had been promised in marriage to a much older man. Her father died in 1887 and the would-be husband claimed her hand. She refused, and the irate fiancé filed a suit demanding her as his lawful property. Ranade and Bhandarkar championed the girl's case. Wolpert, *Tilak and Gokhale*, p. 37.
[4] Agarkar to Bhagwat, 8 September 1888, Agarkar Papers, SIS, Poona.
[5] *Mahratta*, 26 June 1887, RNP (Bombay), 1887.

for putting his ideas before a wider public, complained: 'When we made that arrangement about transferring the Press none of us ever dreamt that those two organs which had done such valuable service to the Institutions in past years would be so conducted as to render disservice because the financial responsibility was, by the consent of the majority, transferred to a single person.'[1] Assisted by his young friend Gokhale (who had joined the Society in 1886), Agarkar decided in October 1888 to start *Sudharak*, an English–Marathi paper, to counteract the influence of *Kesari* and *Mahratta* and to 'regain the lost ground in public estimation'.[2] The attempt to contain differences of opinion within the Society now became even more impossible. Tilak resented the fact that *Sudharak* began to condemn the 'social conservatives' as effectively as he had condemned the reformers, and 'bitterness of feeling increased and each party scandalised the other'.[3]

The conflict in the Deccan Education Society has been seen as one in which the 'Caesarian imperiousness of Tilak dashed itself against the passionate enthusiasm and dithyrambic social fervour of Agarkar'.[4] But differences of opinion need not make men implacable enemies, and this was particularly true of the clash between social reform and social orthodoxy in western India. Unlike the social reformers of Bengal, those of Maharashtra never became cut off from their caste, and to the end Tilak was able to maintain a semblance of friendship with some of his chief opponents.[5] Further, there were limits which even the most extreme social reformer was prepared to abide by. Agarkar was perhaps one of the most radical practising social reformers. He was strongly in favour of Pandita Ramabai's Widows' Home in Poona[6] and refused to shave his head and moustaches on the death of his mother.[7] Yet he had no objection

[1] Agarkar to Bhanu, 6 June 1889, Deccan Education Society Papers.
[2] *Ibid.* [3] Tilak, 'Resignation', p. 13.
[4] N. C. Kelkar, *The life and times of Lokhmanya Tilak* (trans. D. V. Divekar, Madras, 1928), p. 152.
[5] Ranade, who had suffered much from Tilak's pen in 1887, and again in 1891, nevertheless found it possible to sponsor Tilak in 1893 as a candidate for election as Fellow of Bombay University. Letter canvassing for votes from Tilak, 23 December 1893, Tilak Papers, *Kesari* Office, Poona.
[6] Agarkar to his Uncle, 2 September 1891, Agarkar Papers, SIS, Poona.
[7] '... on the ground that it was a shame to the editor of the *Sudharak* to do so.' Agarkar to his Uncle, 25 November 1890, *ibid.*

to his son assuming the sacred thread.[1] For all his radical ideas and their implementation in his personal life, Agarkar was no root and branch reformer, and he never lost caste. The members of the Deccan Education Society were, after all, dons. They fell out over personal, petty issues, and as time went on, they increasingly resented Tilak's attempt to dominate the Society. Although a majority of the members were more akin to Tilak than to Agarkar in their outlook on social reform, it was Tilak who left the Society in 1890.

The years following 1885 were marked by the growth of bitter enmity between Tilak and Agarkar. Perhaps it was that Agarkar was the more able of the two men, and so, when Chiplonkar died, although the mantle did not fall on him because of his radical views, yet it was prevented from adorning Tilak's shoulders. When he resigned, Tilak particularly regretted that there had been 'no one amongst us who, by virtue of his personal character, could have commanded respect and admiration from the rest, thus exercising an effectual control over all'.[2] The situation was exacerbated in December 1888, when Agarkar and Tilak squabbled over the distribution of a purse of money presented to the Society by the Maharaja of Indore. After an acrimonious exchange of letters, Agarkar concluded that throughout the dispute Tilak had aimed at 'self-glorification at the cost of honesty, unity, friendship, public duty, and several other social virtues'.[3] The rift between the two was complete.

Tilak's final alienation from the Deccan Education Society also had to do with money. When the New English School had first opened it was decided that the staff should draw only enough salary for what Tilak termed a 'bare maintenance'. By this he meant a maximum of seventy-five rupees a month.[4] For the first few terms it was possible to draw only forty rupees, though it was proposed that any member who was in desperate

---

[1] Agarkar to his Uncle, 8 June 1894, *ibid*. The significance of the thread-girding ceremony was that it made the boy a full Brahmin. At the completion of the ceremonies his father would say 'Up to this you have been like a Shudra, now you are a Brahman and a Brahmachari'. *Gazetteer of the Bombay Presidency: Poona*, vol. XVIII, pt i, pp. 116–19.
[2] Tilak, 'Resignation', p. 2.
[3] Agarkar to Tilak, 25 December 1888, Tilak Papers, *Kesari* Office, Poona.
[4] Tilak, 'Resignation', p. 15.

financial straits could be given a gratuity.¹ After 1885 the economic position of the Society improved and, not unnaturally, members like Agarkar, who taught at great financial sacrifice, wished to put the whole question of remuneration on a sounder basis.² ' "Equal work and equal pay" was the cry. If anyone had special wants let him meet them by private work. We must all be equally paid.'³

Tilak objected to this idea as he felt that it clashed with the basic principle of self-sacrifice which lay behind the venture, but more particularly he stood against making the arrangement retrospective. In 1885 Agarkar had suggested putting all members on a basis of financial equality. When the school had first started, Tilak had not needed to draw any salary, and he had, moreover, invested in furniture and equipment. Agarkar proposed that those who had drawn more than their salary since 1880 should repay the excess, while those who had taken less should be reimbursed once all the members were drawing equal salaries.⁴ Having failed to emerge as natural leader after Chiplonkar's death, Tilak was not prepared to give up the moral position which his early financial superiority had given him. He refused to countenance 'a proposal to buy up the sacrifice of the older members in former years', and Agarkar's scheme was rejected.⁵ He exalted this point to a principle, stressing that new and younger members, who had not made the early financial sacrifice, had no right to join the Society on equal terms with the founding members.⁶

The question of securing decent salaries remained when Agarkar, to force a decision, carried a motion putting an end to the humiliating scheme of granting special allowances to members in need. On 5 February 1887, Agarkar proposed an increase of five rupees a month to the pittance members drew, and to Tilak's disgust, 'the only reason given for the proposed change was that the financial position of the school permitted it'.⁷ Tilak managed to persuade Agarkar's majority for the

¹ *Ibid.* p. 16.
² Tilak apparently had some private means. Discussing his uncertain financial prospects Agarkar wrote: 'You with your health and your paternal property are probably unable to understand my anxiety on this point.' Agarkar to Tilak, 22 December 1888, Tilak Papers, *Kesari* Office, Poona.
³ Tilak, 'Resignation', p. 17.   ⁴ *Ibid.* p. 10.
⁵ *Ibid.*   ⁶ *Ibid.* p. 17.   *Ibid.*

scheme to disperse by threatening to resign if the Society was to be run on such debased principles. At the cost of shelving the issue indefinitely he was persuaded to stay.

However much Tilak admired the single-mindedness and poverty of missionary organisations, and in particular of the Jesuits whom he thought the young teachers should emulate, it was undeniable that the Deccan Education Society was not a mirror-image of the Jesuit Order. As Agarkar pointed out: 'No jesuit is a married man; no jesuit has a private property, nor is he allowed to make any; the jesuits have a common mess and they live in a common house. Above all they are a religious body in which free thought is strictly forbidden. I think only some of the features of such a body can be imitated by us with advantage.'[1] In order to eke out their salaries the members turned to work outside the Society. Indeed, M. B. Namjoshi became known as the 'Foreign Secretary of the D.E. Society' because of his extra-academical activities. True, he was responsible for raising Rs. 50,000 from the Indian States, enabling Fergusson College to start in 1885; but he also conducted the *Industrial Review*, and *Silpakalavijana*, as well as contributing to the Society's papers. The Reay Museum, the Industrial Conference and the Poona Industrial Exhibition of 1888 owed much to his work.[2] Needless to say, Tilak disapproved of such a variety of activity, as he disapproved of Apte publishing independently of the Society an English–Sanskrit Dictionary.[3]

The question of outside work provided the issue over which Tilak finally resigned. In July 1890 Gokhale accepted the post of secretary to the Poona Sarvajanik Sabha, a post which Tilak claimed would involve two or three hours of work a day.[4] He objected that the appointment was a diversion of energies, and that the principle of private work was carried too far if members were allowed to contract

> such definite engagements outside the body. The Secretary-ship I said was offered to me before but I declined to accept it as long as I was connected with our body and that Mr. Gokhale could do the same. I also stated that there was still ample scope for Mr. Gokhale's energies in the duties of professor of English literature in the Fergusson College and that if we wished

[1] Agarkar's Minute ... 21 May 1889, Deccan Education Society Papers, Poona.
[2] Limaye, *Deccan Education Society*, pt ii, p. 210.
[3] Tilak, 'Resignation', p. 14; Limaye, *Deccan Education Society*, pt ii, p. 118.
[4] Tilak, 'Resignation', p. 23.

to compete with other colleges, we must at least show that we were not behind in reading and work as we admittedly were.[1]

Tilak's arguments went unheeded until a meeting of the Board on 14 October, when it was held that Gokhale's work for the Sarvajanik Sabha was not compatible with his duties to the Society. The motion, moved by Kelkar and seconded by Tilak was passed by six votes to three, Agarkar abstaining. Agarkar then moved that Kelkar's proposition condemning outside work applied much better to Namjoshi 'and equally to Messrs. Patankar, Dharap, Tilak, Agarkar, Apte, Bhanu and Kelkar'. Gokhale seconded the proposition and it was carried in the case of Namjoshi, Tilak, Agarkar and Apte.[2] As soon as the vote was taken, Tilak wrote out his resignation from the Society, promising to send later a detailed statement of his reasons.[3] Two meetings of the Council came to the conclusion that compromise was impossible, and Tilak's resignation was accepted. He left the Society disappointed and embittered at his failure to enforce his ideas and leadership on the association. But he took with him the two newspapers which were to prove invaluable, not only in the vendetta he waged against his old friends, but in developing his political mastery of the Deccan. Tilak the polemicist and casuist was to become a great journalist, and through *Kesari* and *Mahratta* he was to organise his party.

The split in the Deccan Education Society influenced all later political developments in Maharashtra. The controversy was, from an early stage, public property, and each contestant canvassed for his cause in the open.[4] As complete reconciliation was never possible, people had to choose between the protagonists. Moreover, the Poona quarrels interacted with personal rivalries in other towns, and consequently they became generalised.[5] From 1890 Maharashtrians thought in terms of competing

---

[1] *Ibid.* [2] Limaye, *Deccan Education Society*, pt i, p. 118.
[3] Tilak to his colleagues, 14 October 1890, Deccan Education Society Papers, Poona.
[4] This method of face-to-face factional fighting has become an established feature of Indian politics – particularly at the highest levels. Information about jostling for position in bodies like the Congress Working Committee or the All-India Congress Committee rapidly finds its way into the press.
[5] For example, in Amraoti, the capital of Berar, R. N. Mudholkar and G. S. Khaparde, two equally eminent and, at least until 1906, equally prosperous lawyers had resolved while at university in the 1870s 'never to be friends'. (G. S. Khaparde, Diary, 24 February 1879, Khaparde Papers, NAI.) They continued

parties in the Deccan. This imparted a liveliness to public life, and it stimulated discussion of political aims and tactics; but it destroyed all hope of unity. At times of local political crisis people were forced to clarify their loyalties and declare their allegiance, thus driving deeper and perpetuating the bitterness. Joint action became almost impossible as issues of common interest became submerged in factional fighting.

During the last quarter of the nineteenth century, Maharashtrians, and particularly those who lived in the Deccan towns, became more aware than ever before of their common interests and their common identity. In Bal Gangadhar Tilak they discovered a leader to whom they were prepared to swear almost undivided loyalty. Tilak's success as a politician was of a special kind. It sprang in part from the way in which he was able to belittle his competitors, and in part from the image he created of himself as a stern patriot. He certainly convinced the government that he posed a serious political threat to political stability in western India, and the government harassed him more than they did any other Indian politician of his time. Twice Tilak was a political prisoner of the raj, and for other extended periods his freedom of movement and of action was curtailed. The government's fear of him was, perhaps, exaggerated; yet in turn it increased his political importance. To the Bombay government must go a large part of the credit for establishing Tilak as the 'father of Indian unrest'.[1]

Tilak's supporters, and the government officials who regarded him with growing disquiet, were struck by the way in which he

their rivalry in all the institutions of local government in Amraoti, in the committees set up to run the cotton market, in the managing committees of political associations, and on the boards of trustees of charities and the local school. Perhaps their rivalry developed naturally from their profession, for being the best lawyers in the town they invariably appeared on opposite sides in the civil suits that were their daily occupation. Yet the significance of their competition lies deeper: within a small town they could only make their mark, and only display their prowess (and from that win prestige and wealth) by constantly sparring with each other. Apparently trivial personal differences could form the basis of wider factionalism, and as such could play a vital role in politics.

[1] The phrase was Valentine Chirol's. V. Chirol, *Indian unrest* (London, 1910), p. 41. When Chirol wrote this book he was given access to the Bombay government's files on the unrest in the Deccan.

appealed to indigenous religious and political traditions. We hear less from him about Ripon the Good and about the divine dispensation of British rule in India than we do about Ganpati, religious orthodoxy, and the greatness of Shivaji. By making Maharashtrian gods and heroes seem relevant to the contemporary political scene he became more popular than any of his contemporaries. Tilak's speeches and writings had an instant appeal for his audience, and were less remote than the academic debates about British parliamentary procedure and covenanted civil service examinations conducted by his chief opponents in Poona and in the Indian National Congress. His newspapers combined praise of Hindu society and the glories of its past with criticisms of a degraded present, coupled with hopes for the imminent dawn of a golden future. He stood out, therefore, as the guardian of national values. He was the most vehement critic of alien rule, and of the mendicant politics of those associated with it.

Yet care must be taken not to confuse Tilak's style of politics with his purpose. Like any politician, Tilak sought power – the means of controlling men and resources. Judged by this criterion he was to be singularly unsuccessful. Despite his popularity he was excluded from formal governmental politics, and he did not succeed in imposing his will on the national movement. That power was denied him personally was perhaps partly the result of his method of seeking it. His resort to old and new Maharashtrian traditions to mobilise a following in the Deccan may have won him friends: but it also bought influential enemies. They were able to brand him a social reactionary and, less plausibly, the mouthpiece of narrow Brahmin interests only. His style of politics rested on polemic, abuse and satire, disseminated through a news-sheet that was eagerly read by Maharashtrian government servants, teachers and clerks. Not unnaturally, it provoked opposition from government circles which, by the end of the nineteenth century, was strong enough to ensure his exclusion from all regular forms of constitutional politics in India. This also put him at a disadvantage when operating within those nationalist organisations which were built to work in conjunction with the formal apparatus of the raj. Already by the late 1890s Tilak had become an isolated opposition spokesman, and while years spent in the political wilderness often refine a statesman, the experience rarely compensates for perennial exclusion from office.

Social and religious conservatism underlay Tilak's political innovations. While stressing that he personally was in favour of social reform, Tilak did not believe 'in writing or speaking disparagingly about the customs, institutions, habits and ways of his people'.[1] Until 1890 he had not rigidly adhered to all caste customs (and indeed he was never to do so), but in that year he 'determined to gain the support of the orthodox, and with this purpose he proceeded to Allahabad to shave his moustaches and bathe in the Ganges, so that it might not be urged against him that he was unfit to champion the orthodox party'.[2] In the following year the controversy about whether the government should legislate on Hindu family affairs gave Tilak an opportunity not only to come to the defence of Indian traditions but to attack foreign rule and to discredit his former associates in the Deccan Education Society. Further, the vigour with which Tilak conducted his campaign had the effect of forcing people to decide at whose side they stood.

Throughout the nineteenth century Indian social reformers tried to discourage child marriages. Later marriage, they believed, would result in fewer child widows, who were amongst the most deprived classes in Hindu society.[3] As part of this programme, the reformers tried to persuade the government to raise from ten years to twelve the age below which sexual intercourse with a girl, even by her lawful husband, constituted rape. As a result of a campaign by Malabari during the eighteen-eighties Indian opinion was aroused, and at the first National Social Conference, held in 1887, Ranade procured support for a resolution urging that the Age of Consent Act of 1860 be amended. At the 1889 Social Conference he moved a resolution that 'in the opinion of this Conference ... cohabitation before the wife is twelve years old should be punishable as a criminal offence', and that public opinion should be influenced to demand postponement of marriages until the wife was at least

---

[1] T. V. Parvate, *Bal Gangadhar Tilak* (Ahmadabad, 1958), p. 37.
[2] Inspector-General of Police, Bombay, to Govt. Bombay, 15 July 1899, Enclosure 2 in Govt. Bombay to Govt. India, 25 August 1899, Home Public A, September 1899, 5, NAI.
[3] See Pundita Sarasvati Ramabai, *The high-caste Hindu woman* (London, 1888).

fourteen years old.¹ But the lot of the reformers was not easy, for the government was slow to move in legislation which touched the customs of the people it ruled. 'The difficulty of the social reformer is two-fold', Malabari wrote, 'to struggle with the Government and also with the public.'² Following in the steps of the political associations he transferred his agitation to England, where he created a lobby which was powerful enough to prod the Government of India into action.³ A Bill was introduced into the Viceroy's Legislative Council by Sir Andrew Scoble, embodying the reformers' main demand.

Opposition to Scoble's Bill was fierce, particularly in Bengal and Maharashtra. Tilak, supported by the scholarly interpretation of old texts of some Poona Brahmins, argued that for 2,500 years the custom had been to consummate a marriage as soon as a girl reached puberty, whatever her age. Since puberty was often reached before twelve the proposed Bill not only attacked religious custom but it undermined the rights of Hindu husbands.⁴ Although Bhandarkar and Telang drew upon their considerable scholarship to refute Tilak's arguments,⁵ the reformers in Poona found that the debate passed quickly from the study to the streets. When they held a meeting to try to win support for the Age of Consent Bill it was broken up. Before the meeting started a gang of young toughs attacked the reformers as they arrived, and then wrecked the hall were it was to be held. Gokhale, writing in *Sudharak*, saw Tilak's hand in the rowdyism.

¹ C. H. Heimsath, *Indian nationalism and Hindu social reform* (Princeton, 1964), pp. 166–7.
² Malabari to Naoroji, 10 January 1891, Naoroji Papers, NAI.
³ Heimsath, *Indian nationalism and Hindu social reform*, pp. 160–1. Malabari formed a committee in London composed of ex-Viceroys and Governors, the Dukes of Argyll, Westminster and Fife, the poet laureate, Protestant and Catholic Bishops, representatives from the Non-Conformist Churches, the Universities and Law Courts, Herbert Spencer, Max Muller and James Bryce.
⁴ Wolpert, *Tilak and Gokhale*, pp. 52–6. Wolpert says of Tilak's attitude that the 'unstated, though fundamental, premise supporting this otherwise incomprehensible apology for homicidal rape was that men alone were worthy of consideration in marital relations'. *Ibid.* p. 54.
⁵ See, for example, Bhandarkar's essays 'A note on the age of marriage and its consummation according to Hindu religious law with four appendixes' and 'History of child marriage' in Narayan Bapuji Utgikar (ed.) *Collected works of Sir R. G. Bhandarkar* (Poona, 1928), vol. II, pp. 538–602; and K. T. Telang, 'Gleanings from Maratha chronicles', published as an appendix to M. G. Ranade, *Rise of the Maratha power* (reprint, New Delhi, 1961), especially pp. 143–4.

Mr. Tilak's presence in Mr. Kelkar's house during the time of the meeting was a very unfortunate incident and betokened a lamentable error of judgment on that gentleman's part. We are not prepared to charge Mr. Tilak with encouraging or even sympathising with the mob in their shameful work, but we cannot help feeling that *Kridabhuvan* [the place of the meeting] was not the place for him on that day. Mr. Tilak is the leader of that section of the Poona people who have taken up an attitude of uncompromising hostility to the Scoble Bill. He has become recently a kind of demigod to the orthodox community of this place, and we think he knows this. He should have seen that his presence in the *Kridabhuvan*, even as a mere unsympathetic spectator of the meeting, was sure to encourage the mob in its unsympathetic attitude towards the meeting. Mr. Tilak's plea that he went there to escort that reporter of the *Mahratta* and *Kesari* is absolutely and entirely flimsy. Fancy Mr. Gladstone (to compare very very small things with very very great ones), escorting the reporter of a Liberal paper to a Tory meeting or Lord Salisbury conducting a Police notetaker to an open-air demonstration of Irish Nationalists.[1]

Despite the unpopularity of the cause and the government's natural cautiousness in dealing with controversial legislation of this kind, the Bill entered its final stage on 19 March 1891. Sir Andrew Scoble argued that 'the balance of argument and authority is in favour of the supporters of the Bill' and that even were it not so 'were I a Hindu I would prefer to be wrong with Professor Bhandarkar, Mr. Justice Telang, and Dewan Bahadur Raghunath Rao than to be right with Pundit Sasadhur Turkachuramani and Mr. Tilak'.[2] The Bill became law and Tilak loosed a flood of vituperation against the government and prophesied disaster from allowing an alien regime to tamper with Hindu social customs.[3] No effort should be spared, a friend wrote to Tilak shortly after the Bill had been passed, to put 'new life' into the castes and to 'protect our society and our institutions from being crushed under the heels of rampagious free thought and so-called nineteenth-century civilisation'.[4]

But the government was not the only one to be attacked.

[1] *Sudharak*, 2 March 1891, RNP (Bombay), 1891.
[2] Quoted by Heimsath, *Indian nationalism and Hindu social reform*, p. 170.
[3] 'Government rules over us, therefore they have the right to suppress the Hindus by the strength of their fists. This we have to admit if we look at the Age of Consent Bill. The Muhammadans forced the Hindus to grow beards after cutting off the Hindus' locks of hair by taking a sword in one hand and a Koran in the other. So also our subjugation to others gives evidence that our brave English people have the power to send us to "Our Father in Heaven" after making us drink red water [wine] instead of the sacred water of the Ganges.' *Kesari* 24 March 1891. Quoted by Wolpert, *Tilak and Gokhale*, p. 60.
[4] Kirtikar to Tilak, 28 March 1891, Tilak Papers, *Kesari* Office, Poona.

Tilak seized the opportunity to discredit the reformers, all of whom had been connected with the Deccan Education Society in some capacity, in the eyes of Poona. 'We have been shamelessly represented as a nation of savages', he wrote, 'and the *sudharaks* [reformers] have shamelessly testified to it. Let these *sudharaks* therefore form themselves into a separate nationality. ... We ought no longer to allow to be amongst us those of our fellow countrymen who are really our enemies but who pose as our friends.'[1] While Tilak did not succeed in driving the social reformers of Maharashtra out of Hindu society, the Age of Consent controversy made his name. Unlike the high politics of the Sarvajanik Sabha, social reforms intimately affected every family and discussion of them attracted general interest.

The debates about social reforms, and their relation to politics, spilled out of learned papers and editorial columns into popular Marathi literature and the theatre, fields in which university graduates were conspicuous by their absence.[2] By the late nineteenth century Marathi drama had broken away from the 'vulgar and obscene Tamases' favoured by Baji Rao II,[3] and had explored new forms and found an enthusiastic public.[4] Not only were plays and musical entertainments performed depicting events from Sanskrit legends, history and Shakespeare, but the social controversies of the day were presented to amuse and educate the public. Ranade wrote about new plays in 1898: 'The greater part ... refer to the present times with the struggles between the reformers and the orthodox people, on questions of infant, equal and widow marriages and female education. As might be expected, the majority of them cry down the reforms and the reformers.'[5] Since the new Marathi writers

---

[1] *Mahratta*, 22 March 1891.
[2] Out of 511 vernacular authors known to Ranade in 1898, only 75 were graduates. M. G. Ranade, 'A note on the growth of Marathi literature', *Journal of the Bombay Branch of the Royal Asiatic Society*, xx (1902), 78–105.
[3] G. C. Bhate, *History of modern Marathi literature, 1800–1938* (Mahad, 1939), p. 95. Baji Rao II was the last Peshwa.
[4] *Ibid.* pp. 95–6, 244–7; M. G. Ranade, in *Journal of the Bombay Branch of the Royal Asiatic Society*, xx (1902), 99–101.
[5] *Ibid.* p. 101. In June 1892, for example, a group of students from Poona presented a play in Kolhapur about the Age of Consent controversy. In it, a man aged thirty married a girl of eleven and the marriage was consummated. A malignant third party, who was not even related to the couple, lodged a complaint. The husband was brought before the courts and sentenced to transportation for life. The young girl, grieving for the loss of her spouse, took her own life. 'The object

were skilled in satire, political subjects also offered obvious opportunities. Legendary and historical events were used to criticise and ridicule the contemporary scene. When people went to see K. P. Khadilkar's play *Kicakavadh*, for example,

> Kicak appeared to the audience as a fine representative of Lord Curzon. His arrogance, his imperialism, his disregard for everyone, his excessive pride, his love of pomp and power, these are all finely brought out in dialogue and in incidents depicted in the drama. As Kicak was killed by Bhima, it was subtly suggested that Lord Curzon too deserved death. Thus the drama was seditious. But the sedition was too subtle and too remote to be easily discovered.[1]

The new drama shared with the old its close association with the great public festivals of Maharashtra. Tilak saw that these occasions could be used to extend his political influence. Since songs and plays about controversial issues already contributed to entertainments at such festivals, it was a short step to make political speeches to crowds gathered in a holiday mood. Tilak is particularly associated with two festivals: those honouring Ganpati and Shivaji. These festivals were important because they were the means of bringing others besides the Brahmins into politics.[2] The Ganpati festival provided a platform for 'all the Hindus of all high and low classes to stand together and discharge a joint national duty',[3] while the adoration of Shivaji was potentially suitable for reconciling the Maratha castes to Tilak's politics.

Ganpati, in figure a fat, jolly man with four hands and an elephant's head, mounted on the back of a mouse, was one of

apparently is to show that though by rights only a parent or guardian should complain, yet in practice any outsider's complaint would be entertained. There was a very full house and sympathy was all for the accused.' Para. 16 (Kolhapur, 5 June 1892), Bombay Police Abstracts, vol. v, 1892, Bombay HFM.

[1] Bhate, *Marathi literature*, p. 450. The sedition was not, however, subtle enough. Performances of the play were banned by an order of the Bombay government dated 27 January 1910. Supplementary material, Bombay Police Abstracts, vol. XXIII, 1910, p. 240, Bombay, HFM.

[2] 'With the Ganpati celebrations', Chirol wrote, 'the area of Tilak's propaganda was widely increased', while the Shivaji festival was calculated to appeal 'to the fighting instincts of the Mahrattas and stimulate active disaffection by reviving memories of olden times when under Shivaji's leadership they had rolled back the tide of Muslim conquest and created a Mahratta Empire of their own.' Chirol, *Indian unrest*, pp. 44–5.

[3] Kelkar, *Tilak*, p. 284. 'There was no distinction of superiority or inferiority. Brahmans, Marathas, Mahars all took to it and mixed freely with one another.' Parvate, *Tilak*, p. 117.

the Deccan's most popular deities.[1] He was associated with wit, wisdom and success. Ganpati was honoured in particular during Bhadra (August–September). Songs and poems were offered to the god, and at the end of the festival images of him were taken out and immersed in water. Although the Ganpati celebrations held at the Peshwa's court had been on such a lavish scale that they 'bore many of the characteristics of a public festival', and although it was customary for the rich to keep open house during religious holidays, in the nineteenth century Ganpati festivals were primarily family occasions.[2] Naturally, contemporary social and political problems found a place in the petitions addressed to the god,[3] and when the image was taken out to be immersed there was plenty of opportunity for music, processions and merry-making. Yet the festival did not attract particular attention until the eighteen-nineties. Then, strenuous efforts were made to set up Ganpati images in public places, to organise a full programme of speeches, songs and entertainments throughout the period of the festival, and to take out large-scale processions alongside the family ones. The advocates of the change argued that they were trying to use the festival to give Hindus a sense of unity and to make them more aware of some of the social and political problems of the day.

The changing form of the Ganpati festival must be set in the more general context of the spread of Hindu revivalism in India and the sharpening of religious antagonisms that accompanied it. The new spirit of Hindu assertiveness, particularly associated with the cow-protection movements, had already begun to make itself felt in western India in the eighteen-eighties. The purely cultural aspects of these movements became involved with politics when, following the local self-government legisla-

[1] *Gazetteer of the Bombay Presidency: Poona*, vol. XVIII, pt 1, pp. 246–7.
[2] V. Barnouw, 'The changing character of a Hindu festival', *American Anthropologist*, vol. 56, pt 1 (February 1954), 79–80.
[3] In 1887 the *Poona Vaibhav* published four odes requesting him to remedy a variety of wrongs. The first complained about the powerlessness of Indian princes, the employment of Europeans in the Indian states, and the mismanagement of treasuries and public funds. The second mourned the slaughter of cows by non-Aryans and asked Ganpati's protection for cows and Brahmins. The third described the inefficiency of the Poona police in tracking dacoits and prayed that the government would allow people to arm themselves for protection; while the fourth asserted that the material poverty of Indians was due to foreign rule 'and invokes the god Ganpati to emancipate them'. *Poona Vaibhav*, 21 August 1887, RNP (Bombay), 1887.

tion of the 1880s, local boards came to have a larger number of elected members and were able by virtue of their extended powers over local affairs to interfere in religious and semi-religious matters. Inevitably, these powers came to be used for party ends, and sometimes these could be communal in complexion.[1] In Maharashtra, the new organs of local government tended to be dominated by Brahmins.[2] In Poona the main supporters of the various revivalist movements, and men who were closely identified with conservatism and orthodoxy in religion tended to gather round a clique of wealthy sirdars, the most important of whom was Balwant Ramchandra Natu. Associated with him was another prominent sirdar, Wassadeo Harihar Pandit (more usually called Baba Maharaj) and Vinayak Ramchandra Patwardhan, a staunch defender of religion and a leading figure in the cow-protection movement.[3] During the Age of Consent controversy, Tilak had acted as the spokesman of this self-styled orthodox party. They now came to the fore to reorganise the Ganpati festival.

The new festival was not born under very auspicious circumstances. In 1893 the anti-cow-killing agitation culminated in a series of riots. In August there was a major Hindu–Muslim riot in Bombay, and the government were prone to see the anti-cow-killing preachers as the main cause of it.[4] The Poona leaders, and Tilak through his newspapers, resented the government's attitude which they thought was biased towards the Muslims.[5] The net result was a deterioration of Hindu–Muslim relations in Poona itself. Since the Muslims in Poona (as in most of Maharashtra) were 'poor and inoffensive . . . quiet and law-abiding, and much in a minority it was distinctly to their disadvantage to give any cause of offence to the Hindus, who are

[1] See C. A. Bayly, 'Political development in the Allahabad locality', pp. 231–8; F. C. R. Robinson, 'Municipal government and Muslim separatism in the United Provinces 1883–1916', *Modern Asian Studies*, vol. 7, no. 3 (1973).
[2] Memorandum by the Acting Commissioner, Central Division, 2 October 1894, Home Public A, February 1895, 145, NAI.
[3] R. Cashman, 'The political recruitment of god Ganpati', *Indian Economic and Social History Review*, vol. VII (1970), 369–71.
[4] Harris to Lansdowne, 14 August 1893, Lansdowne Papers, IS. 420/16 BM; Lyall to Ardagh, 27 September 1893, *ibid*. See also the papers from the Govt. Bombay to Govt. India, August 1893, filed in Home Public A, October 1893, 34–6, NAI.
[5] Inspector-General of Police Bombay, to Govt. Bombay, 15 July 1899, Enclosure 2, Home Public A, September 1899, 5, NAI.

in many instances their employers and purchasers of their goods'.¹ In April 1894, the organisers of a Hindu religious procession threatened to continue to play music while they passed by a mosque in the city. On that occasion, the rule that noise must cease while processions were going by the place of worship of another denomination was observed.² On 27 June, however, as the Dehu and Alandi Palkis were being taken in procession through Poona, a drummer continued to beat his tom-tom while the procession went by the Madar Chala mosque. Some Muslims retaliated by throwing stones at the procession and a scuffle ensued.³

In consequence the Poona leaders decided to boycott the Moharram festival, due to be held between 5 and 14 July, which until then had been shared by Muslims and Hindus alike.⁴ The municipal commissioners refused to grant licences to Hindus to erect the temporary pavilions needed for the festival, and a combination of intimidation and social blackmail was brought to bear on Hindus to ensure the success of the boycott.⁵ The result was 'No Hindu musicians could be persuaded to play ... most of the Hindu shops were closed and no lamps or illuminations put up. In fact as far as possible the Hindus abstained from either joining in or helping the Muhammadans to celebrate their holiday.'⁶ Similarly, in Satara, as a result of letters sent from Poona advising Hindus not to join in the Moharram, the Muslims found it difficult to get people to prepare or carry the tabuts, and the local authorities refused to allow a municipal tabut as in previous years.⁷

---

¹ District Superintendent of Police to District Magistrate, Poona, 21 September 1894, Home Public A, February 1895, 143, NAI.
² Ibid. ³ Ibid.
⁴ '... in fact, as a rule, there have been more Hindu than Muhammadan Tabuts, and on the last day (the day of immersion) by far the greater part of the procession was entirely Hindu.' Ibid.
⁵ Para. 1150 (Poona, 9 July 1894), Bombay Police Abstracts, vol. VII, 1894, Bombay, HFM.
⁶ District Superintendent of Police to District Magistrate, Poona, 21 September 1894, Home Public A, February 1895, 143, NAI.
⁷ Para. 1230 (Satara, 17 July 1894) and para. 1237 (Satara, 24 July 1894), Bombay Police Abstracts, vol. VII, 1894, Bombay HFM. However, the boycott of the Moharram was far from being complete. The main towns where it was attempted were Poona, Ahmadnagar, Satara and Wai, and even there Hindus were reported joining in the festival (e.g. para. 1230 (Satara 17 July 1894), ibid.). In Sangli, however, where the ruler was a Chitpavan, the Moharram 'went off as usual with

However, Tilak's party did not stop at spoiling the Moharram: they had also planned special arrangements for the celebration of the Ganpati festival, 'which they intend to make very much more of than in former years'.[1] A member of Poona district board and municipality told the district magistrate that

> The proposal is to have a procession, different in many ways and on a very much larger scale than in former years. While pointing out that he and a strong party in Poona were averse to making very great changes in the usual routine of the Ganpati festivities, he said that Mr. Tilak, the editor of the *Kesari*, and his party were advocating that every step should be taken to conduct the procession in such a manner as to make it more effective, that is to say, more distasteful to the Muhammadans.[2]

The festival was celebrated 'with unusual ostentation, as a counterblast to the Muharram, and to compensate the musicians and others who had lost money by not taking part in that festival ... "melas" or gangs of youths were organised in imitation of a similar custom in the Muharram, who paraded the streets in all directions singing and shouting out verses composed for them by the local Hindu talent'.[3] The gist of these verses, which were also circulated as pamphlets, was 'disparagement of the Muharram festival, calling the Hindus "to arms", urging the Marathas to rebel as Shivaji did under the instigation of Ramdas Swami [Shivaji's guru], and declaring that "the dagger of subjection to foreign rule penetrates the bosom of all", and urging that a religious outbreak should be made the first step towards the overthrow of alien power'.[4] Going past a mosque in the city late at night, a procession organised by Hari Ramchandra Natu refused to stop playing music. A small riot ensued in which one Muslim was killed.[5] The Bombay government seemed confirmed in its view that the festival was designed by the Poona orthodoxy to embitter

the ruler himself joining in'. Para. 1200 (SB Bombay, 21 July 1894), *ibid.* The government noted a steady return in following years of Hindu participation in the Moharram. See, for example, para. 831 (Poona, 28 June 1896) *ibid.* vol. IX, 1896 and para. 914 (Bombay, 14 June 1897), *ibid.* vol. X, 1897.

[1] Para. 1271 (Poona, 31 July 1894), *ibid.*
[2] Para. 1486 (SB Bombay, 8 September 1894), *ibid.*
[3] District Superintendent of Police to District Magistrate, Poona, 21 September 1894, Home Public A, February 1895, 143, NAI.
[4] Inspector-General of Police Bombay, to Govt. Bombay, 15 July 1899, Enclosure 2, Home Public A, September 1899, 5, NAI.
[5] District Superintendent of Police to District Magistrate, Poona, 21 September 1894, Home Public A, February 1895, 143, NAI.

communal relations and hence to make government more difficult and British rule more unpopular.[1]

However, although the government disliked some aspects of the festival, they were not inclined to intervene in its development. There was no reason at all why the Hindus should not celebrate Ganpati in a more elaborate way, and only a minority tried to use it for political purposes. During the next few years the festival became more popular. In 1896 fifty public Ganpatis were set up in Poona,[2] and reports from the newspapers and the police records testify to public celebrations being held throughout the Deccan.[3] The new forms for observing the holiday spread to the Maharashtrians living in Bombay city.[4] Regular features of the Ganpati festivals, apart from the purely religious rituals,[5] were dramatic performances, other entertainments ranging from singing competitions to athletics, and a variety of speeches and lectures, some of which were political in content.[6] Tilak certainly used the occasion to talk about national education and the political future of India[7] and in the period following the partition of Bengal, when strenuous efforts were being made to encourage indigenous industries and to boycott British goods, the festivals were accompanied by 'a great deal of swadeshi eloquence in which religion and politics are mingled'.[8]

The greatest innovation, however, was the mela movement. A mela consisted of a group of young men or students, dressed in special costumes, who were armed with sticks and practised

[1] Memorandum by the Acting Commissioner, Central Division, 2 October 1894, Home Public A, February 1895, 145, NAI.
[2] V. Barnouw, 'The changing character of a Hindu festival', *American Anthropologist*, vol. LVI, pt 1 (February 1954), 81.
[3] R. Cashman, 'The political recruitment of god Ganapati', *Indian Economic and Social History Review*, vol. VII, no. 3 (September 1970), 354–5.
[4] *Ibid.* pp. 359–60; para. 1576 (Bombay, 17 September 1894), Bombay Police Abstracts, vol. VII, 1894, Bombay HFM.
[5] These are described by V. Barnouw, in *American Anthropologist*, vol. LVI, pt 1 (February 1954), 75–7, and by R. Cashman, in *Indian Economic and Social History Review*, vol. VII, no. 3 (September 1970), 351.
[6] The best accounts of Ganpati festivals are to be found in G. S. Khaparde's diary. See the entries for 3 September 1894; 25, 26, 29 and 31 August 1900; 5–8 September 1900; 5–21 September 1902; 13–20 September 1904; 3 September 1911. Khaparde Papers, NAI.
[7] *Mumukshu*, 19 September 1907, RNP (Bombay), 1907.
[8] Weekly Report DCI, 19 September 1907, Home Political B, October 1907, 81, NAI.

singing, dancing, drilling and fencing. Each mela was attached to a particular Ganpati, and it would go round the town and neighbouring countryside for some time before as well as during the festival.[1] The melas performed popular verses and songs, and into these songs references to topical political events were inserted.[2] It was such songs in 1894 that were so objectionable to the Muslims, and it was in such songs later on that attacks, often satiric and abusive, would be made on the government and on prominent personalities.[3] Prizes would be awarded for the best songs and for the best drilled melas.

The festival, however, was very loosely organised. A neighbourhood committee, or a family group, or a guild or class organisation, would set up public Ganpatis. It would be responsible to no one for the precise form its own celebration took. This had the advantage that a great many people, from all communities, took part in the Ganpati festivals; but it would be a mistake to think that this spontaneous celebration was in itself of political significance. The main patrons of the movement had no control over the festival as a whole, nor could they ensure that the political complexion given it by some of its participants spread to all of them. Moreover, the political propaganda voiced by some of the melas was not common to all. This aspect of the festival was an addition of which many of the worshippers of Ganpati were either unaware or which they considered dispensable.

The most lavish, and political, celebrations were those organised by the Poona Brahmins. Tilak used the religious festival to attack his opponents. When accounts of the festivities were written up in his newspapers, Tilak argued that while Ranade, Agarkar and Gokhale were betraying Hindu ideals for those of the alien rulers, he watched over a religious revival among the people. In 1896 he wrote, 'with bitter sarcasm', that 'Ranade mixing with the people in the Ganesh festival and lecturing to them in front of that God of learning ... would be inconceivably more useful to the nation than Ranade sitting in the prayer hall of the social reformers with his eyes and lips

---

[1] R. Cashman, in *Indian Economic and Social History Review*, vol. VII, pt 3 (September 1970), 356.
[2] *Ibid.* p. 361.
[3] *Ibid.* pp. 362–3; para. 1305 (Poona, 7 August 1894), Bombay Police Abstracts, vol. VII, 1894, Bombay HFM.

closed in devoted contemplation of their idea of the Almighty!'[1] However, Tilak's opponents did not allow the virtues of the festival to go unchallenged. *Sudharak* observed

> of late years a curious disease 'melases' has made its appearance in Maharashtra. Its origin can be traced to Poona from where it has spread to other places and the time of its recrudescence every year is the month of the Ganpati festival. Young men are specially liable to catch the disease, and when they suffer from it, they show a particular tendency to indulge in silly gesticulations. The attacks of the disease last from a week to ten days and the best means of avoiding it is evacuation i.e., removing from the chawls and other places where public Ganpatis are installed. There are some orthodox persons who trace the disease as far back as Vedic times, but there is no doubt of its very recent origin, and that ours is the true diagnosis of its nature and symptoms.[2]

Yet this remained a minority view, and Tilak's constant propaganda that his opponents were behaving in an anti-Hindu fashion damaged their reputations.

The success of the transformed Ganpati festival encouraged Tilak to start one in honour of Shivaji, the great seventeenth-century Mahratta prince. With the Shivaji festival Tilak hoped to stir Maharashtrian historical imagination. He tried to symbolise in Shivaji's achievements the political aspirations of nineteenth-century India. The festival was inaugurated on 15 April 1896 at Raigarh, Poona, and 'at Brahmin centres' in the Deccan.[3] The main objects of the movement were to raise money for the upkeep of Shivaji's tomb at Raigarh,[4] and to instil a new sense of nationalism into Maharashtrians by holding up the example of their former greatness. *Kesari* told its readers

---

[1] Kelkar, *Tilak*, p. 286. 'No man can deny that our country is badly in want of a religious revival. Well, such a revival is taking place; only it is observable in different phases. Swami Vivekanand and the high philosophy of the Upanishads have appealed to the B.A.'s and M.A.'s of our Universities. The God Ganapati and the vigorous preachings of Ramdas have appealed to the common people. Religion is the main stay, the only prop for a falling nation and some of our friends are committing a national suicide in witholding themselves from a movement which is making us hopeful for the future.' *Mahratta*, 20 September 1896.
[2] *Sudharak*, 1 September 1902, RNP (Bombay), 1902. See also *Kesari*, 2 September 1902 and *Sudharak*, 15 September 1902, *ibid*.
[3] Inspector-General of Police to Govt. Bombay, 15 July 1899, enclosure 2 in Govt. Bombay to Govt. India, 25 August 1899, Home Public A, September 1899, 5, NAI; Parvate, *Tilak*, p. 127.
[4] *Mahratta*, 2 June 1895; Khaparde, Diary, 15 September 1895, Khaparde Papers, NAI. In fact enough money was never raised. Kelkar, *Tilak*, p. 295.

so soon as the memory of Shivaji began to fade away, the Marathas lost their power and greatness, which if they are to regain, they must at once cultivate respect and honour for the memory of Shivaji. We have still among us gatherings for the honour of our religious saints, thanks mainly to the attitude of strict religious neutrality of our foreign Government. But this same Government has unfortunately served to obliterate the memory of our political heroes, and the wholesome education derived by example and inspiration from hero worship in this shape has been denied to us.[1]

The annual festivities, usually held on the anniversary of Shivaji's coronation, were 'on a small scale being attended by a few hundred people only', although every five years a special effort was made to draw a large crowd to Raigarh, Shivaji's inaccessible hill-fort.[2] In form the celebrations resembled the non-religious activities of the Ganpati festival. Ballads were composed in praise of Shivaji and of his Brahmin mentor, Ramdas, *kirtans* and plays were performed, athletic competitions were held, and lectures were given on Mahratta history.[3] The entertainments and speeches infused historical events with contemporary significance, and by praising past deeds encouraged their emulation. It was not Ranade, the greatest living authority on Mahratta history, who gained most credit

[1] *Kesari*, 1 June 1897, RNP (Bombay), 1897.
[2] A very full account of the 1906 celebration was reported in *Mahratta*. Almost 5,000 people went to Raigarh in Kolaba district. The deputy collector and mamlatdar attended as guests. On the morning of 25 April 1906 over 3,000 descendants of the men who 'helped Shivaji in his endeavours to establish the Mahratta Empire' (indicating that 'the festival is getting popular not only amongst the educated but also uneducated classes') and over a thousand Brahmins, Parbhus and other high castes toiled up the hill for the festival. The morning's proceedings were occupied with songs welcoming the guests and extolling the virtues of Shivaji and swadeshi. The assembly then heard a *kirtan* telling how the Sardar of Kalyan, a Muslim, was captured by Shivaji and what honourable treatment Shivaji meted out to the captured man's zenana. The crowd then rested and feasted. In the evening there was more music and singing, followed by a business meeting. The accounts of the Shivaji fund were examined; Tilak and Balwant Ramchandra Natu were re-elected as secretary and treasurer of the fund and a resolution was passed authorising the chairman of the meeting 'to memorialise the Government for granting local facilities and other help in the construction and erection of *Chhatri* on the *Samadhi*'. Votes of thanks were passed and the proceedings were brought to a close by a 'palanquin-torch-procession along the top of the hill from the Royal palace at one end to the Mahadera's temple near the *Samadhi* on the other. Early next morning the large crowd of people who had gone up commenced to come down the hill and the fort assumed its aspect of a deserted place in a few hours.' *Mahratta*, 29 April 1906.
[3] *Kesari*, 15 June 1897, RNP (Bombay), 1897; Khaparde, Diary, 21-4 June 1899, and 6-8 May 1905, Khaparde Papers, NAI.

from the festival, but Tilak. His prominence both as organiser and speaker was widely reported in the press, and by keeping him in the public eye increased his fame in Maharashtra.

Tilak's rising popularity emboldened him to try to capture the Poona Sarvajanik Sabha. This was the most important political association in Maharashtra. It had been founded in 1870 by amalgamating an earlier district association with a committee of Brahmins responsible for the administration of the revenues of the temple of Parvati. Under the influence of Mahadev Govind Ranade it became one of the most authoritative and energetic public bodies in India. The Sabha claimed to voice 'the wants and wishes of the inhabitants of the Deccan' and its members were required to show that they held a mandate from at least fifty adult men 'from any caste or community'.[1] The association comprised 'Sirdars, Land-holders, Sowcars, and other representatives of the people',[2] and most of its members were Poona lawyers, teachers, government servants and journalists.[3] Inevitably, because it was based in Poona, the Sabha was dominated by Poona Brahmins. Indeed, two out of every three of the 125 people who served on the Sabha's managing committee between 1878 and 1897 were Chitpavan Brahmins.[4] But caste and communal distinctions were not really relevant to its operations. Parsi, Muslim and non-Brahmin merchants, bankers and professional men supported its political work.[5] The Sabha established branches in other Deccan towns, and similar associations were later founded in Nagpur and Amraoti.[6]

The Poona Sarvajanik Sabha's main concern was with the effects of government policy on education, taxation, land-

[1] *The constitution of the Poona 'Sarvajanik Sabha'. And its rules* (Poona, 1884), pp. 1, 6.
[2] Address of Welcome to Lord Ripon, 19 June 1880. *Journal of the Poona Sarvajanik Sabha*, vol. III, 2, p. 29.
[3] *Gazetteer of the Bombay Presidency: Poona*, vol. XVIII, pt iii, p. 64.
[4] See table 11 in Johnson, 'Chitpavan Brahmins', in E. R. Leach and S. N. Mukherjee (eds.), *Elites in south Asia*, p. 109.
[5] Parsis, Muslims and Gujaratis living in Poona were represented on the managing committee, and in Gangarambhau Mhaske the Sabha had a prominent Maratha who spoke out against separate non-Brahmin movements. *Ibid.* See also *Dnyan Prakash*, 19 December 1887, RNP (Bombay), 1887.
[6] *Vaidarbh*, 1 January 1887. RNP (Berar), 1887, 8 January, p. 1. Government of Madhya Pradesh, *The history of Freedom Movement in Madhya Pradesh* (Nagpur, 1956), p. 174.

revenue and public employment. The Sabha petitioned and agitated on a wide range of subjects: it organised meetings against Lytton's Vernacular Press Act, it campaigned against the Bombay Forest Regulations, the Licence Tax, famine policy and the government's threatened withdrawal of subsidies from higher education. The Sabha supported the Ilbert Bill, it pressed for an extension of local self-government, it proposed reform of the Legislative Councils and of recruitment to the civil service.[1] Some of these questions interested politicians in other parts of India. In 1878 delegates from the Sabha conferred with other leaders about methods of achieving unity,[2] and in 1880 the Sabha joined the Calcutta Indian Association in sending an appeal to the British public on the eve of the general election.[3] From such alliances grew the Indian National Congress, and the Poona Sarvajanik Sabha played a leading role during the eighteen-eighties and early eighteen-nineties in establishing the Congress and its associated Provincial Conferences.[4]

Until the eighteen-nineties the Sabha had, with some justice, considered itself a voice for all communities alike. It had steered clear of the issues that divided Indians, but the increased tension in some of the Deccan towns during 1893 and 1894 drew it into communal politics. The disturbances in these towns had been connected with the playing of music in public processions. The Government of India's ruling, drawn up to meet the much severer communal situation in northern India, was that musicians must stop playing their instruments when going by the place of worship of another religion. The growth in the number of Ganpati processions had led to these rules being enforced in Maharashtra, and some prosecutions had resulted from consequent infringements of the law.[5]

[1] See the articles in the *Journal of the Poona Sarvajanik Sabha*, vols. I–XIX (1878–97).
[2] J. C. Masselos, 'Lytton's Great Tomasha and Indian unity', *Journal of Indian History*, vol. XLIV, pt 3 (December 1966), 737–60.
[3] Seal, *The emergence of Indian nationalism*, p. 236.
[4] The first four Provincial Conferences in Bombay were little more than open meetings of the Poona Sarvajanik Sabha, which published the proceedings of the 1888 and 1889 sessions in its *Journal*.
[5] Infringements of the music rules were reported from Satara, Wai, Chiplun, Nasik, Yeola and Poona. See, for example, para. 1484 (Satara, 4 September 1894), para. 1488 (Ratnagiri, 5 September 1894), para. 1300 (Satara, 31 July 1894), para. 1584 (Nasik, 18 September 1894), para. 1706 (Nasik, 10 October 1894), para. 2098 (Poona, 16 December 1894) Bombay Police Abstracts vol. VII, 1894, Bombay HFM.

As a consequence of the prosecutions, the Sarvajanik Sabha drew up a memorial in which it argued that the music rules applied not to religious processions, where quiet music was played by devotees, but only to the raucous music performed by hired musicians in marriage and secular processions.[1] In particular, the Sabha protested against the recent rigorous application of the rules in Poona and Wai, claiming that 'This fatal mistake has been at the bottom of all the irritation which has been felt by the Hindoo community all over the Deccan, and the irritation has been aggravated tenfold by indiscriminate prosecutions, under the Police Act, of respectable gentlemen, under the mistaken notion that such prosecutions and punishments would strengthen the authority of the lower executive and police officers.'[2] Inevitably, since Brahmin kin and friends of members of the Sarvajanik Sabha had suffered most from the activities of the police and magistrates, this memorial, so different from the Sabha's earlier work, seemed less than frank. The government responded by demanding to know the communal and caste composition of the Sabha's elected members, and the names of those present when the memorial was approved.[3] Quite properly the Sabha resented this inquisition, but it had to admit that its elected members now comprised 152 Hindus, two Muslims and four Parsis.[4]

At this point Tilak realised that he was powerful enough to grapple directly with his local opponents (particularly Ranade), who had, despite Tilak's growing popularity and his continual attacks on them in his newspapers, retained their control of the Sarvajanik Sabha. In July 1895 Tilak established his supporters in a majority on the Sabha's managing committee. Gokhale wrote:

[1] Secretaries of the Poona Sarvajanik Sabha to Govt. Bombay, 29 November 1894, *Journal of the Poona Sarvajanik Sabha*, vol. XVIII, pt 3, pp. 30–8.
[2] *Journal of the Poona Sarvajanik Sabha*, vol. XVII, pt 3, p. 34. The prosecutions which particularly rankled were those of Hari Ramchandra Natu in Poona, and of thirteen Brahmins at Wai. Ollivant to Woodburn, 10 July 1897, Notes, Home Public A, May 1898, 329–44, NAI. See also para. 1484 (Satara, 4 September 1894), para. 1529 (Satara, 11 September 1894) and para. 1663 (Satara, 2 October 1894), Bombay Police Abstracts, vol. VII, 1894, Bombay HFM. The magistrate at Wai was W. C. Rand, and he had vindictively made his Brahmin prisoners walk, in the heat of the day, the twenty miles from his court to the jail at Satara. Wolpert, *Tilak and Gokhale*, p. 83.
[3] *Journal of the Poona Sarvajanik Sabha*, vol. XVII, pt 3, pp. 42–3, 44.
[4] *Ibid.* pp. 43, 45.

The real object of that revolution was to take the Sabha out of Mr. Ranade's hands. You know of course that for nearly a quarter of a century now, all real work for the Sabha has been principally done by Mr. Ranade. Now some men here, who cannot bear the thought of Mr. Ranade wielding so much influence even in political matters, considered that they might best strike at the root of this influence by taking the Sabha out of his hands. Well, they gained their object by introducing into the Sabha, on the day of the annual general meeting, a large number of new members who practically turned out the old managing Committee and appointed a new one, composed for the most part of men who simply hate Mr. Ranade for his opinions in social and religious matters.[1]

Tilak, who believed that the change had been made in response to popular demand, rebutted the charges levelled against his handling of the election. He maintained that false and exaggerated reports had appeared in the Bombay press. He pointed out that the Sabha had substantially changed its managing committee in 1889,[2] but that there had been no change since then.

For some time past the Managing Committee of the Sabha had come to be regarded as a body of monopolists who were unwilling to take note of what was going on around them. This naturally gave rise to opposition and slowly but surely the latter was gaining in strength during the course of the last twelve months. There is no foundation whatever for naming the two parties as moderate and forward. Both of them hold almost identical views in all matters with which the Sabha is concerned. The distinction is therefore simply imaginary. If it be necessary to name the parties at all we would name them as monopolists and non-monopolists. Both of them were trying to enrol new members with a view to ultimately secure a majority for themselves; and the fight was an open one.[3]

About 125 people had attended the annual general meeting, and Ranade's friends had found themselves in a minority. Of the thirty-five members of the new committee only ten had been on the retiring committee; one of these was Gokhale, who was re-elected secretary.[4] Gokhale, however, could not see himself

[1] Gokhale to Joshi, 8 February 1896, Gokhale Papers, Reel 5, NAI.
[2] This was mainly because the secretary, S. H. Chiplonkar, persisted in supporting the Bombay government's stand against perjured mamlatdars in the Crawford case. See 32 of 1888, para. 6 (Poona, 29 September 1888), 35 of 1888, para. 10 (Poona, 18 October 1888), Bombay Police Abstracts, vol. I, 1888, Bombay HFM; para. 284 (Poona, 12 August 1889), *ibid.* vol. II.
[3] *Mahratta*, 21 July 1895.
[4] *ibid.*

working for the new committee and, after first taking six months' leave, he resigned.[1]

Gokhale's acceptance of the post in the Sarvajanik Sabha had been the immediate cause of Tilak's resignation from the Deccan Education Society. Since 1890 Tilak had taken his revenge on those associated with the Education Society by destroying their influence in public affairs in Poona, and, in particular, by undermining their interest in the Sarvajanik Sabha. With malicious satisfaction the *Journal of the Poona Sarvajanik Sabha*, having recorded its 'high appreciation of the services [Gokhale] rendered to this Journal and the great loss it has sustained in his resignation', continued 'We have, however, the consolation to know that what has been a loss to the Journal and the Sarvajanik Sabha will be a distinct gain to the Fergusson College. Prof. Gokhale will now be able to devote his undivided attention to the work to which he has dedicated his life: and the readers of this Journal will, we hope, feel compensated by the service he might render to the cause of higher education.'[2] Gokhale found the quarrelling in the Sabha, and particularly the attacks on Ranade, so distasteful that he wished to wash his 'hands of all political work in Poona. There is so much that is selfish and ignoble here that I would fly from it to the furthest extremities of the world.'[3]

Tilak's capture of the Poona Sarvajanik Sabha gave him an opportunity of organising his following. His fame and popularity, when compared with those of his rivals, were never doubted. Tilak's appeal to local patriotism and to indigenous Indian traditions had struck a vein of Maharashtrian chauvinism. But he had to find some means of formalising his support and of giving it a regular constitutional shape if he was to be recognised as an effective politician. The spontaneity of the Ganpati and Shivaji festivals had to be translated into the normal political vocabulary of the nineteenth century and had to be made appropriate to the political system within which Tilak sought power. Therefore he set about making the Sarvajanik

[1] Gokhale did not resign at once in deference to Ranade's wishes. Gokhale to Joshi, 8 February 1896, Gokhale Papers, Reel 5; Wacha to Gokhale, 30 January 1896, *ibid.* Reel 11, NAI.
[2] *Journal of the Poona Sarvajanik Sabha*, vol. XIX, 1 and 2, pp. 3-4.
[3] Gokhale to Joshi, 8 February 1896, Gokhale Papers, Reel 5, NAI.

Sabha more active, and he extended its field of operations to districts outside Poona.

When famine loomed over the Deccan in 1897, Tilak decided to send members of the Sabha out into the countryside to investigate agrarian problems.[1] These 'famine agents' were given wide publicity and were reported addressing crowds of villagers and founding Sarvajanik Sabhas wherever they went. They were backed up by students from Poona's colleges who, at a series of meetings held by the Sabha, were instructed, when they returned home in the vacation, to advise the peasants in their village not to pay taxes.[2] This activity was most unwelcome to the government, which construed the Sabha's activities as 'calculated to incite uneducated landholders to withhold payment of revenue due by them to the State, and ... to have resulted in combinations against such payments even in parts of the district where there is no distress'.[3] The Bombay government, disturbed by the general tone of Poona politics, decided that 'The Poona Sarvajanik Sabha as at present constituted must therefore cease to be recognised as a body which has any claim to address the Government on questions of public policy.'[4] Since this had been the Sabha's whole *raison d'être*, the government's notification made it redundant. This cut the ground from under Tilak and it dashed his hopes of using the Sabha as the formal embodiment of Maharashtrian opinion.[5] It also meant that for all practical purposes Tilak's popularity had been neutralised: he had been denied the only way of bringing his extensive support into provincial or national politics.

The government had considered for some time that the new

[1] The Sabha had investigated rural conditions in its very earliest days. See Seal, *The emergence of Indian nationalism*, p. 239.
[2] *Kesari*, 29 December 1896, RNP (Bombay), 1897. See also the numerous police reports, for example para. 7 (Bijapur, 19 December 1896), Bombay Police Abstracts, vol. x, 1897, Bombay HFM; para. 68 (Ratnagiri, 26 December 1896), *ibid.*; para. 71 (Ahmadnagar, 4 January 1897), *ibid.*; para. 141 (Ratnagiri, 13 January 1897), *ibid.*; para. 69 (Kolaba, 3 January 1897), *ibid.*; para. 143 (Khandesh, 11 January 1897), *ibid.*; para. 221 (Nasik, 28 January 1897), *ibid.*; para. 185 (Dharwar, 9 January 1897), *ibid.*; para. 393 (Kolaba, 1 March 1897), *ibid.*
[3] Resolution of the Govt. Bombay, 17 March 1897, *Journal of the Poona Sarvajanik Sabha*, vol. XIX, nos. 3 and 4, p. 69.
[4] *Ibid.* p. 70.
Tilak, of course, was able to use the Sabha's large hall for public meetings and lectures, and the Sabha retained some funds of its own. Para. 697 (Poona, 15 August 1904) Bombay Police Abstracts, vol. XVII, 1904, Bombay HFM.

The politics of western India in the later nineteenth century

style of politics in Poona went beyond acceptable constitutional bounds, and an opportunity occurred later in 1897 for the government to strike at its critics in Maharashtra. Plague followed in the wake of famine, and the Bombay government sent W. C. Rand to supervise sanitary regulations in Poona. He enforced the regulations with such lack of judgement and consideration that he became the most unpopular man in the city.[1] On the night of Queen Victoria's Jubilee, Rand, and an unfortunate young officer riding in a carriage behind him, were shot as they left the governor's residence by two young Chitpavan Brahmins, Damodar and Balkrishna Chapekar. Investigations revealed that the Chapekars were the driving force behind a semi-secret society for the defence of Hindu religion. This society had its headquarters in a room in Khasgiwalla's wada in the heart of the city. Its members advocated 'hostility to the reform party among Hindus, enthusiasm for orthodox Hindu observances, [and] the use of violence towards individuals regarded as obnoxious'.[2] About twenty young men had joined the club and they had spent their time studying old drill-books and practising gymnastic exercises and the use of fire-arms.[3]

The government did not believe that the activities of the Chapekars could be considered in isolation. Bombay reported to Calcutta

there is the clearest possible connection in the eyes of those watching events in the Deccan, between the continual incitement to disaffection, coupled as it is with exhortation to cultivation of physical strength, to imitation of the deeds of Shivaji, to unity and solidarity on the one hand and the doings of

[1] See *Mahratta*, 25 April 1897; para. 508 (Poona, 21 March 1897), Bombay Police Abstracts, vol. x, 1897, Bombay HFM. The Lieutenant-Governor of the North-western Provinces and Oudh wrote later 'If the plague regulations had been enforced in any city of these provinces in the way in which, judging from Mr Rand's letter, they were ... enforced in Poona, there would certainly have been bloodshed here.' Macdonnell to Elgin, 16 July 1897, Keep-with 5, Home Public A, May 1898, 329–344, NAI.
[2] District Superintendent of Police to District Magistrate, Poona, 28 March 1899, Enclosure in enclosure in Home Public A, September 1899, 5, NAI.
[3] *Ibid*. The Chapekars also attended a gymnastic club organised by the Natu brothers. The District Superintendent of Police in Poona had earlier reported that 'The Natu brothers had a following of troublesome and turbulent people, who at their bidding were ready for any mischief and business likely to hamper the authorities and disturb the peace and harmony of the city of Poona'. Quoted by Inspector-General of Police Bombay, to Govt. Bombay, 15 July 1899, enclosure 2 in Home Public A, September 1899, 5, NAI.

such persons as the Chapekars on the other. And while the apostles of the Press, of the Ganpati *melas*, of the Shivaji cult and such movements would repudiate all responsibility and insist on the legality of their pursuits, the Governor-in-Council cannot but realise that the active interpretation of such teaching by the more reckless students therefore is regarded not merely without condemnation, but with feelings which are not far removed from complacency and secret approval.[1]

The first step taken to shake this complacency was to quarter extra police in the town and to require the municipal commissioners to raise taxes to pay for them.[2] The government then proceeded against those it thought morally responsible for the assassinations. Under the provisions of the antique Regulation XXV, it detained Balwant Ramchandra Natu and his brother, Hari Ramchandra, the recognised patrons of the extreme neo-orthodox movement in Poona and attacked their property.[3] More important, however, the government arrested Tilak and charged him with spreading sedition. It produced as evidence a speech he had made at the 1897 Shivaji festival, which had been reported in *Kesari* a few days before the assassinations.[4] Tilak was found guilty of seditious writing and sentenced to eighteen months' imprisonment.[5]

The government's extreme measures had the desired result, and political activity was damped in Poona for the time being.[6]

[1] Govt. Bombay to Govt. India, 25 August 1899, Home Public A, September 1899, 5, NAI.

[2] The immediate cost of the extra police was to be Rs. 32,128, and the annual cost would be Rs. 1,15,207. The government decided to station the police in Poona for two years. Resolution by the Government of Bombay, 29 June 1897, Home Police A, November 1897, 60, NAI.

[3] The Natus were detained in Belgaum district without trial before being finally released on 26 December 1899. Govt. Bombay to District Magistrate, Poona, 26 July 1897. Enclosure in Govt. Bombay to Govt. India, 21 September 1899, Home Public A, November 1900, 92, NAI.

[4] At the Shivaji festival, Tilak had argued that great men were above the common principles of morality. He held that Shivaji had not behaved treacherously when he had killed the Muslim general Afzal Khan while the two sides were parleying together. The government interpreted this as an argument absolving all political assassins from any moral blame See *Kesari*, 15 June 1897, RNP (Bombay), 1897; *Imperatrix* v. *Tilak and another*, Home Public A, May 1898, 356, NAI; Chirol, *Indian unrest*, p. 46; Wolpert, *Tilak and Gokhale*, pp. 85–103.

[5] *Imperatrix* v. *Tilak and another*, sixth day of trial, 11 September 1897, p. 89. Home Public A, May 1898, 378, NAI.

[6] The government also launched a series of prosecutions against the following Marathi newspapers: *Poona Vaibav*, *Pratod*, and *Moda Vritta*. See the reports in the file Home Public A, May 1898, 345–376, NAI. Following these blows, Kelkar, left in charge of *Mahratta* and *Kesari*, viewed the prospect for 1898

The politics of western India in the later nineteenth century

Yet public reactions to the arrests revealed the extent of Tilak's fame. While no one seemed to care about the detention of the Natus, there was considerable sympathy for Tilak, and this seemed to justify the government's stern course.[1] Analysing the volumes of police reports, the inspector-general of police in Bombay was convinced that Tilak had deliberately followed a policy of 'systematically opposing and misrepresenting measures of Government'.[2] He had done so because he had recognised the possibilities of securing widespread and articulate Brahmin support for his leadership in the Deccan. It had been 'clear to him that the surest means of gaining popularity among the people was to take up grievances, supposed or real, and to stand forth as their sympathiser, adviser and champion'.[3] Through his speeches at the Ganpati and Shivaji festivals, Tilak had emphasised, exaggerated, and given wide currency to dissatisfaction with the government. 'By this means he hoped to gain the people to recognise him as their leader, and with their support to create an irresistible public opinion behind him, and so bring pressure on Government to concede the demands put forward by him.'[4] Tilak's newspapers had played upon the anxieties of the educated poor, and had fed them those dreams of grandeur that had underlain Phadke's romantic revolt. Tilak had united under his banner 'the orthodox Brahmins throughout the Deccan and Konkan, so that by carrying out simultaneously at all important centres the programmes mapped out by him, added force, unanimity and popularity might be given to the movement'.[5]

---

bitterly: 'We are still children in the modern ways of political agitation, and are as such liable to commit many excesses and errors. An occasional use of the birch by our masters and the rulers should therefore be welcomed as a salutary corrective which by opening our eyes in time may prevent greater catastrophes.' *Mahratta*, 2 January 1898.

[1] 'The arrest of the Natus is not resented except among the immediate circle of their friends, as they were more feared than popular. Some say that their ancestors betrayed the Peishwa to the British and that the family deserves the disgrace that has overtaken it. As regards the arrest of Bal Gangadhar Tilak, the feeling is different. It is universally disapproved of in the upper circles of Hindu society; the lower classes, however, seem indifferent and the Muhammadans jubilant.' Para. 1152 (Poona, 1 August 1897), Bombay Police Abstracts, vol. x, 1897, Bombay HFM.

[2] Inspector-General of Police to Govt. Bombay, 15 July 1899, enclosure 2 in Home Public A, September 1899, 5, NAI.

[3] *Ibid.*   [4] *Ibid.*   [5] *Ibid.*

The politics of western India in the later nineteenth century

The Bombay government reacted so strongly to Tilak because the eager recipients of his inflammatory propaganda occupied crucial positions in western India: they were the teachers in every school, the journalists manning every printing press, the clerks in every office: even the signalmen on the railway belonged to the communities from which he drew his support.[1] But above all was the threat Tilak posed to the administration itself. The government was in no doubt that he had received 'the sympathy and secret support' of a considerable proportion of those who monopolised jobs in the lower ranks of the civil service and those who were beginning to control the institutions of local government. In sum, the Governor of Bombay had 'no doubt whatever that no Brahmin movement takes place without consultation with him, and that he occupies a position of prominent influence in the Deccan and that his influence is persistently used against the Government, nor does he feel any doubt that Mr. Tilak would not scruple to endeavour to substitute a Brahmin for British rule in Maharashtra, if he could do so'.[2]

The attention the government paid to Tilak showed that they regarded him as a serious trouble-maker. It would, however, be a mistake to think that Tilak was merely a spokesman for a narrow Brahmin clique in Poona. In fact he commanded a wider following, and if the government exaggerated his real influence they also underestimated his independence and his capacity for appealing to a more general constituency. For one thing, Tilak's relationship with the so-called orthodox leaders in Poona was always ambivalent. Although the district superintendent of police in Poona was satisfied that Tilak was simply an exponent of traditional values, the reports on his desk indicated that Tilak was far from being narrowly orthodox himself and that he was not simply a religious revivalist or a reactionary politician. At the same time as Tilak was castigating the supporters of the Age of Consent Bill, a letter bearing his signature alongside those of Ranade and Bhandarkar was circulating the Deccan advocating certain measures of social

---

[1] Para. 720 (Bombay, 23 May 1899), Bombay Police Abstracts, vol. XII, 1899, Bombay HFM.
[2] Govt. Bombay to Govt. India, 25 August 1899, Home Public A, September 1899, 5, NAI.

reform.[1] Although Tilak could appear to be a defender of old Hindu customs, in practice he had no time for their minute observance. He was among the people who were outcasted for drinking tea at the Panch Howd mission in 1891, and he later refused to undergo penances demanded by the Natus and their friends for various breaches of caste discipline.[2]

This makes Tilak a more complex character to understand. Precise analysis of his attitudes and of his actions would not be very rewarding. As in other major public figures, it is easy to discover inconsistencies and, by giving undue weight to them, to dismiss him simply as a self-seeking machiavel. As his later activities were to show, Tilak was able both to use and to discard all kinds of communal and semi-communal elements in his political platform, just as on some issues he was to retain over the decades remarkable consistency. During the 1880s, however, almost everyone he came across in public life in Poona happened also to be a Brahmin; and since so much of his politics consisted of mobilising a following through the Marathi press, he was addressing a primarily Brahmin audience, because they were the readers of that press. Moreover, Tilak's activities in the Ganpati and Shivaji festivals were also capable of being given a purely Brahminical complexion.[3] This had the disadvantage that political movements organised from Poona became characterised as Brahmin inspired and Brahmin dominated. Therefore, political enemies of the Poona leaders, whether within the government or without, would not hesitate to attack them on the grounds of caste exclusiveness. Against the Poona politicians would be made articulate the anti-Brahmin movement.

Most of the early non-Brahmin politicians in Maharashtra who called for an end of 'Brahmin tyranny' were not very convincing people. But the Maharaja of Kolhapur, who unashamedly

[1] Para. 184 (Ahmadnagar, 16 August 1890), Bombay Police Abstracts, vol. III, 1890, Bombay HFM.
[2] *Indu Prakash*, 3 August 1891, RNP (Bombay), 1891; *Kesari*, 17 May 1892, RNP (Bombay), 1892; para. 322 (Poona, 29 February 1892), Bombay Police Abstracts, vol. v, 1892; para. 498 (Poona, 12 June 1904), *ibid.* vol. XVII, 1904.
[3] The case is put in Johnson, 'Chitpavan Brahmins', in E. R. Leach and S. N. Mukherjee (eds.), *Elites in south Asia*, pp. 113–14. However, the general claim made for this argument can no longer be sustained.

deployed anti-Brahmin tactics to achieve his ends, was a politician to be reckoned with. Moreover, at crucial points, his interests impinged on those of the Poona leaders and they became involved in Kolhapur affairs. Shahu Chhatrapati, who was invested with full powers in 1894, came to the Kolhapur throne after a long period of weak and confused government in that state. The first ten years of his reign were spent attempting to master the civil service, to regain control over some of the Kolhapur feudatories, and to bring under survey and scrutiny lands that had been alienated or that were held in return for services rendered to the court. It so happened that many of those most threatened by the reforms in Kolhapur were Brahmins and, inevitably, Shahu's actions were branded as 'anti-Brahmin'. The Maharaja himself responded by standing forth as the saviour of the underprivileged: far from denying that he was persecuting Brahmins, he argued that he was justified in doing so.

In 1896, Shahu began a policy of openly discriminating against Brahmins. He announced that he would employ non-Brahmins in preference to Brahmins in the Kolhapur civil service, and he reinforced his decision by a decree in 1902 that reserved for non-Brahmins 50 per cent of all the vacancies in the administration.[1] Hand in hand with this vindictive policy went schemes for educating non-Brahmins and the establishment of special schools, colleges and hostels for them.[2] Between 1895 and 1910 Shahu proceeded against the special privileges of his feudatories, Vishalgad, Bavda, and Ichalkaranki.[3] The holders of these jagirs were all Brahmins, and, since it was up to the Bombay government to decide the issues between them and the Kolhapur durbar, Shahu presented his case at the Presidency capital in straight caste terms: the Brahmin princelings in their semi-independent enclaves had provided sanctuary on their

[1] A. B. Latthe, *Memoirs of His Highness Shri Shahu Chhatrapati Maharaja of Kolhapur* (Bombay, 1924), vol. I, pp. 152, 220–1.
[2] *Ibid.* pp. 139–48.
[3] Ian Copland, 'The Maharaja of Kolhapur and the non-Brahmin movement 1902–1910', in *Modern Asian Studies*, vol. 7, no. 2 (April 1973), 215–17, 222–4. A fourth large jagir was held directly by the Maharaja's own family. There were, besides these four feudatories, another seven smaller ones which, while recognising the suzerainty of the Kolhapur durbar, possessed some independent legal privileges. *Ibid.*

The politics of western India in the later nineteenth century

estates for fugitive Brahmin terrorists from Poona.[1] The case, although plausible, was not entirely convincing.[2] and the dispute between the durbar and the large jagirdars dragged on into the 1920s.

The Kolhapur Brahmins, seeing that caste was to be a decisive factor in durbar politics, were not slow to use it as a weapon against the Maharaja himself. The most effective way in which they could retaliate was by imposing religious and ritual sanctions on the court. In 1900, Shahu's attendants noticed that the Brahmin who accompanied the Maharaja when he went to bathe in the river Panchaganga did not himself bathe before blessing the ceremony. On being asked why he had omitted to do so, the Brahmin replied that 'it was not necessary for him to bathe as the persons to be blessed were mere Sudras, who had a right to the lower Puranic blessings as distinguished from the Vedic Mantras which alone deserved a preliminary bath'.[3] The Maharaja and his friends were furious at the assertion that they were Sudras and not Kshatriyas, but they could not persuade the Rajopadhye (the court Brahmin) and the Kolhapur priest to change his ruling on this question. The Maharaja thereupon made enquiries into the historical background to the question, employed another Brahmin the following year to perform various rituals for the court, and, finally, confiscated the large estates the Rajopadhye held from the durbar in return for performing religious duties.[4] This expropriation was seen by the press as a flagrant attempt by Shahu to discriminate against the Brahmin community as a whole. More important, it gave credibility to the claim that Kolhapur politics were all about caste.

During the controversies both sides looked beyond Kolhapur – to Bombay and Poona – for support. Both sides, moreover, began to see advantages in putting forward their case in simple caste terms. The anti-durbar press in Kolhapur aligned itself

[1] The ruler of Ichalkaranji in particular gave refuge to fugitives from Kolhapur. He was a Chitpavan Brahmin. *Ibid.* p. 221.
[2] It was inconvenient for the general hypothesis, for example, that the ruler of Sangli, also a Chitpavan Brahmin, pursued a vigorous policy against extremists in the Deccan. In 1905 students in Sangli were prohibited even from taking part in the Shivaji festival. *Kesari*, 3 October 1905, quoted *ibid.* p. 213.
[3] Latthe, *Maharaja of Kolhapur*, vol. I, pp. 186–7.
[4] *Ibid.* p. 194. He was not restored to favour until 1917. *Ibid.* vol. II, p. 459.

with Tilak's newspapers and reproved Shahu for his caste prejudice and his unreasoned hostility towards Brahmins. To the Bombay government, and to the Vicereine herself, the Brahmins in Kolhapur presented themselves as the victims of a ruthless persecution by the Maharaja.[1] Towards Bombay, Shahu showed himself struggling endlessly with wily Brahmin plots, and he traded on the hostility towards that caste known to be found in those quarters. But Shahu's anti-Brahminism was always selective: it was only his enemies he wished to get rid of, and, throughout his reign, 'loyal' Brahmins in Kolhapur had no difficulty in finding jobs or in keeping their land.[2] Shahu looked towards Poona, too, and in that city, where everyone who mattered was a Brahmin, his propaganda against that caste was no asset. Instead, he fell in with the existing party lines: if Tilak was against him, then he was for the other side. His money poured into the Deccan Education Society, of which he was the President; he backed the social reformers, and he rescued their newspaper *Sudharak* when it faced financial ruin.[3]

The Brahmin–non-Brahmin polemic waged between the Kolhapur durbar and *Kesari* concealed, however, a real clash of interests between Balwant Ramchandra Natu, Tilak and the Maharaja. Both Natu and Tilak suffered from the durbar's confiscation of estates in Kolhapur – the first during a quarrel between Shahu and the Shankaracharya of Sankeshwar, the

---

[1] See, for example, *Samarth*, 8 August 1906, quoted in I. Copland, 'The Maharaja of Kolhapur', in *Modern Asian Studies*, vol. VII, no. 2 (April 1973), 218. In 1906 the 'poor helpless women' of Kolhapur petitioned Lady Minto alleging that four Brahmin ladies had been forcibly seduced by the Maharaja and that the Political Agent had refused to act in the matter. Broadsheets were distributed maintaining 'No beautiful woman is immune from the violence of the Maharaja ... and the Brahmins being special objects of hatred no Brahmin women can hope to escape this shameful fate.' The Political Agent commenting on the petition and on the broadsheets wrote 'I am sure as it is possible to be that His Highness leads a clean life. (I believe he had a mistress up to last year, but she died; he has never been a promiscuous fornicator.)' The Agent blamed everything on troublesome Brahmins. Political Agent to Govt. Bombay, 5 August 1906 and enclosures. Appendix to Notes, Home Public A, October 1906, 240–44, NAI.

[2] For example, after nearly thirty years of hostility to Brahmins in public employment, there were still thirty-six of them among the ninety-five posts in the Kolhapur General Department, and forty-three of them among the 153 posts in the Khasgi Department. Latthe, *Maharaja of Kolhapur*, vol. I, p. 152.

[3] Shahu was president of the Deccan Education Society from its foundation in 1884 to his death in 1922. Limaye, *History of the Deccan Education Society*, Appendix II. He financed *Sudharak* in 1906. Latthe, *Maharaja of Kolhapur*, vol. I, p. 255.

The politics of western India in the later nineteenth century

second during a dispute over the adoption of a boy to succeed to the estates of Wassadeo Harihar Pandit.

About half the revenues of the Sankeshwar math came from villages in Kolhapur state.[1] In 1902, the Shankaracharya, as was the custom, nominated his successor. He made his choice on the advice of the Poona leaders, especially the Natu brothers to whom he was indebted. The Kolhapur durbar saw in the adoption an attempt to manoeuvre in the Vedokta controversy and so the Maharaja claimed that the durbar must approve the succession before it was legally valid. The Shankaracharya at first refused to accept this condition and, as a result, Shahu confiscated the estates held by the math in Kolhapur.[2] Balwant Ramchandra Natu immediately suffered from this move because he held the Shankaracharya's Kolhapur villages as security for his loan.[3]

The second case concerned the lands of Wassadeo Harihar Pandit. This sirdar was a Deshastha Brahmin whose family had long ago held office in Kolhapur as religious advisers to the raja. Better known as Baba Maharaj, he had been a leader of the reformed Ganpati movement. He died in Poona during the cholera epidemic of 1897.[4] His will established a board of

---

[1] The revenues of the math derived from tribute from disciples, fines levied on those who broke caste-discipline, and the revenue from thirty villages. Fifteen of these were in Kolhapur, five in Belgaum district, three in Hyderabad, and the rest scattered over southern Maharashtra. In the early 1880s the annual income from the thirty villages was estimated at Rs. 30,000. *Gazetteer of the Bombay Presidency: vol. XXI: Belgaum* (Bombay, 1884), p. 601. By 1910 it was estimated that the total annual revenue from Kolhapur alone was of the order of Rs. 25,000. Para. 144 (SB Bombay, undated January 1910), Bombay Police Abstracts, vol. XXIII, 1910, Bombay HFM.

[2] *Ibid.* See also, para. 412 (Kolhapur, 21 May 1904), *ibid.* vol. XVII, 1904; para. 508 (a) (Kolhapur, 25 June 1904), *ibid.*

[3] Natu had lent the Shankaracharya Rs. 75,000 in the late 1880s. Para. 388 (Poona, 14 May 1904), *ibid.* vol. XVII, 1904. The affairs of the math, and the Shankaracharya's relations with both the Kolhapur durbar and the Poona leaders, became incredibly tangled over the next six years as all parties tried to make the most of the situation. The story is fairly clearly set out in para. 144 (SB Bombay, undated January 1910), *ibid.* vol. XXIII, 1910. But see also para. 367 (Poona, 30 April 1904 and SB Bombay, 7 May 1904); para. 388 (Poona, 14 May 1904); para. 412 (Kolhapur, 21 May 1904); para. 508 (Kolhapur, 25 June 1904 and Satara, 21 June 1904); para. 438 (Poona, 4 June 1904); para. 479 (Satara, 13 June 1904); and para. 692 (Kolhapur, 20 August 1904), *ibid.* vol. XVII, 1904; and also para. 428 (Belgaum, 31 May 1906); para. 696 (Kolhapur, 1 September 1906), *ibid.* vol. XIX, 1906; and para. 1407 (Kolhapur, 4 July 1909), *ibid.* vol. XXII, 1909.

[4] He died on 7 August 1897. The Poona authorities reported 'His death is a blow

trustees to manage the estate and, if necessary, to arrange the adoption of an heir. In 1899 the infant son of Baba Maharaj died, and the complicated process of adoption began.[1] The widow, Tai Maharaj, together with two of the trustees, Tilak and G. S. Khaparde of Amraoti, eventually arranged for a boy in Aurangabad district to be adopted.[2] The trustees then fell out among themselves. Tai Maharaj attempted with the connivance of one of them to take over direct administration of the estate.[3] She went to Kolhapur, claimed that she had been forced to adopt the Aurangabad boy against her will, and agreed with Shahu to put up a rival candidate for the succession. In the process, Shahu took over those estates that lay within his jurisdiction and Tilak and Khaparde had no redress.[4] As a result of this quarrel, the Bombay government actively encouraged the widow and her party to pursue Tilak through the civil courts in order to gain possession of lands lying in British territory. The government even intervened to bring a criminal prosecution against Tilak in connection with the case.[5] In fact the courts eventually ruled that Tilak and his party of trustees

to the Shivaji and Ganpati movements.' Para. 1204 (Poona, 9 August 1897), *ibid.* vol. x, 1897. See also *Dnyan Prakash*, 9 August 1897, RNP (Bombay), 1897.

[1] See the entries in Khaparde's Diary, 31 May 1901, Khaparde Papers, NAI. Khaparde, whose son was married to a daughter of Baba Maharaj (para. 441 (Poona, 21 April 1901), Bombay Police Abstracts, vol. XIV, 1901, Bombay HFM) was fully preoccupied with the affairs of the estate and a detailed account of the whole business is recorded in his diary for April, May, June and July 1901.

[2] G. S. Khaparde, Diary, 29 June 1901, Khaparde Papers, NAI.

[3] G. S. Khaparde, Diary, 9 July 1901, 15–20 July 1901.

[4] Latthe, *Maharaja of Kolhapur*, vol. I, pp. 271–7.

[5] On 29 July 1901, Tai Maharaj began the case against Tilak to upset the Trustees. The Agent for the Deccan Sirdars supported her, and in his court the probate granted to Tilak and Khaparde was revoked, the adoption of the Aurangabad boy overturned, and several criminal charges were framed against Tilak. On 24 August 1903, Tilak was convicted of perjury in the Poona Magistrate's court. He was sentenced to eighteen months' imprisonment and fined Rs. 1,000. On 4 January 1904 the sessions judge confirmed the conviction but reduced the sentence. Tilak was imprisoned, but released pending an appeal to the Bombay High Court on 8 January 1904. The Bombay High Court allowed Tilak's appeal and quashed his conviction. In June 1904 he therefore resumed the civil case. In 1906 it was transferred to the Privy Council who resolved in favour of Tilak's side. The case was, however, to drag on for another decade before, in February 1917, the decision of the Privy Council was executed. See, *All about Lok. Tilak with a foreword by Mr Joseph Baptista* (Madras, 1922), pp. xxiv–xxix; N. C. Kelkar, *Landmarks in the Lokmanya's Life* (Madras, 1924), pp. 62–110, 125–30. Tai Maharaj herself died in September 1903. Para. 1034 (SB Bombay, 2 October 1903), Bombay Police Abstracts, vol. XVI, 1903, Bombay HFM.

had the law on their side, and the Bombay government's unscrupulous use of the case to harass and occupy one of its political opponents is not very creditable.

The Maharaja of Kolhapur's declared intention of employing non-Brahmins in his state, his moves against his feudatories, and his action over the properties of the Rajopadhye, the Shankaracharya of Sankeshwar and Baba Maharaj were the fuel with which the anti-Brahmin movement in western India was fed. The Bombay government, for its own ends, made selective use of the Kolhapur intrigues: it was convenient to be able to show from an independent Indian source that Brahmins as a class were not to be trusted in politics. The wrangling extended to Poona and the leaders there became embrangled in Kolhapur quarrels. Yet it would be fanciful to see in these events evidence of serious caste-conflict in Maharashtra, or the formation of a genuine non-Brahmin political platform. They were, once again, an expression of factional fighting among elite groups; a few rounds of shadow boxing between those who were, or sought to be, the spokesmen of Maharashtra.

So far, Tilak has emerged as the central figure in Maharashtrian politics. By the end of the nineteenth century he had achieved wider fame than any of his contemporaries, and he had been credited, by friends and enemies alike, with organising a major political movement in Maharashtra. There can be little doubt, from all the evidence available, that from the mid-1890s until his death in 1920, the way in which Tilak caught the imagination of Maharashtrians was unequalled by any of his rivals, and it can be argued that no other Indian of his generation strove so successfully to muster such a committed and loyal following as Tilak did: not in Bengal, and neither in the northern heartland nor in the southern Madras Presidency was any leader so widely known, regarded with such devotion, or so utterly accepted. Yet what part did Tilak play in the politics of the continent? And how, in the face of his popularity, did his opponents try to curb his influence?

To begin with, some qualifications must be made about Tilak's success as a politician. Mere popularity is a fickle political attribute. Unless it could be turned into solid voting power, or organised and disciplined within the existing institutional and constitutional machinery, it risked becoming irrelevant to the struggles for power conducted within it. How could the euphoria of the carnival be made a realistic political asset? What use to Tilak were the Ganpati crowds, or the avid readers of his editorials, if their influence could not be brought to bear upon the government or upon the Congress? In fact it could not. The legislatures and local boards were still elected by a handful of men; the organisation of the Congress barely existed. Tilak's success in whipping up enthusiasm in Maharashtra counted against him in more formal political arenas. The government decided in 1897 that brutal firmness was required when dealing with him. By sending Tilak to jail in that year, and again in 1908, and by its continual antipathy towards him, the government made sure that never, to his life's end, would he participate directly in the formal councils of state, or in the politics of municipalities and district boards. Tilak had therefore put beyond reach that power which he as a politician sought. This made him an ineffective broker between Indian interests and the government, for who, except those whose causes were already lost, would hitch their wagon to his star? Further, the uniquely Maharashtrian elements in Tilak's appeal threw doubt upon his capacity to act as a mediator between wider Indian interests. Thus, in the Bombay Presidency, what could he offer to men in Gujarat or Sind, whose historical traditions made them wary of Mahratta imperialism or of fervent Hindu proselytising? And, in an all-India context, what did Ganpati and Shivaji mean to men in the Punjab, or Bengal, or Madras? Was not Tilak's nationalism Maharashtrian rather than Indian?

Moreover, although Tilak's triumphs in Poona seemed to be complete, it does not do to underestimate the skills and resources of his opponents. In Poona itself, Gokhale and his friends had stayed in command of the Deccan Education Society, with its valuable college and its network of affiliated schools. Once Tilak had taken over the Sarvajanik Sabha, they had formed the Deccan Sabha 'to secure a well-conducted political organisation, which will subserve, in these more advanced times, the interests identified with moderate and liberal public opinion'.[1]

[1] Advertisement describing the aims of 'The Deccan Sabha', Tilak Papers, *Kesari* Office, Poona.

The politics of western India in the later nineteenth century

Although this body might not have been very active, its members were men of weight in Maharashtra. When the Sarvajanik Sabha ceased to be recognised by the government of Bombay, the field was left open for the Deccan Sabha to become the sole mouth-piece of responsible opinion in Poona. It functioned also as the centre for official Congress work in Maharashtra.[1] After Gokhale retired from the Deccan Education Society in 1902, he decided to devote his life to politics. With this end in mind, the Servants of India Society was founded in 1905 to draw together a band of graduates, dedicated to full-time educational charities and political work.[2]

Lacking the spontaneity and show of Tilak's festivals, and the fire of his journalism, the institutions in Poona with which Gokhale was intimately connected were far better placed to play a part in the formal political life of India. The Education Society, the Deccan Sabha, and later the Servants of India Society,[3] were precisely the kinds of open institution that were capable of standing forth as intermediaries between governed and governors and between one Indian interest and another. Gokhale himself was an ideal candidate for municipal and legislative council work, and his Servants of India busied themselves throughout the next twenty years touring the country and acting as fact-finders and political middle-men. Not only was this style of politics fully in line with the constitutional developments taking place within the government, but it was the very life-blood of organisations like the Congress.

Although it is usually argued that Tilak cared nothing for the government and thought its deliberative bodies farcical,[4] there can be little doubt that despite his depreciation of them the politician in him was aware of their importance and the lawyer in him relished every opportunity for constitutional obstruction

---

[1] See, Deccan Sabha, Poona, Correspondence File, 1896–1920, Servants of India Society Papers; *The Deccan Sabha, Poona: Golden Jubilee Celebration* (Poona, 1947).
[2] See, Servants of India Letter Books, Servants of India Society Papers, Poona.
[3] The Servants of India Society was founded by Gokhale on 12 June 1905. Its aim was to 'train men for the work of political education and agitation, and to promote by all constitutional means the national interests of the Indian people'. See the original constitution of the Society in D. G. Karve and D. V. Ambekar (eds.), *Speeches and writings of Gopal Krishna Gokhale*, vol. II – Political (London, 1966), pp. 181–6.
[4] For example, Parvate, *Tilak*, p. 72; Kelkar, *Life of Lokhmanya Tilak*, pp. 273–4.

which the machinery of government afforded. When in 1895 the government of Bombay decided to accept a nomination for the provincial legislature from the district boards of the Central Division, Tilak did not think it beneath him to stand and he was elected easily.[1] When his term of office came to an end in 1897 he was returned a second time. His imprisonment deprived him of his seat, but no sooner was he released in 1899 than he began canvassing for re-election. During that year vigorous lobbying went on among the district boards that made up the constituency.[2] Only when Gokhale had secured the promise of a majority of the votes did Tilak withdraw from the contest.[3] The fact that Tilak showed so badly was, no doubt, because some of the voters were not sure whether the government would allow his nomination: but the incident illustrates well some of the limitations on his political appeal. When votes were cast it would be on the basis of hard-headed calculations as to who would be the best man, not necessarily the most popular.[4]

However, perhaps the most decisive check on Tilak's influence was the fact that Maharashtra was no longer a self-contained political unit, nor was Poona, its natural centre, any

[1] *Ibid.* p. 271.
[2] *Ibid.* p. 275; para. 955 (Ahmadnagar, 25 June 1899), Bombay Police Abstracts, vol. XII, 1899, Bombay HFM; para. 1511 (Satara, 10 October 1899), *ibid.*; para. 1515 (Poona, 10 October 1899), *ibid.*; para. 1588 (Ahmadnagar, 21 October 1899), *ibid.*; para. 1626 (Nasik, 30 October 1899), *ibid.*; para. 1628 (Sholapur, 30 October 1899), *ibid.*; para. 1652 (Poona, 30 October 1899), *ibid.*; para. 1681 (Satara, 6 November 1899), *ibid.*; para. 1711 (Ahmadnagar, 21 November 1899), *ibid.*
[3] 'After his release from jail in 1899, Tilak again wanted to get elected. But for one reason or another Tilak did not take any resolve to stand or not to stand, and when at last he decided on the first alternative, his friends and supporters themselves thought his candidature too late in the day.' (Kelkar, *Life of Lokhmanya Tilak*, pp. 275–7.) 'The Inspector-General of Police learns that Bal Gangadhar Tilak sounded his constituents and finds that they are not disposed to support him, so [he] has decided not to stand for election. Professor Gokhale is said to have secured the promise of 45 or two-thirds of the votes and is therefore sure of being elected.' (Para. 1714 (SB Bombay, 21 November 1899), Bombay Police Abstracts, vol. XII, 1899, Bombay HFM.)
[4] Gokhale told the district magistrate in Satara that 'he [Gokhale] is practically certain of the support of all the Satara electors, for although some of them are in favour of Mr Tilak, who is apparently also going to stand, they think that it would be wasting their votes to give them to him, as they expect that Government would refuse to sanction Tilak's election, even if he received a majority of votes.' Para. 1511 (Satara, 10 October 1899), *ibid.*

longer the mainspring of power in western India. The establishment of British rule had radically changed the political geography of the whole region. The most important parts of Maharashtra had been absorbed into the Bombay Presidency and Poona had become a simple divisional headquarters. After the defeat of the Peshwa, the political future of Poona and the surrounding Marathi-speaking districts was bound to the development of the Bombay Presidency and subordinated to rulers based on an off-shore island. This shift in the balance of power in western India created new unities, weakened some old ones, and set up tensions between them. As the economic and political weight of Bombay began to be felt on its hinterland, the strains between the old order and the new became more telling. For, while the nineteenth century brought fresh opportunities for Maharashtrians living in the Bombay Presidency, the framework of rule also imposed limitations on their ambitions. In the new Presidency, Maharashtra was thrown in with parts of Gujarat, Sind, and the Karnatak. At the new seat of authority Maharashtrians were not the only, or the most influential, groups.

The economic and political importance of Bombay city grew with the nineteenth century. Between 1818 and the 1850s road and rail links were established between the town, which was once isolated, and the mainland. Its fine natural harbour, and the opening of the Suez canal, made it the most important international port in India. Between the 1840s and 1900 Bombay's economic development was prodigious: not only did shipping and commerce grow, but supporting services and industries were established. By the turn of the century, Bombay city was one of the five biggest textile producing areas in the world.[1] Apart from its economic role, Bombay developed as a great administrative, military, and educational centre. All the main government offices and the highest courts of law for the whole Presidency were located there. In 1857, one of India's first universities was opened in Bombay, and in 1901 the city boasted the highest number of adult male literates in western India, the

[1] For Bombay see O. H. K. Spate and A. T. A. Learmonth, *India and Pakistan* (3rd edition, London, 1967), pp. 656–65; M. D. Morris, *The emergence of an industrial labor force in India: a study of the Bombay cotton mills, 1854–1947* (Berkeley and Los Angeles, 1965), pp. 10–21; *Census of India 1901*, vol. X, pt IV (Bombay, 1902).

highest number of English literates in the Presidency, and three of the region's seven English Arts Colleges.[1]

The opportunities afforded by the progress of trade, local industries and better communications drew people to Bombay from all over western India. The population of the city increased nearly nine times in as many decades: between the early nineteenth century and the census of 1911 the number of people living in the city had risen from 160,000 to over 900,000.[2] Moreover, most of this increase was from immigration: in 1901 less than a quarter of Bombay's citizens had been born there.[3] Bombay was thus not only a new but a very cosmopolitan city. The European element played a much smaller and a much less powerful part in Bombay than it did in other British settlements in India. In both traditional and new trades, in traditional and new industries, as well as in the administration and the professions, it was Indians who primarily benefited from the growth of Bombay.

But which Indians were able to take the best advantage of the transformation of Bombay from an unimportant island into an economic, commercial, administrative and political powerhouse of the British raj? Bombay attracted enterprising and mobile social groups: families who were prepared to change their occupations and their place of residence in order to accumulate wealth and power. These free-floating communities were usually small. Further, arriving at Bombay, immigrants naturally sought the friendship and patronage of people of their own kind. The population of the city thus retained or developed strong communal identities.[4] But the newcomers were also

[1] At the turn of the century Bombay city's three colleges had 976 pupils. Poona had two colleges with 400 pupils; Ahmadabad one college with 243 pupils; Karachi one college with 157 pupils. *Supplement to the Director of Public Instruction's Quinquennial Report for 1897/98 to 1901/02*, pp. 8–9.
[2] Morris, *The emergence of an industrial labor force in India*, p. 20.
[3] *Census of India 1901* (Bombay, 1902), vol. IX-A, pt vi, table XI; *ibid.* vol. X, pt iv, p. 152.
[4] The census commissioner noted 'all the tribes in Western India seem to have flocked to Bombay... The poorer Parsi sought the home of his ancestors in the North Fort or Dhobi Talao; the Yogi, the Sanyasi found a resting place near the Shrines of Lakshmi, Kali, or the God of the Sands; the Goanese, the Native Christians were never absent from Cavel, the old home of early converts to Roman Catholicism; the Jolaha, weaver of silk, sought Madanpura; the grain merchants were a power in Mandvi; the Bene-Israel owned their Samuel Street and Israel Moholla; the dancing girls drifted to Khetwadi, "the scarlet woman"

people who were practised in dealing with more numerous neighbours and both the need and scope for co-operation between them, in economic and political affairs in the city, was very great. Paradoxically, one of the main features of life in Bombay was the development of caste or communal solidarity simultaneously with the growth of strong cross-communal affiliations, secular in nature and based on economic interest or political advantage.[1]

While Maharashtrians constituted the bulk of the populations of Bombay,[2] it was men from Gujarat and Kathiawar who best exploited the economic potential of the city and who came to dominate its affairs. Parsis, Hindu and Jain Banias from Gujarat, tiny Muslim merchant communities like the Khojas, Memons and Bhoras, Bhatias from Kathiawar and Kutch, Lohanas and Bhansalis from the north and west, all displayed their enterprise and achieved riches and fame in the city.[3] The success of individuals and families from these communities gave the wealth of Bombay a particularly Gujarati complexion. By contrast, Marathi-speakers in Bombay were not especially renowned for their prosperity.[4] Of course, Maharashtra had its adaptable, mobile, elite groups too, but they were not so much concerned with trade as with letters, and their skills were professional rather than commercial. In the nineteenth century, eager Prabhu and Brahmin lads had flocked to the new city. There they learned the skill of the rulers; there they filled the schools and offices; there they became reconciled to the fact that in the competition for power the sons of the Peshwa were no longer alone.

The inhabitants of Bombay city were at once more parochial

to Kamathipura; in the Nall Bazaar lived the progeny of men who fought under Sidi Sambhal; in Parel, Nagpada and Byculla were mill-hands from the Konkan and labourers from the Deccan; many a Koliwadi, from Colaba to Sion, gave shelter to the descendants of earliest settlers; the Mussulman was a power in B Ward, the Arab haunted Byculla; and in Girgaum the Brahmin had made his home.' *Census of India 1901*, vol. x, pt iv, p. 152.

[1] Christine Dobbin, 'Competing elites in Bombay city politics in the mid-nineteenth century (1852–83)', in E. R. Leach and S. N. Mukherjee (eds.), *Elites in south Asia*, pp. 79–94; idem, *Urban leadership in western India: politics and communities in Bombay city 1840–1885* (Oxford, 1972), *passim*.
[2] *Census of India 1901*, vol. ix, pt i, table iii, p. 158.
[3] Dobbin, *Urban leadership in western India*, pp. 2–6.
[4] The only Maharashtrians who matched the wealth of Gujarati families in the city were from the tiny Sonar and Kasar communities. *Ibid.* pp. 6–7.

and more cosmopolitan in their outlook than many of those living on the mainland. The Parsis had made the city their own; the trading and industrial families looked to no other as their homeland. Those doing well in Bombay considered the city their permanent abode: a house on Malabar Hill rather than an estate in the country was what they most desired. The Maharashtrians might look to the mainland as their real home: the labourers would return to their villages in the Konkan and the Deccan for the harvest, marriages and religious festivals, while the clerisy would look to Poona as its spiritual haven. But even by the middle of the nineteenth century such desires were mainly nostalgia for a dead past: the city conferred too many benefits, and too many individual freedoms, to be given up lightly for the more closed and regimented world of the Deccan. So Bombay's relations with the regions lying around it remained eclectic and ambiguous. It developed its own identity; it retained its own independence.

Moreover, Bombay did not grow solely upon its immediate neighbourhood. From the early nineteenth century it developed strong ties with those areas producing for overseas markets, and with the main centres for the distribution of foreign merchandise. This meant that Bombay interests extended a great distance from the town, but it did not follow that its local or regional economic impact was of a similar order. The development of communications from Bombay, for example, ignored some nearby local economies. The railway lines connecting the island to the mainland were almost exclusively designed to serve the import–export trade. The main trunk lines concentrating the trade of Gujarat, Rajputana, the United Provinces, the Central Provinces, the Deccan and Hyderabad at Bombay were opened early; yet 'the needs of internal trade were long neglected'.[1] The banking and commercial facilities of Bombay were also developed to meet the needs of foreign trade, and even in the nineteen-twenties organised banking had not advanced far from the ports and inland cities to the rural areas.[2] This begins to explain another paradox of the city. Its economic influence and its political importance extended to Delhi, to Jubbulpore,

[1] Bombay Provincial Banking Enquiry Committee Report, in *Report of the Provincial Banking Enquiry Committees, 1921–30*, vol. I (Calcutta, 1931), p. 21.
[2] *Ibid.* p. 20.

The politics of western India in the later nineteenth century

and into Mysore and Madras; yet it bypassed many closer districts because they were irrelevant to the city's economic interests. Bombay's ties with Hindustan, for example, were arguably stronger and more important than its links with the Konkan and parts of the Deccan.

The uniqueness of Bombay and its far-reaching economic and political influence must be seen not only in relation to its immediate neighbourhood but to India as a whole. Because Bombay was such an important trading metropolis, outward-looking and dealing with national and international markets, so its particular interests could be construed as general Indian ones. Where else in India was there such a concentration of vested interests in national and imperial policies? Where else would people be so immediately affected by changes in tariff policy? Who else matched Bombay's interest in the daily fluctuations in the value of the rupee? A town which had benefited so much from the new raj was also one which would be called upon to support it financially. Already by the eighteen-nineties the inhabitants of the town and island of Bombay paid almost as much in income-tax as did those of the whole of the North-western Provinces and Oudh,[1] so what other place would be so concerned with the taxation policies of the government? Bombay men had long realised the need to have the ear of the policy-makers, and nowhere else in India had Indians won so much political power so early as they had in Bombay. It was Bombay men, too, good at aggregating political support, who realised early the need for adequate representation of their views in England, the ultimate source of all political power in India.[2] The parochial issues of Bombay were thus elevated at once to the highest political plane: the interests of the city were those of the nation as well.

---

[1] For example, in the tax year 1892–93, in Bombay city 25,834 people paid Rs. 18,16,888 in income tax; in the North-Western Provinces and Oudh, 75,611 people paid Rs. 22,34,379. *Reports on the operations in connection with the income tax in the Bombay Presidency for the year 1893–94* (Bombay, 1894), p. 58; *Report on the administration of the income tax under Act II of 1886 in the North-Western Provinces and Oudh for the financial year ending 31st March 1894* (Allahabad, 1894), Appendix p. iv. By 1910 Bombay city paid more in income tax than any other province save Bengal. Only Calcutta's residents produced more revenue. I am indebted to Mr. C. Emery for this information.

[2] Dobbin, *Urban leadership in western India*, p. 79. Seal, *The emergence of Indian nationalism*, pp. 229–30.

The politics of western India in the later nineteenth century

Bombay, a microcosm of India itself, would clearly play a special role in all-India politics. Its local history particularly qualified its politicians for organising those large alliances necessary for pursuing national goals. Just as important, Bombay's wealth and its own interests enabled it to pay for such activity. No wonder that the Indian National Congress, from its earliest days, was so bound to Bombay; no wonder that, when the Bombay economy came under stress in the second decade of the twentieth century, the Home Rule Leagues, the Khilafat movement, and Gandhi, found such a response in the city. It was easy for Bombay to behave as if it were itself the embodiment of all-India since it dealt with so many truly all-India concerns. To many of those in the Deccan this state of affairs would be far from satisfactory. They would be coerced into mendicant politics when they least wanted to be; they would be dragged into non-cooperation when it suited them not at all. Maharashtrian frustration against the rising power of Bombay – the city of parvenus and Gujaratis, without a history and tied to alien rule – was voiced early. 'How different, indeed, would Bombay be, if the Maratha element were richer and more influential', lamented *Indu Prakash*, a moderate English–Marathi newspaper, in 1865. For Maharashtrians 'have a strong national feeling, and an ennobling literature, and had we a more influential position here, Bombay would become the intellectual, as well as the commercial capital of India'.[1]

Yet the lament was in vain, for while Bombay was not properly part of Maharashtra, Maharashtra was tied inescapably to Bombay. Hence also, Maharashtrians who wished to be effective in the Presidency or in national affairs could not avoid the journey to Bombay to achieve their rise to power. And so, while Tilak presided at Shivaji and Ganpati festivals and pondered Mahratta greatness, Gokhale became a member of the Bombay Presidency Association – the city's most important political society – which functioned as the nerve-centre of the Indian National Congress.[2] Gokhale's alliance with the Bombay politicians became his great political strength.[3] It was Bombay

[1] Quoted in Dobbin, *Urban leadership in western India*, p. 217.
[2] Gokhale was elected to the Council of the Bombay Presidency Association on 17 June 1893. Council Minutes, 17 June 1893, Bombay Presidency Association Papers, Bombay.
[3] Gokhale was reported in 1909 saying that 'he was of opinion that he had no

The politics of western India in the later nineteenth century

friends on the provincial legislature who decided in 1902 to send him as their representative to the Viceroy's legislative council;[1] it was the Bombay Presidency Association which raised money for his visit to England in 1905,[2] and which supported his next two trips in 1906 and 1908. Through the Bombay connection, Gokhale not only became recognised by the government as the main Congress spokesman, but he became a key figure in maintaining the all-India alliance which constituted the Congress itself. This was why Tilak's triumphs in Maharashtra did not mean the end of the Poona struggles. For Gokhale, using Bombay and all-India to redress the balance of Poona and Maharashtra, and Tilak, thwarted in provincial and national politics by Gokhale, became locked in a struggle that almost succeeded in destroying the Congress at Surat in 1907.

sympathisers or supporters among the ignorant masses who had no idea of him and his work. In the mofussil he counted 2 per cent of the educated classes as his supporters and sympathisers, 15 per cent in Poona, and 50 per cent in Bombay.'
Weekly Report DCI, 20 February 1909, Home Political B, June 1909, 104, NAI.
[1] Gokhale was elected the Bombay representative, in succession to Pherozeshah Mehta, in 1901.
[2] Council Minutes, 15 February 1905, Bombay Presidency Association Papers, Bombay.

3
TILAK, GOKHALE AND THE INDIAN NATIONAL CONGRESS, 1895 to 1906

But for an outbreak of cholera the first session of the Indian National Congress would have been held at Poona.[1] The sitting was moved at short notice to Bombay, a city which, by comparison with Poona, led a placid political life. During the middle years of the nineteenth century its inhabitants seemed too occupied with trade, with domestic reforms, and with the municipality to bother much about national politics. It was not until 1885 that its own political club, the Bombay Presidency Association, was founded.[2] Yet within a few years Bombay effectively took command of Congress politics in western India, and members of the Presidency Association supervised the general strategy of the whole movement.

To begin with, Poona retained its early prominence in the Congress. When it was decided in 1888 to hold a provincial conference to 'strengthen the hands of the great National Congress', it was the Poona Sarvajanik Sabha which called it.[3] Bombay city 'held herself aloof' as Poona had not deigned to consult her prior to calling the Assembly'.[4] Indeed, Bombay did not join the provincial conference until the fifth meeting in 1892, but then the city's dominating role became clear. Pherozeshah Mehta went to preside over the sitting in Poona. A partial observer recorded that a 'good deal of new blood and new spirit' was infused into the proceedings. 'The previous Conferences were more like vestrydom. Pherozeshah . . . at once lifted it up from the narrow platform of parochialism to something higher and nobler and more national.'[5] But in Indian

[1] *INC 1885*, p. 6.
[2] For an account of earlier attempts to found political associations in Bombay city see Seal, *The emergence of Indian nationalism*, pp. 226–32.
[3] Proceedings of the Bombay Provincial Conference, 2 November 1888, *Journal of the Poona Sarvajanik Sabha*, vol. XI, 3 and 4, January and April 1889.
[4] Wacha to Naoroji, 2 November 1888, Naoroji Papers, NAI.
[5] Wacha to Naoroji, 12 November 1892. *Ibid.*

politics the parochial often interacted with the national in a manner neither high nor noble. Once the Congress visited an area with strong regional politics or a town with lively local politics, there was, inevitably, a danger that it would become prey to them. Maharashtra was such a province, and Poona such a town, when it was decided to hold the eleventh session of the Indian National Congress in the old capital of the Peshwas in 1895.

When the Congress came to Poona, Tilak was engaged in taking over the Sarvajanik Sabha. He was able to transfer his local vendetta to all-India politics, and at the same time he tried to reassert the influence of Poona, already undermined by Bombay, in the National Congress. In previous years, after the Congress had closed, the same pandal was used for the National Social Conference. Although Ranade's official position prevented him from participating fully in the Congress, he dominated the Social Conference. Tilak, to reduce Ranade's prestige beyond Poona, agitated for the total separation of the Congress from the Conference. He stirred up local feeling against the Conference in his newspapers. 'Poona is essentially a conservative town', he wrote, 'and it is natural that public opinion should not be in favour of the Social Conference.'[1] The association of Congress and Conference, he argued, 'kept back the masses from joining the Congress', and he urged that 'this defect should be removed at the Poona sitting'.[2] Throughout October and November, Tilak and his friends organised public demonstrations in Poona to put pressure on the Congress. The Bombay city leaders' sympathy lay with Ranade. They were well aware that social reform was an issue likely to divide Indians, and as such had no place in the deliberations of the Congress. But they also realised that it was impolitic to allow Congress to become identified with social orthodoxy. As *India* reported after the controversy was over, 'It may be doubted whether any single thing could be more detrimental to the Congress than the growth of a belief that its supporters were for the most part opposed to social reform.'[3] The old arrangement whereby the two organisations had existed independently side by side had been ideal: conservatives could be told that the

[1] *Mahratta*, 29 September 1895.　　[2] *Ibid.* 13 October 1895.
[3] *India*, January 1896.

Conference had nothing to do with the Congress; reformers could see in the sharing of a meeting place an association between the two.

To counter Tilak's influence the Bombay Provincial Congress Committee reorganised the Poona working committee, adding four new secretaries, one of whom was Gokhale.[1] Tilak was infuriated by the intrusion of the Bombay leaders and resigned from the committee, declaring the new appointments to be 'unconstitutional'. His followers stopped working for the Congress and stepped up their programme of public meetings. On 22 October a meeting of some six thousand 'subscribers and sympathisers of the Indian National Congress' assembled behind the Reay market and passed a resolution, moved by Tilak, regretting that 'the work of the Congress is drifting into the hands of a small clique and . . . unless the work of the 11th National Congress be entrusted to the gentlemen as are prepared to work for the Congress and for the Congress alone, it cannot be carried out as successfully as is expected from the people of a historic city like Poona'.[2] The names of about sixty-five 'leading gentlemen' of Poona were recommended for the Congress Reception Committee, to replace those likely to be nominated by the Provincial Congress Committee. Namjoshi moved that 'In the opinion of the Poona public the Social Conference is not popular owing to its sectional character and time has now come when public confidence in the National Congress should not be allowed to be shaken by the cognate relation which is now believed to exist between the Congress and the Conference.'[3] In his editorial comment on the meeting Tilak stressed that the Congress would fail simply because the Social Conference was so unpopular, and headed his column 'Whose is the Congress? Of the Classes or of the Masses?'[4]

By resigning from the working committee, Tilak had left Congress preparations in the hands of his opponents. He now sought to destroy their credentials as representatives of Indian opinion.

---

[1] Wolpert, *Tilak and Gokhale*, p. 72. The original committee had consisted of the managing committee of the Poona Sarvajanik Sabha and about forty other people. Tilak and Baba Maharaj were among the executive officers. Para. 749 (Poona, 25 May), Bombay Police Abstracts, vol. VIII, 1896, Bombay HFM.

[2] *Mahratta*, 27 October 1895.   [3] *Ibid.*   [4] *Ibid.*

Tilak, Gokhale and the Indian National Congress, 1895 to 1906

Bombay ought to have no voice in the matter at all [he wrote], because Bombay has never shown the least desire to consult public opinion in Congress matters. Guzarat has remained indifferent and we do not know what right it can claim. Ultimately the question reduces itself to Maharashtra and it is Maharashtra that must speak... Let... Maharashtra make its voice ring... in deciding whether the Congress shall be an institution of the people or whether it would be an institution of a clique who make the people their sport and declare that they shall speak to order.[1]

Yet however much Tilak might have wished Poona to dominate the Congress, it was clear that the Congress could not function without Bombay. The city was to contribute Rs. 15,000 out of the Rs. 40,000 needed to hold the session.[2] Pherozeshah Mehta, controlling the Bombay Presidency Association, and Dinshaw Edulji Wacha, the Congress secretary, were too essentially part of the Congress fabric to be more than polemical targets for Tilak, and they steadfastly refused to take any notice of Tilak's public meetings. By the end of October it appears that Tilak had been negotiating a return of his friends to Congress work. While some agreement had been reached,[3] the crucial issue whether the men elected at the public meeting on 22 October could be recognised as members of the Reception Committee was unresolved. The Bombay people saw only disadvantages in legitimising Tilak's meeting.[4] Pherozeshah Mehta called a meeting of the Bombay Congress Committee on 26 October, which Tilak attended, and they decided not to recognise Tilak's Reception Committee.[5] Then, without more ado, the Bombay leaders elected Surendranath Banerjea president of the Poona Congress.[6]

At this point Tilak began to receive support from other provinces. Repaying *Kesari* and *Mahratta* for services rendered during the Age of Consent controversy, the Bengal press came to Tilak's aid in the Congress–Conference wrangle. The *Amrita Bazar Patrika* wrote:

The Congress leaders should indeed know their position. They are, most of them, quite unfit, on account of their Anglicised ideas, to discuss the subject of Hindu reform in the right way, much less to offer suggestions. Besides,

---
[1] *Ibid.*   [2] *Ibid.* 29 September 1895.
[3] Ranade to Mehta, 5 November 1895, Pherozeshah Mehta Papers, NAI.
[4] Wacha to Mehta, 29 October 1895, *ibid.*
[5] Para. 1448 (Bombay, 28 October), Bombay Police Abstracts, vol. VIII, 1895, Bombay HFM.
[6] Wacha to Gokhale, 6 November 1895, Gokhale Papers, Reel 11, NAI.

the sensitiveness of the Hindoos to such outrageous suggestions as were embodied in the resolutions of the Social Conference of the last year cannot but make the National Congress, of which the Social is a branch, odious to all right-minded Hindoos. We are very glad that the Hindoos of Poona ... have practically protested against the Social Conference being held in connection with the Congress.[1]

Tilak was encouraged privately by Moti Lal Ghose, the *Patrika*'s editor. Ghose naturally thought that the 'selection of Babu Surendra Nath Banerjee as president ... is a fatal blunder which, I fear, will hurt the Congress very vitally. I am afraid no man of position in Bengal will come to Poona this time.'[2]

Emboldened by this support, Tilak organised a meeting in Poona on 10 November when, it was said, ten thousand people attended. It condemned outright the activities of the Bombay and Poona Congress committees 'setting at naught popular voice in Congress work', and maintained that the Social Conference gained 'fictitious importance' from being connected with the Congress. In a covering letter sent with the resolutions to the Congress committees, it was made quite plain that while 'the people of Poona and the Deccan are all in favour of the Congress ... they do not wish to lend their support directly or indirectly to the reform movement which calling itself national, is, in the opinion of the public, likely to do more mischief than good'.[3]

The renewed agitation in Poona and the hostility of some Bengalis showed Ranade that it would be impolitic to ask for the Congress pandal for his Social Conference. Tempers in Poona were running high, and some feared that physical violence might result from the controversy.[4] While only a dozen of the Congress committees stated definitely that they were against the continued association of the Congress and the Conference,[5] Ranade agreed to compromise and announced that he would not hold the Social Conference in the Congress

[1] Quote in *Mahratta*, 3 November 1895.
[2] Ghose to Namjoshi, 16 November 1895, Tilak Papers, *Kesari* Office, Poona.
[3] *Mahratta*, 24 November 1895.
[4] *Ibid.* 17 November 1895. About this time the Chapekar brothers sent letters threatening Congress workers with violence if the plan to hold the Social Conference was not abandoned. Autobiography of D. H. Chapekar, pp. 13–14, Enclosure 6 in Inspector-General of Police Bombay, to Govt. India 25 August 1899, Home Public A, September 1899, 5–6, NAI.
[5] Ghose to Tilak, 27 November 1895, Tilak Papers, *Kesari* Office, Poona.

pandal.[1] Tilak, having forced Ranade to capitulate on this issue, no longer pressed for recognition of his public meetings as electing bodies to Congress committees, and preparations for the Congress were resumed. Banerjea, who as president-elect had a stake in the success of the session, wrote to Tilak that now 'the chief difficulty has been got over, I trust minor matters will not be permitted to stand in the way of the harmonious working of all parties with a view to make the Congress at Puna the success it deserves to be'.[2] The *Mahratta* certainly found cause for satisfaction. Banerjea's address 'in spite of its inordinate length',[3] gave a 'complete catalogue of Indian grievances' and he confirmed that the ideal Congress was a political, not a 'socio-political' one. The Deccan, it was claimed, now had the credit of having effected the divorce between the Congress and the Conference, the marriage of which had 'kept away a large body of our orthodox and sober countrymen'. It had thus taken the 'first step towards putting the Congress on a real popular basis'.[4]

Although the Congress at Poona turned out to be 'a greater success than what even the most sanguine expected',[5] Tilak's activities had fluttered the dovecots. While nominally a contest about the Social Conference and its relation to the Congress, it was inconceivable that the controversy would have been carried to such lengths had not Poona been the scene of bitter conflict for the past five years. The association of Ranade and Gokhale with Mehta and Wacha, besides the jealousy between politicians in Bombay and Poona, automatically drew the Congress committees into the quarrel. Finding that he could not persuade the Bombay city leaders to agree to dissociate the Conference from the Congress, Tilak appealed to popular feeling outside the committees to compel them to do so. As a result the controversy spread and politicians in other provinces began to take sides. The majority had no strong feelings on the subject but

[1] *Ibid.*
[2] Banerjea to Tilak, 2 December 1895, Tilak Papers, *Kesari* Office, Poona.
[3] *Mahratta*, 5 January 1896. The speech took six weeks to prepare and over four hours to deliver, 'and I think I was able, during the whole of that time, to keep up, undiminished and without flagging, the attention of a vast assembly of over five thousand people'. Banerjea, *A nation in making*, p. 129.
[4] *Mahratta*, 5 January 1896.
[5] Wacha to Naoroji, 4 January 1896, Naoroji Papers, NAI.

were prepared to compromise for the sake of unity in the Congress. Since Tilak's tactics would have made it impossible to hold the Congress in Poona unless the Conference was not held in the same tent, Congress leaders had not much option but to give in to his demands. But Tilak's pre-occupation with his local quarrel was an unwelcome irrelevance in the business of Congress. The 1895 session had been too keen and stirred too many controversies to bear frequent repetition, and even those men who might have agreed with Tilak about social reform became suspicious of him.

Further, Tilak's much publicised conduct and utterances in Poona embarrassed the Congress in other ways. If Anglo-Indian officials were allowed to make charges of sedition adhere to Congressmen, then all the latter's hopes of influencing government, parliament and the British public would come to nothing. Congress leaders held that the events in Poona in 1897, and in particular Tilak's journalism, had been directly responsible for a tightening of the press laws and pointed to a further strengthening of despotic government. Tilak was a 'mischief maker' and an individual who should

find no place in the Congress camp. . . It is a pity that Tilak and his party do not perceive the potentiality of the mischief that their own rash acts are leading to. . . Tilak is already spoilt. They have made a hero of him and he has grown giddy. He thinks he is the coming saviour of India. When people have got such notions into their head you can understand to what limits they may go. Altogether his conduct is inexcusable and he is using his talents to a most objectionable and mischievous purpose.[1]

Thus, to keep the Congress united, and to maintain the image of the nationalist movement as a constitutional body making comprehensible and just demands, it was safer to avoid controversy; safer to avoid Maharashtra. Significantly, the Congress never met in Poona again during Tilak's lifetime, nor did he ever preside at one of its annual sessions.

Following the excitement in Poona, interest in the Congress flagged during the later 1890s. In part this was a reflection of the success of the 1892 Councils Act, and in part it was because there seemed little opportunity for further work in England. Attendance at the annual sessions dropped, and the proportion

[1] Wacha to Naoroji, 15 April 1899, Naoroji Papers, NAI.

Tilak, Gokhale and the Indian National Congress, 1895 to 1906

of local delegates increased.[1] After the 1900 session even Dinshaw Wacha lost enthusiasm and considered giving up his post as Joint-Secretary. He complained to Dadabhai 'Your big leaders nowadays don't care to attend the Congress, so we have a minor crew – most of whom try to boss themselves without judgment and wisdom.'[2] Curzon saw no need to take the organisation seriously, for all his information suggested that it was 'tottering to its fall'.[3] The 1902 session held at Ahmadabad, was attended by fewer delegates than any Congress since 1886, and almost nine out of ten delegates came from the Bombay Presidency.[4]

However, from 1903 the Congress began to slough off its apathy. In part this was a reaction to developments in England. During that year a change of government seemed imminent. The Congress had been founded with the idea of laying India's case before the English electorate, and its leaders had always hoped, however mistakenly, that they would benefit from the policies of a Liberal government. In this the Congress had been unlucky, for the Liberals' fall from office in February 1886 happened just after the first meeting of the Congress had been held, and, apart from a weak ministry between August 1892 and June 1895, the Liberal party was in opposition until December 1905.[5] But by 1903 the Conservative government was in difficulties. The cabinet was split over tariff policy and the government began to lose by-elections in the country.[6] To Liberal onlookers the signs were distinctly hopeful. Sir William Wedderburn, the former Bombay Civilian who was now a

[1] Between 1894 and 1903 the proportion of local delegates ranged between 64·7% and 88·6%. This compares with a range of 43·5% to 59·5% for the period 1885–1893. Calculated from attendance figures in Ghosh, *Indian National Congress*, pp. 25–6.
[2] Wacha to Naoroji, 16 February 1901, Naoroji Papers, NAI.
[3] Curzon to Hamilton, 18 November 1900, Curzon Papers, Mss. Eur. F. 111/159, IOL.
[4] The attendance was 471, the lowest since the second Congress, and the proportion of local delegates was 88·6%, the highest at any Congress during this period.
[5] See the list of cabinets in R. C. K. Ensor, *England 1870–1914* (Oxford, 1936), pp. 608–12.
[6] In September 1903 five cabinet ministers resigned. They were Chamberlain, the Colonial Secretary, Ritchie, the Chancellor of the Exchequer, Hamilton, the Secretary of State for India, Lord Balfour of Burleigh, the Secretary of State for Scotland, and the Duke of Devonshire, the Lord President of the Council. *Ibid.* pp. 371–6.

Liberal MP and the principal organiser of the British Committee of the Congress, wrote to India that for the past eight years England had been ruled by the party standing for aggression abroad and selfish class interests at home. 'Now the political pendulum is about to swing strongly in the opposite direction, towards national righteousness abroad, and care for people at home.'[1] As in December 1885, so again in 1903, Indian politicians must prepare for the coming of a Liberal government by presenting England with united, comprehensible and just demands framed by a revitalised Congress.

Stimulated by the news from London, Congress leaders began their work of refurbishing the organisation in India. The founder-members, whom Wacha had criticised for their absence, re-appeared at the 1903 session in Madras. The most significant results were first that Pherozeshah Mehta and his Bombay city friends invited the Congress to their city for its next session (despite the fact that the Bombay Presidency had played host to the Congress as recently as 1902), and secondly that Gopal Krishna Gokhale was appointed an additional Joint-Secretary to take over effective command of the organisation.[2]

During 1904 the Bombay city leaders and their allies gave a firm lead to the Congress. They sought to achieve the appearance of organised and widespread support, and to emphasise the unity of the movement by controlling not only its main critics but those personally hostile to the leadership. Besides working in Bombay and Poona, Gokhale visited Bengal, Madras, the Central Provinces and Berar to stimulate interest in the Congress.[3] However, criticism of the leadership's activity was not slow to emerge. The Bombay city men and Gokhale had to cope with Bal Gangadhar Tilak.

Towards the end of 1904 Dadabhai Naoroji, the veteran

---

[1] W. Wedderburn, D. Naoroji, W. C. Bonnerjee and A. O. Hume, *The Indian National Congress: a call to arms* (reprinted from the *Hindustan Review* for December 1903), p. 2. The pamphlet, sent to the Secretaries of the forthcoming Congress at Madras, lamented India's apathy and indifference. Hume was particularly critical: 'most of you alas! it seems to me, are never more than half earnest in *your* fight.' *Ibid.* p. 10.

[2] Resolutions XV and XVI, *INC 1903*.

[3] Gokhale to Natesan, 19 May 1904; Gokhale to Krishnaswami Iyer, 11 July 1904 and 2 August 1904, Gokhale Papers, Reel 5, NAI.

Congress campaigner, tried to get a guarantee of Tilak's good behaviour. Tilak replied to Naoroji's approach at great length, assuring him that 'I have never been, nor am I in any way against the Congress. Constitutional agitation, I shall be the last person to decry.'[1] At the Congress session, Tilak seconded the resolution about the need to send delegates to England to try to influence the election, thus making public his promise to stay in line with the expressed orthodoxies of Congress strategy. He said in his speech that the resolution was 'one of the most important resolutions in our programme today'. The work of the annual session was to focus opinion in India, but 'our principal purpose and our principal hope to carry out the programme that we prepare lies not here – (Hear, hear) – but in England'.[2]

Not only did the 1904 Congress adopt the old strategy: it listed again the old demands. The resolutions which had been ignored were reiterated; those where concessions had been won were widened and reformulated. Reform of the civil service; increased government expenditure on higher education; an enlargement of legislative councils in India and greater power for them; the appointment of Indians to the Secretary of State's council in London and to the executive councils in India; Indian representation in the House of Commons: all were aired and approved. The firm deliberation with which Mehta had brought the Congress to Bombay, and which guided the session, not only marked the re-awakening of the Congress and the return to Congress politics after some years' absence of the principal Congress figures, but it underlined the supremacy of Bombay city politicians in the all-India movement.[3] After the Congress Wacha wrote 'there was not a man in the entire country who could successfully *lead* men as P.M.M. [Pherozeshah Mehta]. He proved to the hilt that for Congress under

[1] Tilak to Naoroji, 6 December 1904, copy, Tilak Papers, *Kesari* Office, Poona.
[2] *INC 1904*, pp. 149–50. His speech, however, may have been less than candid, since the resolution, if implemented, would have sent all the main leaders to England leaving Tilak a free hand in India.
[3] 20% of the delegates had been elected by the council of the Bombay Presidency Association at a meeting held in Pherozeshah Mehta's chambers. The council approved 256 names at a meeting on 14 December 1904 (Minutes of Council Meeting, 14 December 1904, Bombay Presidency Association Papers, Bombay). 202 of them actually attended the Congress. *INC 1904*, Appendix A.

present conditions there is only one leader – a *born* one and that is P.M.M.'[1]

However opportune the situation in England might have appeared for the successful conclusion of Indian demands, it was less clear that the Congress commanded undivided loyalties in India itself. In general terms the effect of governmental policies towards the end of the nineteenth century was to stir into activity several areas of India hitherto quiescent, and vitally to affect the interests of some of those most concerned with the Congress. Despite the triumph of the Bombay session of 1904, the fundamental unity of the movement had never been put under such strain as it was to endure over the next four years. Undoubtedly, the politicians who thought they had most to gain by putting new life into the Congress and advancing the old demands were those based at the capitals of the maritime provinces: Bombay, Bengal and Madras. It was in these Presidencies that provincial government was most developed, and it was at their capitals that the new politicians were most in evidence. It was they who, in 1904, would stand to gain immediately from any extension of power to provincial (and by implication imperial) legislative and executive councils, by any modest decentralisation of the powers of the administration to elected bodies, and by any widening of the terms on which the government consulted 'representative bodies' of unofficial Indian interests.

However, all three Presidencies had not developed in the same way, and their politicians did not stand to gain equally from reforms. By the early twentieth century the men in the cities of Bombay and Madras were moving into closer collaboration with government and they were beginning to exert their influence over their respective Presidencies. But what of Calcutta? Had not Bengal been in the lead in founding associations? Did not Bengalis as a race know more about Parliament than the average English voter? Were not Bengalis the mainstay of the Congress? In terms of similar development, did not Calcutta lead in a class composed of Bengal, Bombay and Madras? Yet it was the Bengalis who found it most difficult to continue the Congress along the old lines. This was because the government of Bengal, backed by the government of India, had

[1] Wacha to Gokhale, 23 January 1905, Gokhale Papers, Reel 11, NAI.

launched a series of policies that sought to undermine the position of the new political leadership built up in Calcutta from the 1870s. At first, the new Bengali leaders, connected with the Indian Association and the Congress, had been quite successful in acquiring power in the municipalities, the legislative councils and, above all, in the university senate. From the mid 1890s, however, government and other Bengali interests moved against them. In 1898 a legislative council seat, usually held by some lawyer or journalist, came to be reserved for a zemindar.[1] In 1899 Calcutta corporation was summarily reformed by reducing the number of elected members by half.[2] Curzon's proposed university reforms brought official interference into the sanctuary of educated Bengalis, the senate of Calcutta University, while the government's policy of tightening up educational standards affected the bhadralok more than any other social group.[3]

The partition of Bengal, under active consideration from 1903 and implemented on 16 October 1904, was the culminating blow. The new boundaries of Bengal separated the Muslim-majority districts of east Bengal from Bengal proper. But these districts were also where the dominant minority of high-caste Hindus – Brahmins, Baidyas and Kayasths – lived. They saw partition as a move to divide the Bengali-speaking population, to lessen the influence of Calcutta politicians in east Bengal, and to deprive the Hindu high-castes there of the opportunities which Calcutta and an undivided province afforded for education and employment. Petitions and memorials were organised in Calcutta and the eastern districts against the partition, but they had no effect.

The failure to prevent partition drove Bengalis to adopt more vigorous political techniques. They advocated a boycott of English manufacturers to mark their protest. However, boycott might be extended from foreign cloth to all things British,

[1] Govt. of Bengal to Govt. of India, 8 October 1898, Home Public A, November 1898, 113, NAI.
[2] Curzon to Hamilton, 11 October 1899, Curzon Papers, Mss. Eur. F. 111/158, IOL. A majority of non-official members was, however, preserved. Surendranath Banerjea was among those who resigned from the corporation in protest, and he never worked on it again.
[3] For the effect of the partition on the bhadralok see G. Johnson, 'Partition, agitation and Congress: Bengal 1904 to 1908', *Modern Asian Studies*, vol. 7, no. 3 (July 1973), 546–50.

including the government. The agitation against the partition among the east Bengal bhadralok, and among students in the city, took on a life of its own.

The established Bengali Congress leaders were in a cruel dilemma. They were interested in reforms from government; but to collaborate with the government unless partition was annulled was to lose support in Bengal. Moreover, the agitation stirred up fighting among Bengali factions. For, while all Bengalis opposed the partition, less recognised politicians could afford to be more extreme in their propaganda. Thus, as well as the long-standing wrangles between Calcutta men, there were now new challengers for the role of spokesmen of Bengal. Some of these new men, like Bipin Chandra Pal and Aurobindo Ghose, had no previous influence in the politics of Bengal. They tried to undermine the recognised leaders, like Surendranath Banerjea and Bhupendranath Basu, by using the unrest to advocate a more extreme boycott amounting to non-cooperation and passive resistance. By keeping pace with the extremists Bengali leaders retained some local support, but there were drawbacks: they further alienated the good will of the government and they lost the sympathy of their all-India colleagues. The latter, finding the Bengali agitation a liability to their campaign for reform, took every opportunity to dissociate themselves from it. Hence conflict within the Bengali leadership was exacerbated, and tension arose between Bengali and other Congressmen. As fights developed for influence in the Congress, the difficulties in Bengal upset the balance and alignments within the Congress leadership.

The Congress in Bombay in December 1904 had endorsed the strategy of putting its main emphasis on campaigns in England. With his passage and expenses paid by the Bombay Presidency Association,[1] Gokhale went to London in 1905 to present the Congress case before the British public. He stayed at the National Liberal Club, and campaigned amongst the Liberal Party. The British Committee of Congress arranged for him to address forty-five meetings during his seven-week stay.[2] He wrote: 'My visit, you will be glad to know has been success-

[1] Council minutes, 15 February 1905, Bombay Presidency Association Papers, Bombay.
[2] Gokhale to Natesan, 13 October 1905, Gokhale Papers, Reel 4, NAI.

ful beyond my wildest dreams. Friends here are putting a lot of pressure on me that I should return to this country for a few weeks at least next year, as soon as the next Liberal Ministry is formed, and I fear I shall have to come again in April next for about three months.'[1] As a reward for his work he returned home as India's 'Grand Young Man'[2] to preside over the Congress at Benares.

Meanwhile, however, in India the partition of Bengal had been accomplished and the agitation against it was reaching its height. Before the Benares session opened, a group of Bengal delegates asked Gokhale for his approval of 'agitation by Boycott' and requested that the 'present Congress should express its opinion in unmistakable terms as to whether or not boycott is a legitimate means of constitutional agitation and as such deserving of sympathy'.[3] At the same time, Tilak and Khaparde, his friend from Amraoti, told Gokhale that if a resolution welcoming the Prince and Princess of Wales to India was not dropped from the Congress agenda, then they would be 'constrained to raise an opposition in the Congress Pandal'.[4] The last thing the Congress wished to appear was disloyal, and it was also reluctant to sanction the more extreme agitations that had begun in Bengal.

But Tilak's intention was to put pressure on the Bombay leaders. In the Subjects Committee he made a bargain: if the Congress would pass a resolution supporting boycott in Bengal, then he would withdraw his opposition to a telegram of greeting being sent to the Prince of Wales.[5] He had embarrassed the Bombay city leaders while making himself prominent in the cause of Bengal: and by playing a major part in the negotiations he laid foundations for an opposition party within the Congress.

In this, the opening stages of his campaign against the Bombay leadership, Tilak was able to present an attractive alternative to others besides the Bengalis and his own committed Maharashtrian supporters. For, while the Congress waited patiently for changes in England, the situation in India was moving much more rapidly. In particular, events in the

[1] Gokhale to Natesan, 17 November 1905, Gokhale Papers, Reel 4, NAI.
[2] Wacha to Gokhale, 28 October 1905, Gokhale Papers, Reel 11, NAI.
[3] Ray and others to Gokhale, 27 December 1905, Gokhale Papers, Reel 3, NAI.
[4] Tilak and others to Gokhale, 27 December 1905, *ibid.*
[5] Khaparde, Diary, 28 December 1905, Khaparde Papers, NAI.

Punjab were making Congress support from that province uneasy. It was increasingly evident to the Hindu townsmen there that if the Punjab government was to reform it was more likely to do so in order to associate big country interests and some Muslim and Sikh communal representatives with the local government.

The Punjabi Congressmen therefore hoped to gain some leverage on their provincial situation. Yet it seemed likely that the moderate reforms for which Gokhale and his friends were working would end by benefiting other local groups. Moreover, Punjabi Congressmen during this period felt that the Hindu communal position was worsening, that their alliance with Congress was not helping them to protect it, and that it was necessary to retreat from the secular platforms of the Congress. One result of this growing anxiety was that Punjabi representatives at the Congress faced a similar dilemma to that of the Bengali leaders: they needed, for domestic reasons, to press a more active and aggressive line than suited the Congress leadership as a whole.[1] In particular Lala Lajpat Rai was keen to see the movement adopt a less mendicant attitude. He, however, was a great friend of Gokhale, and his importance between 1904 and 1908 lies in the fact that he, more than any other politician, attempted to bridge the growing differences within Congress. In fact along with Tilak and Khaparde, Lajpat Rai was mainly responsible for persuading the Subjects Committee to recognise the importance of the Bengali agitation.[2]

Gokhale handled a difficult situation well, and his presidential address at Benares was a brilliant exposition of the traditional role of Congress.[3] In it he also dealt efficiently with the whole question of the boycott.[4] Even Tilak had to admit that

[1] In this, Punjabi leaders mistook their best course. What happened in the end was that they decided that the best way to protect Hindu communal interests in the province was not wider agitation against the government, but closer collaboration with it. The leaders of the extremist period, therefore, found themselves cast into the political wilderness after 1909, bearing the blame for the unsatisfactory communal arrangements in the reforms.

[2] Khaparde, Diary, 1 January 1906, Khaparde Papers, NAI.

[3] The speech is reprinted in Karve and Ambekar (eds.), *Speeches and writings of Gopal Krishna Gokhale*, vol. II, pp. 187–209.

[4] Gokhale condemned the partition and approved of the boycott in Bengal, with the qualification that 'a weapon like this must be reserved only for extreme occasions'. *INC 1905*, p. 11.

Tilak, Gokhale and the Indian National Congress, 1895 to 1906

'Mr Gokhale's speech was much bolder than was expected from him.'[1] Yet the speech was specific enough for Congressmen to see themselves as either moderate or extremist judged by Gokhale's standards. Mahomed Ali, already showing his talents as a publicist, recorded 'Mr Gokhale's precision has made possible that which makes us regard Messrs Pal and Tilak as the apostles of Extremism.'[2] The terms 'moderate' and 'extremist' became popular with the various politicians engaged in the struggle for supremacy, and they served as rallying points for the different factions.

During 1906 the initiative passed into the hands of the extremists. This was partly because they had greater freedom of manoeuvre than the moderates, and partly because the new Liberal government did not effect a major change in British Indian policy overnight. The latter's decision to stand by the partition of Bengal acted as a cold douche on Indian leaders who had been hoping for more than expressions of sympathy from the Liberals.[3] Tilak was jubilant. 'At last Mr. Morley has disappointed his Indian admirers. I expected nothing better from him and have said so in the *Kesari*, but I am surprised that our so-called leaders here have hopes still! I don't know when we shall learn to depend on ourselves and ourselves alone.'[4] The immediate disillusionment with the Liberals gave Tilak the chance he needed to discredit the Bombay leadership further, and to offer himself as an alternative. His first step was to go with Khaparde to Calcutta in June 1906. For a fortnight he surveyed the political scene there, appearing in the role of peace-maker to the factious Bengalis. 'There are three parties at Calcutta', wrote Khaparde with uncharacteristic understatement. 'One led by Babu Surendranath Banerjea. It is the

[1] Tilak to Krishnavarma, 9 February 1906. Reprinted in *Mahratta*, 26 July 1936.
[2] Mahomed Ali, *Thoughts on the present discontent* (Bombay, 1907), p. 13.
[3] In reply to an amendment moved in the House of Commons by Herbert Roberts and Sir Henry Cotton on 26 February 1906, John Morley, Secretary of State for India, while being sympathetic to the demand for reuniting Bengal, said 'But the redistribution of Bengal is now a settled fact. At this moment there is a great subsidence – it may be only temporary – but there is a subsidence of feeling against the redistribution; and in face of that it would be very unreasonable to ask the Government to start afresh to redistribute the areas and incur what, to my mind, would be a new outlay of taxation.' *Parliamentary debates, fourth series*, vol. CLII, col. 844.
[4] Tilak to Krishnavarma, 16 March 1906. Tilak Papers, *Kesari* Office, Poona.

Moderate party. Then Moti Babu [Moti Lal Ghose] has a party of his own, and the party led by Bapu Bipin is the real popular party and corresponds to Tilak's party in Poona. Our advent smoothed the differences of these parties and led to their amalgamation to some extent.'[1]

This visit to Calcutta, to seek and cement alliances, was followed by the publication of a letter by Khaparde in which he outlined a programme for the Congress. The crux of his plan was that Congress should have a proper organisation so that it could run a more effective campaign in India. This, of course, was precisely what the Congressmen had avoided for the past twenty years. Yet, at this time, it seemed that the only way of winkling the Congress out of the Bombay shell was to propose the establishment of a formal constitution for which there could be open jockeying for power. Khaparde concluded his letter by suggesting that as Punjab had not provided a president for the Congress, it might be appropriate to elect Lajpat Rai to the office.[2] A more active line in India, together with a Punjabi as President, were the last things the Bombay leaders wanted to befall the Congress.

Sir William Wedderburn, who financed the work of the British Committee, and to whom Gokhale turned for advice, was disposed to consider Khaparde's plan 'a sort of grumble-all-round, with a proposal that Lajpat Rai should be the next President'.[3] Critics of the movement had from the very start trotted out the hobby of the constitution, since this was the only way of attacking those who voted by informal means. The *Times of India* was less sanguine, reporting that it was the first open move to oust Mehta from his position in Congress; while the *Mahratta* responded by saying that it was ridiculous to suggest that Tilak and Khaparde were trying to wrest control of the Congress from Mehta and Gokhale,[4] nonetheless

the Congress may and must be amended... The senior Congress leaders here, however, have been somewhat unwisely and almost obstinately

---

[1] Khaparde, Diary, 12 June 1906, Khaparde Papers, NAI. See also the entries for 31 May to 11 June 1906.
[2] *Hindu*, 9 July 1906.
[3] Wedderburn to Gokhale, 8 August 1906, Gokhale Papers, Reel 12, NAI.
[4] Tilak's 'constant pilgrimage to the shrine of the Congress, his unswerving loyalty to its unwritten laws, his scrupulous homage to the senior Congress leaders – all these are public knowledge'. *Mahratta*, 15 July 1906.

resisting the demand for this amendment . . . Sir P. M. Mehta may keep the Congress as the undisputed domain of his leadership of it. But even leaders have at times to allow themselves to be led if they want to keep pace with public opinion. As a senior Congresswalla he is the undisputed leader of the Congress movement. But he is only a trustee of it for the people whose opinion Congress must reflect.[1]

This was not calculated to reassure the Bombay leaders: 'Behind all is Tilak', complained Wacha, 'who, knowing how he is regarded by the sober section of the Congress party, has been moving heaven and earth to get Lajpatrai elected for the Presidentship! Today Lajpatrai and tomorrow Tilak! Where will the Congress be?"[2] Even the *Hindu*, which at this time was edited by Kasturi Ranga Iyengar who had no special liking for the Bombay leaders' friends in Madras, assured its readers that it did not rejoice in the prospect of a change in Congress leadership.

We should regard it as a calamity for India, if at the present juncture, when the annual deliberations of the Congress are being regarded with an earnest attention never accorded to them in the past, Sir Pherozeshah Mehta and those who think with him were supplanted by a band of virulent extremists. Such an unhappy result would deprive the Congress of those opportunities for useful and effective influence which are likely to open out before it in the near future; and it would kill the new spirit of toleration and respect with which the Congress is now being contemplated.[3]

Symbolising the new opportunities for useful and effective influence, Gokhale left India for England in April 1906. By June he was able to report that he had established 'excellent relations with Mr. Morley . . . He has agreed to go over the whole field of Indian administration with me point by point.'[4] Although the discussions between Morley and Gokhale were informal, they nonetheless represented a significant development in Indian politics. Morley was prepared to give him more than one interview,[5] and the beginning of July found Gokhale hopeful that his 'tug-of-war with the officials of the Indian

---

[1] The article continued: 'Will he or will he not, therefore, consent to such modifications of the movement as a large majority of the Congressmen, including dozens of leaders in the rank next to him and a very large body of the rank and file of the Congress forces, have decided upon as desirable and inevitable?' *Mahratta*, 15 July 1906.
[2] Wacha to Gokhale, 21 July 1906, Gokhale Papers, Reel 11, NAI.
[3] *Hindu*, 11 July 1906.
[4] Gokhale to Krishnaswami Iyer, 8 June 1906, Gokhale Papers, Reel 5, NAI.
[5] Gokhale to Natesan, 10 May 1906, Gokhale Papers, Reel 4, NAI.

Council as to who should capture Mr. Morley's mind' would bear fruit in the dismissal of Sir James Bampfylde Fuller, the unpopular Lieutenant-Governor of Eastern Bengal. Between visits to the India Office, Gokhale was 'coaching different members of Parliament in connection with the forthcoming Budget speech'.[1] Gokhale felt that his whole visit had been worth while. In his Budget speech, the Secretary of State had

> definitely promised a further reform of our Legislative Councils, and has re-iterated the Queen's proclamation... The Salt Tax is now doomed and Military Expenditure will be kept under vigorous control if not materially reduced... the expenditure on elementary education will be substantially increased and the separation of Judicial from Executive functions soon effected. Then Sir B. Fuller will not remain in the new Province beyond September... Well, considering the tremendous difficulties of Mr. Morley's position, we need not be altogether dissatisfied with what we have got in the first year of his administration. I for one look forward to a period of progress while he is at the India Office.[2]

However, the political situation in Bengal was exacerbated by the refusal of the government to reconsider the partition. Surendranath Banerjea wrote to Dadabhai Naoroji in July

> Mr. Morley's inaction and his unwillingness to modify partition have produced deplorable results in Bengal. The party of constitutional agitation is losing ground; while the anti-constitutional party which has been opposed to the Congress is gaining in strength and numbers. People are fast losing confidence in the British Government; and a strong feeling of discontent is abroad. God only knows what the upshot of it all will be. The Liberal administration has been a grievous disappointment so far. The Liberals must have their own men to carry out their own policy. Lord Minto is a failure.[3]

Surendranath and his friends had found that they had little control over the agitation in east Bengal, and their embarrassment was increased by the speeches and journalism of Bipin Chandra Pal and Aurobindo Ghose, who were seeking to depose them.

The tradition by which Congress toured the sub-continent and which had previously proved so useful, now worked against the interests of its leadership. The 1906 session had been

---

[1] Gokhale to Natesan, 6 July 1906, *ibid.*
[2] Gokhale to Krishnaswami Iyer, 27 July 1906, Gokhale Papers, Reel 5, NAI.
[3] Banerjea to Naoroji, 12 July 1906, Naoroji Papers, NAI. Surendranath was unwilling to give up his faith in the Liberals. He clung to the vain hope that all would be well if India had a Liberal Viceroy. Lord Minto was a Tory appointment.

Tilak, Gokhale and the Indian National Congress, 1895 to 1906

arranged for Calcutta, since meetings had been held in the United Provinces, Bombay and Madras the previous three years. Inevitably, just as it had fallen foul of the Poona quarrels in 1895, the Congress became embroiled in the Bengali factions. The Bombay city leaders had adopted a strategy of inactivity,[1] but when Gokhale returned from England he realised that more positive measures would have to be taken. A week was spent reading back-numbers of the newspapers and in 'frequent consultations with Bombay friends as to what could be done to extricate the Congress from the dangers which threaten it in Bengal'.[2] Gokhale sent Deodhar, a member of his Servants of India Society, to Calcutta for first hand information.[3] From Deodhar's report it was clear that

Calcutta has been for some time past a regular pandemonium. Surendranath's inexcusable excesses, the *Patrika's* vindictive pursuit of Mr. Surendranath, the fierce quarrel between Surendranath and Bipin Chandra Pal and the latter's unscrupulous ambition to play at all cost the role of a new leader, Anglo-Indian ferocity let loose against Indians, Mahomedan ill-will stirred up against the Hindus, and last the offence given by the Hindu–Mahomedan dinner to orthodox Hindus – all of these have created in Calcutta a situation from which the Congress cannot hope to escape without serious injury. The only man who seems to retain a head on his shoulders is Mr. Bhupendranath Bose. But for the past two or three years his influence has been rapidly on the wane, and his position is a most difficult one – Bipin Chandra Pal unscrupulously assailing him on one side and Surendranath resenting the curbs which he puts on him on the other. The preparations for the Congress have not yet been taken in hand, though we are now at the end of September. A huge unwieldy so-called reception Committee, consisting of anybody and everybody was no doubt formed two months ago, but no care was taken in regard to the men that were put on it, any name that was handed in being accepted. The result is that neither Surendranath nor Bipin Chandra knows which side has a majority on the reception committee and they are both postponing the election of an executive or

---

[1] 'Sir P.M.M. is as firm as ever in his policy of sitting tight over the present situation. My brother was organising a certain memorial which might have given an opportunity for some plain speaking but Sir P.M.M. put an extinguisher over it. He has put an absolute embargo upon all movements.' V. K. Bhatavadekar to Gokhale, 27 September 1906, Gokhale Papers, Reel 1, NAI.

[2] Gokhale to Krishnaswami Iyer, 29 September 1906, Gokhale Papers, Reel 5, NAI. Gokhale even persuaded Tilak to attend a meeting in Bombay with Pherozeshah Mehta but 'Nothing tangible resulted from this conference', *ibid.*

[3] Deodhar was sent on 16 September and reported back by telegrams on 19 and 20 September. Gokhale to Krishnaswami Iyer, 29 September 1906, Gokhale Papers, Reel 5, NAI.

working committee out of this body, as that means the first open trial of strength between the two parties.¹

Even if the difficulties of actually getting the Congress to meet were overcome, Gokhale foresaw trouble at the session itself.

Bipin Chandra Pal and his party are working hard to get a large contingent of delegates on their side and they want to sweep the present programme of the Congress clean off the board and substitute in its place only three resolutions, the first, declaring our inherent right to govern ourselves and demanding autonomy, absolute, immediate, free from foreign control; the second calling upon all Congress men to withdraw their sons and wards from all Government institutions and make independent provision for their education, so that the rising generation should grow up full of determination to wrest complete autonomy from England; and the third advocating not only Swadeshism in the industrial field but a comprehensive boycott against everything English – English goods, Government Schools and Colleges, Government Service, honorary offices and so forth – so that the only points of contact between the Government and the people should be those of violent hatred. This is the programme of the new Bengal Party and they profess that they will make no compromise with anyone who proposes to agitate for mere reforms as the success of such agitation would mean an improved and therefore prolonged foreign rule. They are claiming Mr. Tilak as their leader, though we all know that he does not believe in the practicability of their belief that he is their leader. When the Congress meets, if it meets at all in Calcutta, we must be prepared for violent scenes and disorderly attempts to make its work on old lines impossible. It is sad, inexpressibly sad that all this should occur at the very moment when the Viceroy and Secretary of State are contemplating an important step forward. It may be that we are after all, as an ancient writer says, 'the mere sport of aimless destiny'.²

Gokhale recognised two main criticisms of the Congress. The first was the agitation for some sort of constitution. On this he believed that the leadership should give ground, if only to prevent the extremists using it as a rallying cry. The second was the more general attack being launched by some extremists against the whole strategy of the Congress. On that front no compromise was possible. Gokhale estimated that 'the whole of Madras, two-thirds of Bombay, the whole of United Provinces, two-thirds of Punjab, two-thirds of Central Provinces

¹ Gokhale to Krishnaswami Iyer, 29 September 1906, Gokhale Papers, Reel 5, NAI.
² Gokhale to Krishnaswami Iyer, 29 September 1906, *ibid*.

Tilak, Gokhale and the Indian National Congress, 1895 to 1906

and about half of Bengal are with us in this matter'.[1] There was, therefore, a chance that the leadership would be able to maintain its control.

The first trial of strength came with the choice of the President. If either Lajpat Rai or Tilak were elected, then it would appear that the opposition had triumphed. To avoid that, Surendranath Banerjea, in consultation with Bombay, telegraphed to Dadabhai Naoroji, offering him the Presidency of the Calcutta Congress.[2] The other side urged Dadabhai to refuse an offer which had been made 'without consulting the Reception Committee or the Standing Congress Committee', and which came only from Surendranath Banerjea and Bhupendranath Basu.[3] Bipin Chandra Pal tried to upset the arrangement by writing to Dadabhai that unless the latter stood down from the Presidency, he would run Tilak against him openly.[4] This move was scotched by Tilak himself, who preferred to delay any trial of strength until the Congress met. He wrote with less than total candour to Dadabhai:

> You may have learned by this time why they are fighting in Bengal. I have not the least connection with it, nor is the quarrel there encouraged by me in any way. They are, no doubt, using my name, without my consent or authority, to serve their own purposes; but I cannot prevent it in any decent way. I can however assure you this much that the Congress would not suffer on this account. Babu Motilal, if not Bipin, may be fully relied upon for this purpose.[5]

The possibility of collusion between Tilak and the Bengal extremists was very serious from the Bombay leaders' point of view. Gokhale and Wacha began to rally support from their friends in other provinces.[6] They announced that the Standing

---

[1] Gokhale to Krishnaswami Iyer, 29 September 1906, *ibid.*
[2] Banerjea to Naoroji, 7 September 1906, Naoroji Papers, NAI. Banerjea and Basu to Naoroji, 13 September 1906, *ibid.*; Wacha to Naoroji, 10 September 1906, *ibid.*
[3] Ghose to Naoroji, 20 September 1906, *ibid.*
[4] Gokhale to Krishnaswami Iyer, 29 September 1906. Gokhale Papers, Reel 5, NAI.
[5] Tilak to Naoroji, 21 September 1906, Naoroji Papers, NAI.
[6] An unexpected misfortune occurred at this time in Madras. On 22 October Arbuthnot and Co., an old banking firm, failed without warning, ruining thousands in Madras Presidency. On hearing a report from the south of the extent of the losses, Gokhale wrote to Krishnaswami Iyer 'It will be a great misfortune if this crash reduces largely the contingent of delegates from your Presidency to the next Congress, because we on this side have all been depending largely on the solid

Congress Committee, appointed at Benares the previous year,[1] would meet in Bombay on 17 and 18 November to discuss the crisis.[2] In order to attend this meeting, Surendranath Banerjea brought forward the date fixed for the meeting of the Calcutta Congress Reception Committee from 18 November to 11 November.[3] The Reception Committee was to elect formally the President of the Congress and to appoint an executive committee to attend to the organisation of the Calcutta session. The change of date had an added attraction for Surendranath Banerjea: because such short notice was given, members of the Reception Committee living far from Calcutta would not have time to attend it. Not unnaturally Bipin Chandra Pal was furious at this manoeuvre since many of his supporters lived in east Bengal.[4] 148 members of the Reception Committee met in the Indian Association's rooms in Calcutta on 11 November. They successfully defeated a motion by R. N. Ray that the meeting be held on the 18th, confirmed Dadabhai Naoroji as President of the Congress, and appointed an executive committee in which Surendranath's party were 'in an overwhelming majority'.[5]

At the Standing Congress Committee in Bombay the following week, Pherozeshah Mehta conceded that the Calcutta Congress would have to discuss more thoroughly than hitherto the question of a constitution for the organisation. Apart from agreeing to leave the details of the controversial resolutions to the Subjects Committee, and some preliminary discussion about the location of the 1907 Congress, the meeting came to an end

and clear-headed common-sense of Madras to keep down the fights of the dreamy and imaginative element from Bengal. You must come in any case yourself and I hope that at least a hundred delegates from the different parts of your Presidency will be able to attend.' Gokhale to Krishnaswami Iyer, 30 October 1906, Gokhale Papers, Reel 5, NAI. In fact the political associations in Madras, and many of Krishnaswami Iyer's friends and political allies, lost very heavily. D. A. Washbrook, 'Politics in the Madras Presidency 1880–1920' (Trinity College Fellowship Dissertation, Cambridge, 1971).

[1] *INC 1905*, p. 96.
[2] *Hindu*, 2 November 1906.
[3] *Ibid*.
[4] Bipin Chandra Pal denied that the Standing Congress Committee had any right to meet at all since its 'existence ... had never been practically demonstrated before'. *Hindu*, 7 November 1906.
[5] *Hindu*, 16 November 1906. According to the *Hindu's* correspondent the moderates had twenty-one seats on the executive committee compared to the extremists' four. *Ibid*. 17 November 1906; see also *ibid*. 21 November 1906.

without any major decision being taken.¹ Its significance was that it was the first occasion on which such a committee had met.

The Bombay leaders had every reason to feel that their intervention had been productive of good in Bengal. However, they were still apprehensive of what might happen, and it became clear that a Maharashtrian–Bengali axis had been formed. Mudholkar wrote to Gokhale:

> the situation in Calcutta is still anything but reassuring. The tone of New India shows that Bipin Chandra Pal is still intent on mischief. As to what your townsman [Tilak] – the tribune of the people – the new Sivaji – has planned out can more be imagined than discerned. My respected townsman and colleague on the municipality and elsewhere [Khaparde] is arranging to go very early to Calcutta if possible before the 20th to see what action should be taken 'to put down the moderates who have stolen a march upon the true patriots' recently. This is no mere gup. Whether he will do all he threatens is more than I can say.²

The proceedings of the 1906 session of the Indian National Congress were very lively. The Bombay leaders came in force. Mehta arrived to take charge of the proceedings. Khaparde wrote: 'He was very gushing, put his arms round my neck and did other things which surprised me. This means war to the knife between the old and the new school. He is said to be adept at imposing his will on others both by cajoling and threatening.'³ But it was to require more than force of personality to influence this Congress. As Satyananda Bose had written to Gokhale 'You are well aware that Bengal is very keen about the swadeshi, boycott, Partition and National Education. The feeling is not confined to the Extremists but is shared by the Moderates also.'⁴

In fact, these were the four main planks to the Bengali platform. First of all, Bengali leaders intended that the Congress should condemn the partition of Bengal; related to this was a resolution, first passed in 1905, that the boycott movement practised in Bengal was a legitimate political technique. The boycott was primarily aimed at foreign goods, and the

---
¹ Khaparde, Diary, 21 November 1906, Khaparde Papers, NAI. Tilak and Mehta had a tiff: see Tilak to Mehta, 21 November 1906, Mehta Papers, NAI.
² Mudholkar to Gokhale, 14 December 1906, Gokhale Papers, Reel 8, NAI.
³ Khaparde, Diary, 24 December 1906, Khaparde Papers, NAI.
⁴ Satyananda Bose to Gokhale, 16 December 1906, Gokhale Papers, Reel 2, NAI.

swadeshi movement to encourage indigenous industries was linked to it in the Bengali campaigns. After the tightening up of government educational facilities the Bengalis had also started a scheme for an independent structure of schools and colleges, and in these great emphasis was placed on scientific and technical learning. Of course all these issues were subject to a wide range of interpretation within Bengal – did the boycott include government schools, offices and titles for example? Some of the resolutions bore different interpretations outside Bengal – to a Punjabi or a man from the United Provinces, the development of indigenous industries had been vigorously championed by both local governments and local politicians since the mid-nineteenth century. It was about these issues that the fiercest controversy arose.

Bipin Chandra Pal and Tilak, unsure of their actual power within the Congress, convened a meeting of their supporters before the sessions began.[1] Tilak presided, and he and his followers resolved that if the Subjects Committee of the Congress would not accept their resolutions, then they would move amendments in the open session of the Congress. Since the main object of the Congress was to present unanimous demands to the government, all the speakers usually supported the resolutions. Tilak's plan thus threatened to destroy the unanimity of the movement in public. Moreover, in the open session he and his men would be able to deploy local feeling to a greater extent than on the Subjects Committee, where they would be constrained by delegates from other provinces. However, in the event the draft resolutions 'show a clear advance on the proceedings of the previous Congresses'[2] and Tilak, Pal and their followers were able to wield considerable influence on the Subjects Committee.

At all previous meetings of the Congress the informal procedure by which the Subjects Committee was chosen meant that anyone of importance gained a place on it and a great deal of influence was concentrated in the hands of a few men. The informality of the process was consequently attacked by those

[1] Khaparde, Diary, 24 December 1906, Khaparde Papers, NAI.
[2] Khaparde, Diary, 31 December 1906, *ibid.* Khaparde wrote his diary for 25–31 December in one connected piece. He was here referring to events on 25 December.

who stood to gain by formal elections. *Bande Mataram*, Aurobindo Ghose's newspaper, complained that previously the appointment of the Committee had 'been an operation carried out irresponsibly by a small number of men in authority. On this occasion it was evident that such a method could not be adopted without challenge.'[1] The result was chaos and confusion. Over six hundred delegates managed to force their way on to the Subjects Committee[2] – more people than had attended some of the previous Congress sessions.

The Committee met in the Maharaja of Dharbanga's palace. Most of the resolutions were old stalwarts and were accepted without question. The resolution about government in India was slightly modified: it was explicitly stated that the Congress hoped for the extension to India of the kind of government 'obtaining in the self-governing British Colonies'.[3] The importance of an independent system of education 'Literary, Scientific and Technical' was recognised and the Congress gave its blessing to the organisation of educational facilities 'suited to the requirements of the country on national lines and under national control'.[4] But quarrels developed over the phrasing of the resolutions about the partition of Bengal, the swadeshi movement, and boycott.

The first discussion on 26 December was taken up by the partition resolution. In draft this resolution asked for an enquiry by the government into partition. Motilal Ghose, Tilak's old friend and Surendranath Banerjea's old enemy, argued that the time had come to give up petitioning for government enquiries and he moved that this clause be struck out. Dadabhai Naoroji decided that the feeling of the house was against the amendment, but wisely refused to put it to a vote.[5] In the end, Surendranath Banerjea decided to accept the amendment, and speaking in the open session he said that 'all reference to

---

[1] Quoted in *Hindu*, 1 January 1907.
[2] Khaparde, Diary, 31 December 1906, Khaparde Papers; NAI; *Hindu*, 1 January 1907. The difficulties of accommodating such a large number were immense. Pherozeshah Mehta insisted on sitting next to the President; there was not enough room on the platform for the Bombay delegates. Surendranath moved some Bengalis to make way for the Bombay people. They in turn displaced some newspaper reporters and there were minor scuffles. *Hindu*, 1 January 1907.
[3] Resolution IX, *INC 1906*.
[4] Resolution XI, *ibid*.
[5] Khaparde, Diary, 31 December 1906, Khaparde Papers, NAI.

the commission of inquiry will be deleted' from the final wording of the resolution.¹

After partition was discussed, the Committee turned to the swadeshi resolution. This too provoked heated exchanges. A poll was demanded, but Naoroji refused to grant it, saying that there was a majority against the Pal–Tilak party. Khaparde insisted that they had a right to divide the house. A procedural wrangle then ensued 'and the President showed an attitude of hostility and would not consent to divide the house'.² Thereupon, Khaparde and some two hundred followers left in a body. Tilak stayed to watch over further proceedings in the Committee while Khaparde drafted his party's amendments, sent them to the press, and gave notice that they would be taken up again the following day.³ However, compromise was again reached. Ananda Charlu, who had been a constant supporter of Congress since 1885, moved the swadeshi resolution in the Congress:⁴ it was seconded by Madan Mohan Malaviya from the United Provinces. He stressed, however, that the swadeshi movement had nothing to do with the agitation in Bengal: 'As you have been told, the Swadeshi movement is an *old* movement in this country. It is not born either of Partition or after Partition and it is extremely desirable that this should always be looked upon as entirely independent of any political considerations.'⁵ Tilak, speaking after Malaviya, insisted that the swadeshi movement involved more than simply encouraging

---

¹ *INC 1906*, p. 72. The Resolution ran: 'This Congress again records its emphatic protest against the Partition of Bengal and regrets that the present Government, while admitting that there were errors in the original plan and that it went wholly and decisively against the wishes of the majority of the people of Bengal, is disposed to look upon it as a settled fact, in spite of the earnest and persistent protest of the people and their manifest disinclination to accept it as final.

'This Congress composed of representatives from all the Provinces of this country, desires earnestly to impress upon the British Parliament and the present Liberal Government that it will not only be just, but expedient to reverse or modify the Partition in such a manner as to keep the eastern Bengali-speaking community under one undivided administration and thus restore contentment to so important a province as Bengal.' Resolution VI, *ibid*.

² Khaparde, Diary, 31 December 1906, Khaparde Papers, NAI. ³ *Ibid*.

⁴ The Resolution finally read: 'This Congress accords its most cordial support to the *Swadeshi* movement and calls upon the people of the country to labour for its success by making earnest and sustained efforts to promote the growth of indigenous industries and to stimulate the production of indigenous articles by giving them preference over imported commodities even at some sacrifice.' Resolution VIII, *INC 1906*. ⁵ *INC 1906*, p. 107.

Tilak, Gokhale and the Indian National Congress, 1895 to 1906

Indian industries: it also involved self-help, determination and sacrifice on the part of those who consumed foreign goods.[1] In plain words it involved boycott, and this was precisely what the moderate leadership disliked.[2] But Tilak never succeeded in permanently joining boycott to swadeshi, and his followers never managed to appropriate the swadeshi movement to their cause.

The real conflict came on the wording of the boycott resolution itself. At the 1905 Congress, under pressure from Bengal, the Congress leaders had accepted that boycott of foreign goods was a legitimate and constitutional technique for use in Bengal. Tilak and Pal now attempted to widen the concept by arguing that boycott applied to everything British, not just manufactured goods, and that it was a perfectly acceptable form of agitation in any province at any time. The Congress leaders were particularly anxious to disown such an interpretation since it would inevitably be associated in England with Irish tactics and would consequently damage the Indian cause. The resolution passed at Benares had been quite limited and specific,[3] but as it emerged from the Calcutta Subjects Committee, the resolution laid before the Congress was capable of much wider interpretation.

A. C. Mazumdar, in a speech which managed to ignore any discussion of boycott,[4] moved in the open session of Congress

[1] *INC 1906*, p. 111.
[2] In the Subjects Committee Tilak had originally wanted to use the word 'boycott'. After protracted negotiations Mehta and his allies were prepared to accept the phrase giving indigenous articles 'preference over imported commodities even at some sacrifice'. But, as Tilak intended, this could be interpreted as approval of boycotting foreign goods. 'Mehta was very annoyed and said "you would not and could not have treated me so in Bombay." Tilak replied "if provoked to it we could show you a sample even in Bombay."' Khaparde, Diary, 31 December 1906, Khaparde Papers, NAI.
[3] 'That this Congress records its earnest and emphatic protest against the repressive measures which have been adopted by the authorities in Bengal after the people there had been compelled to resort to the boycott of foreign goods as a last protest and perhaps the only constitutional and effective means left to them of drawing the attention of the British public to the action of the Government of India in persisting in their determination to partition Bengal in utter disregard of the universal prayers and protests of the people.' Resolution XIII, *INC 1905*.
[4] Mazumdar, a supporter of Surendranath Banerjea from Faridpur in east Bengal, rambled on about the evil effects of partition, the dilemma of political leaders and the enthusiasm of the young, ending with a statement that he hoped the Resolution would be supported. *INC 1906*, pp. 81–3.

that 'Having regard to the fact that the people of this country have little or no voice in its administration, and that their representations to the Government do not receive due consideration, this Congress is of opinion that the Boycott Movement inaugurated in Bengal by way of protest against the partitition of that province was and is legitimate.'[1]

The Congress leaders had agreed to accept this formulation of the resolution in the hope that, like the one on swadeshi, it met the demands of the extremists without making them explicit. But if they expected to get the resolution through without a split, their hopes were rudely shattered when Bipin Chandra Pal rose to second it. He began by making pleasantries about Mazumdar, to whom he was usually opposed.[2] Then he began his speech in earnest:

> As regards the resolution that has already been read out to you, you will have observed that the word 'boycott' is attached to the word 'movement'. The word 'boycott' is left alone, left severely alone, and the only qualification that the authors of this resolution have attached to the word 'boycott' is, that it shall move, move from point to point (hear, hear), move from city to city (hear, hear), move from division to division, move, I hope you will allow me to add, from province to province (cheers and hear, hear), and the omission of any other qualifying expression in regard to this term is significant. It is not, you will observe, a mere boycott of *goods*. It is a boycott of something else. Do not be afraid. We have done that something in that part of Bengal which I have the honour in my humble way to represent. We, in Eastern Bengal and Assam, have not only tried to boycott, so far as it has lain in our power, British goods, but all honorary offices and associations with the Government.[3]

Pal went on to argue that by making the administration impossible in east Bengal, the agitators (and not Gokhale) had secured the dismissal of the Lieutenant-Governor of the new province. The message was clear: 'Sir Bampfylde Fuller is gone, but our boycott has come to remain and it will remain until every grievance, that we have, is redressed.'[4]

The Congress leaders were furious, and disputed Bipin Chandra Pal's interpretation. L. A. Govind Raghava Iyer from Madras was the first to speak. He warned that boycott must be used with caution and 'that while the necessities of Bengal do require the use of this weapon, such a necessity has

[1] Resolution VII, *INC 1906*.
[3] *Ibid.*, p. 83.
[2] *INC 1906*, p. 83.
[4] *Ibid.*, p. 84.

not arisen elsewhere'.¹ Madras was sympathetic to Bengal, but, he argued, Madras delegates would have nothing to do with boycott as a regular political tactic.²

Asutosh Chaudhuri then had the unenviable task of reassuring the other provinces that nothing more was intended than that the Congress should support the boycott in Bengal, without at the same time antagonising the large number of Bengali supporters of Bipin Chandra Pal.³ Pandit Madan Mohan Malaviya, however, was standing for no strained interpretations. He argued that the Congress did express its approval of the adoption of boycott in Bengal, for there all other political techniques had failed to move the government on the burning issue of the Partition. So, as a last resort, Bengal had 'declared a boycott of British goods ... to invite the attention of the English people to the grievances under which they [sic] laboured'. Congress endorsed this action, but within severe limits. There was no question of using boycott as a regular technique, and there was no question of deploying it outside of Bengal. Therefore, 'the Congress does not, I am certain, – speaking certainly for a large number of delegates of different Provinces – I declare emphatically that the Congress does not associate itself with the remarks of Mr. Bipin Chandra Pal'.⁴

At this there were cries of 'yes, yes' and 'no, no', and 'great disorder prevailed'.⁵ Malaviya however held his ground and in a running exchange with his audience affirmed on behalf of a large number of delegates present – not only from the United Provinces – that his interpretation was correct. Gokhale con-

---

¹ *INC 1906*, p. 86.
² *Ibid.* At this point there were cries of 'no, no', 'not all' from the Madras delegates. Raghava Iyer went on: 'Those of you who were in the Subjects Committee last night must have recognised that even in Madras there is difference of opinion, (voices: "There is"). But he will be a bold man who will contradict me when I say that the general body of opinion in Madras is decidedly in favour of the view that I put forward. Gentlemen, I simply say that what we mean by this resolution, is, as I understand it ... exactly the same as was done at last year's Congress in Benares.' *Ibid.* Khaparde had earlier (on 25 December) recorded that Madras was solidly against boycott. Khaparde, Diary, 31 December 1906, Khaparde Papers, NAI.
³ He said 'We want you to say that Bengal was right and we want you to adopt this resolution simply with regard to Bengal. We all express the pious hope, every one of us, that if and when circumstances make it necessary, the other Provinces in their own time will adopt it.' *INC 1906*, p. 87.
⁴ *Ibid.* pp. 87–8.   ⁵ *Ibid.* p. 88.

cluded the debate with a simple statement that whatever interpretation individuals put on specific resolutions, official Congress policy was that the boycott applied only to British goods, and it involved only Bengal.[1] The resolution was put to the Congress by the President and passed.[2]

The Calcutta session of 1906 was a notable landmark in the history of the Indian National Congress. The resolutions were more radical than ever before. The Congress had urged more activity in India, and more self-help. National education and swadeshi were endorsed by the delegates. The Congress had re-affirmed the legitimacy of boycott as a political weapon in Bengal, and the widely reported speeches of Pal and Tilak showed that to some delegates it meant much more. The Congress had given a new twist to some of its old demands. The claims that the superior civil service examinations should be held in India as well as in England; that Indians should sit on the councils of the Secretary of State, the Viceroy and the Governors of Madras and Bombay; that the legislative councils be reformed; and that local government bodies should have more power, were now linked together to form a general demand that the system of government in India be similar to that in other self-governing colonies.[3] Dadabhai Naoroji picked up the theme in his closing address. Congressmen now had before them 'a clear goal, a clear star, as Sir Henry Campbell-Bannerman would have called it, of Self-Government or Swaraj'.[4]

Of course there would be many interpretations of 'self-government' in the debates that followed, but there was no doubt that the alliance between Tilak and some of the Bengalis had given a new direction to Congress affairs. Tilak later wrote to Shyamji Krishnavarma that

---

[1] *Ibid*. p. 89. Gokhale went on to say 'Beyond this, if any of you want to go, go by all means but do not go in the name of the Congress. You go forward as individuals; you have every right to do that; we do not question that by any means, but do not drag the rest who do not want to go with you.' *Ibid*.
[2] *Ibid*. p. 89.
[3] *Ibid*. Resolution IX. Most of these demands had, in some form or other, found a place in Congress resolutions from the very earliest meetings.
[4] *Ibid*. p. 139. Khaparde wrote 'The President made an excellent though very brief speech last of all and said that Self-Government was the goal and the younger generation should work for it. The Moderates could not have liked it. I saw them wince.' Khaparde, Diary, 31 December 1906, Khaparde Papers, NAI.

Tilak, Gokhale and the Indian National Congress, 1895 to 1906

in spite of Mr. Mehta and his party who mustered strong this year, we were able to carry out 3/4 of our programme in the Congress. I must say that Dadabhai was sympathetic towards the aspiration and programme of the new party, though in his Presidential address he did not go in for it completely. His concluding speech was much better, however, his placing Swarajya as a goal before the Congress in distinct terms was some advance on old ideas.[1]

Khaparde was jubilant at their success. He recorded in his diary that 'Sir P. Mehta and all old leaders generally had lost their influence. Sir P. Mehta tried to lecture the delegates but they would not stand it ... Madan Mohan Malaviya made an exhibition of himself and Gokhale walked about and talked like a woman with a complaint.'[2] The Congress, *Mahratta* trumpeted, had emerged from Calcutta 'triumphant and rejuvenated'.[3]

Tilak's famous speech 'Tenets of the New Party', given in Calcutta after the Congress, must be considered against this background. His success at the Congress, and the situation in Bengal, led him to try to draw party distinctions within the Congress, and, by formulating alternative strategies for Congress, he laid the foundations for the split that followed. In his speech, he tried to explain the distinction between moderates and extremists in Indian politics. Both parties, he said, shared a fundamental premise: 'that this government does not suit us'.[4] The technique of appealing to England had failed, and it was an impossibly difficult task to convert the whole electorate of Great Britain.[5] The new party did not believe in an appeal to the British nation. The remedy lay closer to hand, 'not petitioning but boycott'.[6] Tilak pointed out that the entire administration 'which is carried on by a handful of Englishmen, is carried on with our assistance'. The rulers should be made aware of the power of Indians to co-operate with each other, and to

[1] Tilak to Krishnavarma, 18 January 1907. Reprinted in *Mahratta*, 23 May 1941.
[2] Khaparde, Diary, 31 December 1906, Khaparde Papers, NAI. At the railway station when the Congress was over, Khaparde discovered that 'Sir P. Mehta had engaged the half compartment next to the one in which I got accommodation, but it appeared that all his gushing friendship had disappeared and he tried to ignore me. Not knowing his inner feelings I spoke to him once and then guessing what was passing in his mind, I ignored him too all the way and we never exchanged a single word.' *Ibid.*
[3] *Mahratta*, 6 January 1907.
[4] *Tilak: his writings and speeches* (Madras, no date), p. 38.
[5] *Ibid.* pp. 43–4. [6] *Ibid.* p. 48.

withhold collaboration from the government. Active resistance was out of the question, but,

> you have the power of self-denial and self-abstinence in such a way as not to assist this foreign Government to rule over you. This is boycott and this is what we mean when we say boycott is a political weapon. We shall not give them assistance to collect revenue and keep peace. We shall not assist them in fighting beyond the frontiers or outside India with Indian blood and money. We shall not assist them in carrying on the administration and justice. We shall have our own courts, and when the time comes we shall not pay taxes. Can you do that by your united efforts? If you can you are free from tomorrow.[1]

Tilak's speech found a receptive audience and it was widely discussed in the Indian press. Yet its content was not strikingly original. What Tilak was trying to do was to rearrange some of the current slogans of Indian politics (especially the calls for self-help, swadeshi and passive resistance, all of which had long pedigrees) into a plausible alternative to the strict constitutionalism and limited strategy of his opponents.[2] This explains in part the masterly ambiguity of the speech: Tilak and his supporters argued at once not only the differences but the similarities between the parties. Indeed, politicians of every hue recognised that much of the ground on which they stood was common to them all. Moreover, the very precise limits within which any all-India politics were viable restricted the politicians' options. Of course as an opposition politician within Congress, Tilak had less to lose by stepping outside the bounds of conventional political propriety. This merely confirmed the moderates' distrust of him, for they felt that Tilak was putting at risk the common programme for personal ends.[3]

[1] *Ibid.* pp. 49–50.
[2] A detailed discussion of the speech can be found in *Panjabee*, 12 January 1907 and 16 January 1907.
[3] R. N. Mudholkar argued strongly that beneath the extremist froth lay the moderates' own programme. Moderates also relied on their 'demands being strengthened, and enforced by a large volume of effective popular opinion. Popular education, organization of public opinion, greater keenness in political matters, effective self-reliance, assertiveness, are the things on which the constitutional party rely. Now this is precisely the thing which the extremists claim they advocate.' Moreover, the moderates had been grossly misrepresented by Tilak's party. 'Take for instance the Resolution about "autonomy on the self-governing system." Past Presidents and speakers on the Congress platform have proclaimed this ideal of his over and over again. Sir Henry Cotton made pointed reference to it at Bombay and you [Gokhale] did the same at Benares and yet

At Calcutta, it looked as though the Congress was being diverted from its old course. However, it would be a mistake to think that the extremists had had everything their own way. For all Khaparde's triumphant crowing about the eclipse of the moderate party, and for all the gloomy prognostications about extremist success from the moderates, the Congress leaders had managed to lay the foundations for Tilak's eventual downfall. The first step was to frame a new constitution for the Congress; the second was to arrange that the 1907 session be held in Nagpur.

Before the 1906 session, a Congress constitution had been loudly demanded by the critics of informal control. So it is at first sight surprising that the proposals for a constitution presented at Calcutta went by unremarked. This was partly because the moderate leadership agreed that it was necessary to make concessions on this issue.[1] Having done so, however, the moderates found that the various problems associated with framing a constitution worked in their favour. For, having disarmed criticism by accepting the need for a constitution, the moderates were able to exploit to their advantage the dilemma that faced Congressmen of every shade of opinion: what form should the constitution take? However much argument there might be among Congressmen about political attitudes, there was very little scope for a real quarrel about the constitution. If the all-India body was to survive, everyone could see that the shape of the Congress had to be as flexible and informal as possible. If it was made too rigid the organisation itself would be destroyed and all sides would find that the disadvantages outweighed the advantages.

The special committee set up at the Benares Congress in 1905 had met once during 1906[2] and it presented a report to the Subjects Committee at Calcutta. This report made 'tentative' proposals, and the Subjects Committee decided unanimously –

our excellent typical patriot is not ashamed of writing in his paper that no past President noticed this point or laid any emphasis on it. Only a few months ago these same people the Tilaks Pals and Aravind Ghoses were abusing us for proclaiming the ideal of the self-governing colonial system, and now they claim victory because we compelled them to adopt our ideal.' Mudholkar to Gokhale, undated, January 1907. Gokhale Papers, Reel 8, NAI.
[1] Gokhale to Krishnaswami Iyer, 29 September 1906, Gokhale Papers, Reel 5, NAI.
[2] *INC 1906*, p. 132.

and that after all the divisions over the resolutions about swadeshi and boycott – to recommend the adoption of the report. The main difficulties facing would-be constitution makers were well illustrated by the circumlocution of the speeches proposing the measure on the floor of the Congress session: 'we have grown free and easy', said D. A. Khare, 'and we have seen how we have gone on and it is thought that the time have [sic] now come when a sort of elastic and tentative constitution may be placed before you for acceptance this year'. Urging the Congress to accept the proposals, Khare pointed out that they were 'to be tried strictly for one year, so as to enable us to see how they suit our requirements'.[1]

In brief, the proposals suggested the establishment of Provincial Congress Committees, to be set up either by Provincial Conferences or by special meetings, to pursue Congress work throughout the year. The second main provision was for the establishment of a Central Standing Committee of the Congress, to be elected by the delegates assembled at the Calcutta meeting. This committee would carry out the resolutions of the Congress 'and deal with urgent questions which may arise and which may require to be disposed of in the name of the Congress' during the year.[2] Two possible procedures were laid down for the selection of the Congress President[3] and the Subjects Committee was to be much reduced in size.[4]

[1] *INC 1906*, p. 132.   [2] Resolution XVI, *INC 1906*.
[3] The first procedure was that the Reception Committee established by a Provincial Committee should elect the President. If it was not possible to achieve a majority of at least three-fourths of the Committee, the matter was to be referred to the Central Congress Committee whose decision was binding. The alternative method was that the Reception Committee should consult all the Provincial Congress Committees and, if it approved of the nominee of a majority of the Provincial Congress Committees, it should elect that man. However, the Reception Committee was not obliged to accept the advice of the Provincial Committees and again the matter could be referred for final decision to the Central Congress Committee. Resolution XVI, *INC 1906*.
[4] It was agreed that the Subjects Committee should consist of: 25 representatives of Bengal, Bihar, Assam and Burma, 15 representatives of Madras, 15 representatives of Bombay, 10 representatives of United Provinces, 10 representatives of Punjab, 6 representatives of Central Provinces, 4 representatives of Berar, and 10 additional representatives from the host province; together with the President, the Chairman of the Reception Committee, the General Secretaries of the Congress, the local Secretaries of the province arranging the session, and all past presidents and past Chairmen of Reception Committees as *ex-officio* members. Resolution XVI, *INC 1906*.

Tilak, Gokhale and the Indian National Congress, 1895 to 1906

The two latter proposals had arisen to avoid any repetition of the confusion surrounding the Calcutta Congress, while the first two proposals did not differ materially from earlier suggestions. The motion was put to the house where it was carried, and, in the turmoil of delegates leaving the pandal, Gokhale collected the names of men to serve on the Central Congress Committee for 1907.[1] The difference between the 1906 constitution and its predecessors was that during 1907 its provisions were acted upon and changed the history of the Congress. Moreover, the people who turned this modest exercise in making the Congress administration more formal were those who had long controlled it by informal methods.

Almost all the Congress leaders were agreed that it had been a great mistake to send the Congress to Calcutta in 1906. The local crisis had endangered the smooth running of the all-India movement. It was therefore very important that the error should not be repeated in 1907. This would be the crucial year for discussion of reforms, and it was essential that the Congress should keep to its proper task – the influencing of English public and governmental opinion. A reasonable and impeccably constitutional line had to be taken, and the radical implications of some of the Calcutta resolutions had to be toned down. Above all, Tilak, the leader of the extremist party, must be prevented from presiding over the 1907 session.

There was not much choice about where to hold the 1907

---

[1] The names of the Central Congress Committee for 1907 were not in fact published in the Congress Report. They were however:

Bengal: S. N. Banerjea, Moti Lal Ghose, Bhupendranath Basu, Narendranath Sen, Asutosh Chaudhuri, Baikunthanath Sen, Ambica Charan Mazumdar, Aswini Kumar Dutt, Bipin Chandra Pal, K. K. Mitra, A. Rasul and S. Sinha

Madras: Ananda Charlu, C. S. Nair, Nawab Sayed Mahomed, G. Subramania Iyer, C. Vijayarajhavacharia, N. Subba Rao, V. Krishnaswami Iyer, V. Ryar Nambiar

Bombay: P. M. Mehta, Gokuldas K. Parekh, D. A. Khare, M. A. Jinnah, B. G. Tilak, R. P. Karandikar, Ambarlal Sakarlal Desai, Harish Chandra Vishnudas

Punjab: Lala Muri Dhar, Lala Hans Raj, Lal Harkishen Lal, Sheikh Umar Bakhsh

Central Provinces: G. M. Chitnavis, Dr H. Gour, Roop Govind, W. M. Kolhatkar

Berar: G. S. Khaparde, R. N. Mudholkar

United Provinces: Gangaprasad Varma, Madan Mohan Malaviya, Hafiz Abdur Rahim, Pandit Prithi Nath, Dr Tej Bahadur Sapru, Pandit Gokarnath Misra

Source: *Panjabee*, 12 January 1907.

Congress. Bengal, the United Provinces, Bombay and Madras had all recently played host: this left the Punjab, which had not seen the Congress since 1900, and the Central Provinces, which had last held a session in 1897.[1] Of these two, the Congress leadership preferred the Central Provinces. Punjab was suspect because none of the main Congressmen lived there or had interests there. Moreover, Punjabi delegations to Congress between 1904 and 1906, although small in size, had played an important part in pushing the movement into a more radical posture. And there was a risk that a party could be organised in Lahore to run Tilak for President.

On the other hand, the Central Provinces had much to recommend them. Congress support there was drawn from a wealthy elite of landowners, bankers, merchants and lawyers, who were closely associated politically, professionally, and socially with the government of the province. Men who had turned years of administrative service to good account, contractors and revenue farmers who had become great landlords, and lawyers who had grown rich on the civil suits springing from the wealthy cotton-growing lands, were unlikely to find the extremist platform at all enticing. 'Most of the purse-proud pleaders of Berar never cared much for politics', wrote a correspondent to the *Panjabee*, while 'What are called public men at Nagpur were so far some Government pensioners, pettyfogging lawyers and not overeducated but titled Zamindars. These gentry necessarily belong to the Moderate school.'[2]

The political opinions of the Nagpur leaders were in fact well known. Addressing the second Central Provinces and Berar Provincial Conference, held at Jubbulpore in April 1906, G. M. Chitnavis, the first citizen of Nagpur,[3] had stressed the need for constitutional agitation, but had roundly condemned the 'irresponsible agitation and extravagance' of some of the extremists. On no account, he argued, must official sympathy

---

[1] The 1897 Congress had been held at Amraoti, the chief town of Berar. Until 1906, Congressmen considered the Central Provinces and Berar as one unit. At the Calcutta Congress, however, they decided to make two separate provinces out of the region.

Panjabee, 26 October 1907. For an official comment on the loyalty of Nagpur Congressmen see Lyall to Elgin, 17 July 1897, Home Public A, May 1898, 329–44, KW V, NAI.

[3] *Central Provinces District Gazetteers: Nagpur District* (Bombay, 1908), pp. 97–8.

be alienated from Congress. As befitted one of the great cotton magnates of western India, he warmly welcomed the swadeshi movement 'But very few amongst the well-wishers of India will have a kind word to say of the *Swadeshi* Movement used as a political weapon against England, and degraded into a Commercial Boycott.'[1] In fact an agitation involving boycott was unlikely to find supporters among the rich of the Central Provinces.

The Provinces were not, however, an ideal place to hold the Congress. For one thing, the Marathi-speaking areas in the west were susceptible to influence from Poona. Tilak had several connections with Berar in particular, and there was a real possibility that the factional strife in Poona could be extended to Amraoti and Nagpur. Further, since the Central Provinces were outside the Bombay Presidency, there was no formal bar to Tilak being elected President of the Congress; and there were several purely local grievances that could be taken up by politicians and used in the struggle for control of the 1907 Congress. The first of these was the recent amalgamation of the administrations of Berar and the Central Provinces. In particular, the Berar people risked losing their high court in Amraoti. Leading Berar lawyers now had to journey to Nagpur to plead in the superior court. This meant that the hitherto discrete factional politics of Amraoti and Nagpur began to mesh. Secondly, Nagpur had a large student population.[2] Already under pressure from overcrowding, the students were particularly vulnerable to the high prices of 1907 and could easily be enlisted in agitation. Nagpur also contained another coherent social group with a long history of riotous behaviour during the periods of high prices: the Koshti community. The Koshtis were the weavers of the region. They had been hit hard during the 1890s by the opening of the mills in Nagpur, and, although some of them had found employment in the new factories, they remained a volatile wage-earning group who were particularly sensitive to fluctuations in the price of food.[3]

But these threats to the placid politics of the Central Provinces were concealed when the decision was taken to send the Con-

---
[1] *Speeches and writings of Sir G. M. Chitnavis KCIE* (Printed for Private Circulation in 1927), p. 330.
[2] *Nagpur Gazetteer*, pp. 269–71.   [3] *Ibid.* p. 83.

gress to Nagpur. The Bombay leaders hoped that in Nagpur they could rely on G. M. Chitnavis and B. K. Bose, a successful Bengali lawyer, to keep the Congress out of difficulties, while they could also depend on Maharashtrian friends in Amraoti, like R. N. Mudholkar, to contain discontent there. In December 1906, it seemed that Nagpur had the fewest disadvantages of any town for holding a moderate session of the Congress; so an invitation was engineered from Nagpur and the Congress resolved to hold its 1907 meeting there.[1]

[1] Bose to Chitnavis, 1 January 1907; Bapu Rao Dada to Chitnavis, 1 January 1907, Chitnavis Papers, Nagpur.

4

TILAK, GOKHALE AND THE INDIAN NATIONAL CONGRESS, 1907 to 1915

As soon as the delegates began to disperse from the Calcutta Congress in December 1906, Indian politicians began to plan their strategy for the coming year. Both sides realised that the next twelve months would be crucial. On the one hand, the Congress leadership had to reassert its hold over the organisation. On the other hand, Tilak and his allies were aware that they had been given an unprecedented opportunity to try to wrest the Congress from the hands of Gokhale and the Bombay Presidency Association clique.

On his way back to Poona from Calcutta, Tilak visited his daughter in Allahabad and made speeches there similar to his 'Tenets of the New Party' address. He aimed at making the United Provinces 'as much a portion of his dominions as Satara and Belgaum'.[1] But the local politicians, apart from some expatriate Bengalis and some students, were unimpressed by his oratory.[2] Nevertheless, the Bombay moderates had to secure their allies in northern India. With Bengal so unstable, and the Punjab such a dubious ally, Gokhale and Mehta realised that the best hope for checking Tilak's campaign lay in close association with the leaders of the United Provinces. Malaviya in particular had proved a pillar of strength at the Calcutta Congress and his support for the Bombay group was soon to be endorsed by his local rival, Motilal Nehru.

In some ways, this alliance between the United Provinces and Bombay city was unexpected. Until now, the northern region had never, except when actually visited by the Congress, participated very much in the all-India movement. Yet its political leaders saw advantages in supporting a moderate Congress movement at this time. The United Provinces were one of the most closely administered regions of British India.

[1] Mudholkar to Gokhale, undated, January 1907. Gokhale Papers, Reel 8, NAI.
[2] Bayly, 'The development of political organisation in the Allahabad locality 1880–1920', pp. 274–6.

As the provincial government developed, it devolved more power on Indians. Politicians in the United Provinces, therefore, like those in Bombay and Madras, were trying to work in association with the government. They saw an opportunity for securing greater control over the provincial budget and its expenditure which decentralisation of the administration and increased power to the legislature could be expected to bring. In this area of fairly close rule 'When ... the local and provincial governments were forthcoming with, or were expected to be forthcoming with, advance in the legislative councils or educational patronage and subvention, the local leadership in the United Provinces would hesitate to alienate its greatest benefactor.'[1] Moreover, the government of the United Provinces had for long been faced with well-organised demands for a share of its power from several distinct groups which had never coalesced. A provincial leadership that was able to combine all before dealing with government had not emerged: but the balance between the parties meant that none could afford to antagonise the government. However, since some interests, such as 'Landlords' and 'Muslims', seemed to have more opportunities of gaining the ear of the provincial government without external alliance,[2] other politicians had to find some outside help to support their case, but not such that would discredit them at home. Thus, predominantly Hindu interests, already working with local government in industrial concerns, actively negotiating the charter for the Benares Hindu University, fresh from considerable successes in the Nagri campaign and on the text-book committees, saw that, in any adjustment of government in their area, they needed a prominent but impeccably respectable public platform; one that would help them add to what they had already won. In short, they saw Bombay and Madras Congressmen as admirable associates.

At the invitation of the United Provinces' leaders, Gokhale followed Tilak's sojourn in Allahabad with a much more thorough tour of the whole province. Leaving Calcutta on 2 February 1907, he visited Allahabad, Lucknow, Cawnpore,

---

[1] Bayly, 'The development of political organisation in the Allahabad locality', p. 299.
[2] See F. C. R. Robinson, 'Consultation and Control: the United Provinces' Government and its allies, 1860–1906', *Modern Asian Studies*, vol. 5, no. 4 (1971), 313–36.

Aligarh and Agra, putting the Congress case for reform of the legislative councils and decentralisation of governmental administration.[1] Unlike Tilak's appeal to the more excitable residents of Allahabad, Gokhale's conciliatory tone and his acute awareness of the dangers that would spring from unleashing communal and sectional politics in northern India meant that his visit strengthened the hands of his local allies.[2] In return, the contract between Bombay and the United Provinces within the Congress was firmly sealed.

The early tours across northern India were to set the pattern for political activity during 1907. Politicians embarked on campaigns of stump oratory on a wide scale. Shyamji Krishnavarma gave Tilak money to finance lecture tours in Bengal, Bombay, and Madras, to print pamphlets, and to set up for the extremists a similar organisation to that of the Bombay Presidency Association.[3] In the event, Tilak was unable to implement his plan fully. He was ill for much of April and May, but Khaparde made a tour of the Central Provinces,[4] and Bipin Chandra Pal visited Madras.[5] Moreover, the agitation against the partition of Bengal reached a new peak, and the Congress leaders in Lahore became involved in serious peasant unrest in the Punjab colonies.[6] The wide spread of political agitation, and the fact that several local trouble spots seemed to be getting rapidly out of control, made events in Nagpur all the more important.

To begin with all went well with the preparations for the forthcoming Congress. The moderates' strategy was to keep tight control of the Congress organisation, to limit participation in the movement, and to associate it with the local government.[7] On 12 January a small meeting of Chitnavis' friends was held which decided to summon representatives from the districts to elect a Provincial Congress Committee. The Provincial Committee could then elect a Reception Committee, which would

[1] Some of the speeches are reprinted in Karve and Ambekar (eds.), *Speeches and writings of Gopal Krishna Gokhale*, vol. II, pp. 215–35.
[2] See reports of his tour in *Indian People*, 17 February 1907 and 21 February 1907.
[3] See Tilak to Krishnavarma, 4 April 1907, reprinted in *Mahratta*, 26 July 1936.
[4] Khaparde, Diary, 3 May to 3 June 1907, Khaparde Papers, NAI.
[5] See reports in *Hindu*, 20 April 1907–10 May 1907.
[6] V. C. Joshi (ed.), *Lajpat Rai, autobiographical writings* (Delhi, 1965), pp. 118–22, 223–40.
[7] Chitnavis to Craddock, draft, 5 February 1907, Chitnavis Papers, Nagpur.

in turn appoint an Executive Committee.¹ On the following evening, friends of Tilak and Khaparde, Moonje amongst them, were invited to endorse this decision. They did so and a meeting was called for 27 January.² Although the meeting to elect the Provincial Congress Committee for the Central Provinces was described as a 'good gathering', the only districts outside Nagpur to send representatives were Bhandara and Wardha.³ Congressmen from neighbouring Berar sent word that they considered themselves a separate province, and that they would have a committee of their own.⁴ The separation of Berar from the Central Provinces meant that Nagpur would have to bear the expense of the Congress, but this was considered a small price to pay: the separation meant that Khaparde was excluded from any formal part in arranging the Congress.⁵

Previous divisions in the Congress had centred on the choice of president. It had been decided at Calcutta that three-quarters of the votes of the Reception Committee were necessary to elect a president, and consequently the composition of the Reception Committee underlay the first tussle in Nagpur. The Provincial Committee met on 22 February to elect the Reception Committee and the moderates had a decisive majority.⁶ Moonje had hoped to swamp the Reception Committee with his friends by making admission to it cheap. His party suggested a fee of Rs.25. The moderates, on the other hand, were for charging Rs.100. This would not only raise funds for the Congress quickly, but it meant that control of Congress affairs would be restricted to persons 'of experience and position', and that

[1] Bapu Rao Dada to Chitnavis, 14 January 1907, *ibid*. [2] *Ibid*.
[3] Bapu Rao Dada to Chitnavis, 28 January 1907, *ibid*. [4] *Ibid*.
[5] *Ibid*. The separation of the two provinces for Congress purposes was decided at the 1906 Congress. At the time Khaparde wondered why Mudholkar, his great rival in Amraoti, had supported him in pressing for a separation of Berar and the Central Provinces. He thought that Mudholkar, who was party to sending the Congress to Nagpur, had done this solely to exclude him from Congress activities during 1907. Khaparde, Diary, 31 December 1906, Khaparde Papers, NAI.
[6] Chitnavis, in his absence, was elected President, Ghatake, Vice-President, and Padhye, Secretary of the Provincial Congress Committee. The two latter offices had been provisionally held by extremists, Moonje and Naidu, and when they were replaced they left the meeting in a rage. They returned later. The moderate majority meant that 'the preaching of the boycott propaganda or the formation of District Associations on any similar lines, which is entirely the work of the P.C.C., is beyond the range of possibility from any authoritative source.' Pandit to Chitnavis, 23 February 1907, Chitnavis Papers, Nagpur.

responsibility for the election of the President would not lie with 'any and every man in the street who can pay Rs. 25 or any schoolboy who wants to get in'.[1] Despite their preponderance, the moderates found that when the vote was taken, many of their supporters, weary from their journey to Nagpur, had slipped away without being noticed, and Moonje managed to win a majority. The latter took advantage of the favourable position, and, before allowing the meeting to be adjourned, passed another resolution giving one man one vote on the Reception Committee, however much he contributed to Congress funds.[2]

The following morning the moderates were unable to reverse the decisions, although they succeeded in ameliorating the situation.[3] At this meeting fifty-six people were present; they voted themselves to be the Reception Committee, and appointed an executive committee on which the moderates had an overall majority.[4] 'It was very fortunate for the Congress', a friend wrote to Chitnavis, 'that the moderates have won the day and having you at the helm of affairs, the Congress is bound to be an unqualified success.'[5] But it was not clear whether Chitnavis, who all this time was in Calcutta for the Imperial Legislative Council, would consent to chair the executive committee. Moonje, realising Chitnavis' importance, tried to persuade him to be the figure-head for Congress in Nagpur;[6] but this did not prevent Moonje from campaigning for Tilak, whom he knew to be completely unacceptable to Chitnavis. The moderates began to lose interest in the Congress, and the initiative for its preparations passed to Moonje. Rather self-righteously he complained to Chitnavis that although he had called three meetings of the Executive Committee since 23 February, the

[1] *Ibid.*
[2] *Ibid.* 'We had made stupendous efforts to avoid this calamity, but by some of our friends slipping away . . . we were unnecessarily defeated on this point.'
[3] For example they managed to raise the fee for committee members to Rs. 55. Pandit to Chitnavis, 23 February 1907, Chitnavis Papers, Nagpur.
[4] Chitnavis (moderate) was elected Chairman, Patwardhan (moderate) and Moonje (extremist), were appointed secretaries; Bapu Rao Dada and Waman Rao (moderate) and C. V. Naidu and V. R. Limaye (extremists) were made Vice Chairmen. There were 14 out of 27 moderate Committee men. *Ibid.*
[5] Illegible to Chitnavis, 25 February 1907, *ibid.*
[6] Moonje to Chitnavis, 14 March 1907, *ibid.* It is clear, however, that Moonje did not wish Chitnavis to be more than a figurehead.

people of the Moderate party were conspicuous by their absence and now I am told that this absence is studious and fully intentional and that it should be taken as an indication that they are not prepared to co-operate with us until, as one of them told me, we give an undertaking that neither Mr. Tilak nor Lajpat Rai will be elected President of the Congress and that we will not oppose the invitation to be sent to the C[hief] C[ommissioner] to open our Exhibition.[1]

This Moonje considered a disloyal and unconstitutional way to behave, and he solicited Chitnavis' help to bring the moderates back into Congress work.

Yet, although it was Maharashtrian extremists in Nagpur who were active, they could not manage to run the Congress by themselves. The point was clearly underlined when, at the end of March, the Provincial Congress Committee held a Conference at Raipur – well away from the Marathi-speaking area. Presided over by Dr Gour, the conference was aggressively moderate in tone. Khaparde recorded 'I was sorry to see that Waman Rao Kolhatkar and others of his party had so arranged things as to cause as much annoyance as possible to the new party. Bande Mataram is not written in the entrance arch. In its place is put the motto "Moderation is our watchword".'[2] And, of course, the resolutions discussed made no reference to any of the more radical propositions aired at Calcutta. At the conference, the Congressmen of the Central Provinces fell openly into two warring factions.[3]

Preparations for the Congress were put into cold storage for the hot weather. The summer saw the all-India situation reproduced in microcosm in Nagpur. Two parties had aligned and were deadlocked. Without a majority on a full committee, and unable to raise enough money by their own efforts,[4] Moonje and his friends, spurred on by Khaparde, resorted to public

---

[1] Moonje to Chitnavis, 22 March 1907, Chitnavis Papers, Nagpur. Every year an Industrial Exhibition was held in connection with Congress. At Calcutta it had been opened by the Viceroy. The Nagpur people not only intended that their Chief Commissioner should open the 1907 Exhibition, but that the government should help to organise it. Moonje was very hostile to this on the grounds that "a Swadeshi Exhibition should be opened by a Swadeshi man." We will fight for giving effect to this principle to the bitter end. We will not allow, under any circumstances, a European to open our Exhibition.' Moonje to Chitnavis, 2 February 1907, *ibid*.
[2] Khaparde, Diary, 29 March 1907, Khaparde Papers, NAI.   [3] *Ibid*.
[4] The extremists had collected only Rs. 500 by the end of March. Bose to Chitnavis, 26 March 1907, Chitnavis Papers, Nagpur.

meetings (much as Tilak had done in 1895) in an attempt to bring pressure to bear on the moderates. The students of Nagpur were mobilised to agitate for Tilak as president. This upset the moderates whose sense of commitment to the Congress was not strong enough for them to think it worthwhile to act in its defence. The dedicated men held up their hands in despair; the district support stayed at home. Chitnavis wished to wash his hands of the whole affair, and wrote to Mudholkar intimating his desire to resign from the committees. Mudholkar replied that Chitnavis had only to make a personal appearance in Nagpur to set things to rights.

> You have to grapple with the situation which though complicated is by no means beyond your strength and resources. It would be a serious loss to your prestige, position and credit with Government and people if you submit in such an ignominious fashion as your letter would lead one to believe ... If violence obtains the upper hand then all end to our hopes for years to come.[1]

But outsiders could do no more than exhort. The sentries of the Central Provinces who had been relied upon to keep the Congress moderate did not want to get involved in public quarrels. As a result, the extremist faction under Moonje exerted the most influence. By voluble meetings, Moonje's followers made it clear that if they were not to have Tilak for president, then Congress leaders must be prepared for a troubled session.

Chitnavis was in a dilemma. He wrote to Gokhale that it was doubtful which party would win in Nagpur, and he considered it an 'unseemly spectacle to work for the same object with [illegible] two such directions'. He advised the holding of a small Congress at Nagpur, composed of just the leaders. 'I sincerely think that we must be prepared for an unprecedented row.'[2] Gokhale replied that it would be impossible to decide how to select delegates for a restricted Congress.

> No, the only way before us is to face the crisis in December next. That this year's crisis is the greatest that has so far confronted us is without doubt. My own reading of the situation is that it will be impossible to avoid a split this year. But if the split must come, let it come. I think that almost anything is preferable to the present situation, in which wild and irresponsible men,

[1] Mudholkar to Chitnavis, 26 April 1907, Chitnavis Papers, Nagpur.
[2] Chitnavis to Gokhale, 18 July 1907, Gokhale Papers, Reel 2, NAI.

who can think and talk daily of nothing but turning the 'Feringhee' out of the country, seem to be dragging us along with them! I fear the tail has been allowed to wag the dog too long and those who think with us must put their foot down this year.¹

Throughout August and September the crisis deepened. By September, it was clear that the extremists did not command sufficient votes on the Reception Committee to elect Tilak president.² They therefore devoted all their time to hampering Congress work. But on his side Chitnavis was unable to stiffen the moderates. After some particularly rowdy meetings in late September they had had enough, and Bipin Krishna Bose wrote to Gokhale that since a compromise between the two parties was impossible the inevitable conclusion was 'no Congress at Nagpur this year'.³ The Congress leadership was reluctant to allow the locals to admit defeat, but had to give in at the end of October when visits to Nagpur by neutral negotiators had failed to mediate successfully.⁴

At this point the Bombay leaders decided to put an end to the shilly-shallying at Nagpur. The Central Standing Congress Committee, set up at the Calcutta session to 'deal with urgent questions which may arise' was summoned to Sir Pherozeshah Mehta's house in Bombay on 10 November. Eleven members attended, eight of them from the Bombay Presidency, the other three from Amraoti and the Central Provinces.⁵ Mehta 'carefully arranged to send the Congress to Surat. A deputation was waiting in his house and it was introduced. They asked for and got the Congress.'⁶ Using the constitution, the leadership of the Congress had regained control of the wayward movement.

¹ Gokhale to Chitnavis, 7 August 1907, Chitnavis Papers, Nagpur.
² *Panjabee*, 1 September 1907.
³ Bose to Gokhale, 28 September 1907, Gokhale Papers, Reel 1, NAI.
⁴ See Mudholkar to Mehta, 2 October 1907, Gokhale Papers, Reel 8, NAI, and Mudholkar to Wacha 29 October 1907 *ibid.*; Chitnavis to Chief Commissioner Central Provinces, 1 November 1907, enclosure to Chief Commissioner to Viceroy, 3 November 1907, Home Public Deposit, November 1907, 22, NAI.
⁵ The members who attended were: Khaparde, Tilak, Khare, Gokhale, Mehta, Jinnah, Wacha, Mudholkar, Kolhatkar, Desai, and Parekh. Khaparde, Diary, 10 November 1907, Khaparde Papers, NAI. There were thus no delegates from Bengal, Punjab, Madras or the United Provinces. The missing Bombay delegates were Karandikar and Vishnudas.
⁶ Khaparde, Diary, 10 November 1907, Khaparde Papers, NAI. The voting was nine to two in favour of Surat, Khaparde and Tilak voting against. *Panjabee*, 23 November 1907 and 30 November 1907. Gokhale had been in favour of sending the Congress to Madras (Gokhale to Krishnaswami Iyer, 7 October 1907).

Tilak, Gokhale and the Indian National Congress, 1907 to 1915

Surat was a considered choice. It was in the Bombay Presidency, which meant that the Bombay leaders could take personal charge of the arrangements. Moreover, the 1907 Bombay Provincial Conference had been held at Surat, so there remained some vestigial organisation that could be used to arrange the session at short notice. But above all, having the Congress in Bombay Presidency, Tilak could not become the president of it since the tradition had been established that the host province did not elect a President from its own region. Not unnaturally the extremist press bitterly attacked the change.

The Reception Committee at Surat, 'composed largely of Sir Pherozeshah's followers',[1] had little more than a month in which to make arrangements for the Congress. On 24 November, the Committee unanimously elected Dr Rash Behari Ghosh, who had been the Chairman of the Reception Committee at Calcutta in 1906, President of the forthcoming session. Although disappointing to those who had wanted Tilak or Lajpat Rai, Rash Behari Ghosh was an ideal compromise candidate. He was a Bengali, and his election was bound to ensure the attendance of some Bengali delegates. Moreover, he was a prominent member of the National Council of Education and as such was closely associated with the politically neutral ideal of self-help. From the start, Tilak and his party opposed Ghosh's election as a matter of principle. They argued that the decision to move the Congress to Surat was illegal and therefore the decisions of the Surat Reception Committee were also illegal.[2] They continued to hold meetings to press Lajpat Rai's claim.[3] However, Lajpat Rai himself announced at the beginning of December that he would not stand for election.[4] Granted Tilak's ineligibility to stand, this decision deprived the extremists of their most likely candidate.

Gokhale Papers, Reel 5, NAI) but he was eventually persuaded that Bombay was the safest province.
[1] B. G. Tilak et al., *The 23rd Indian National Congress, Surat. An account of the proceedings* (Surat 1907), p. 1.
[2] Weekly Report DCI, 21 December 1907, Home Political B, January 1908, 26 NAI.
[3] Khaparde held a meeting for the purpose in Amraoti on 24 November (Khaparde, Diary, 24 November 1906, Khaparde Papers, NAI), and Tilak held one in Poona on 11 December. At the latter an appeal was made 'to the generosity of Dr. Rash Behari Ghosh to retire in favour of the Lala'. *Hindu*, 13 December 1906.
[4] Lajpat Rai to Gokhale, 3 December 1907, Gokhale Papers, Reel 7, NAI.

165

Tilak, Gokhale and the Indian National Congress, 1907 to 1915

Throughout December, Mehta and Gokhale worked to secure a majority at Surat. The Bombay Presidency Association elected 219 delegates to go to the Congress.[1] The Surat Reception Committee pitched its charges for accommodation at the Congress higher than usual. The extremists claimed that the fees were made purposely high 'in order to embarrass their party'.[2] However, they were not without their own devices. Funds raised by the extremists at Nagpur were now switched to 'manufacturing delegates who will otherwise not be able to come to Surat'.[3] They also decided to rally their following. Khaparde, choosing an auspicious hour to leave his house,[4] arrived at Surat shortly after dawn on 17 December to take matters in hand. His strategy was first to conjure up some local following in the town and secondly to organise a rival Congress encampment. An 'All-India Nationalist Gathering' was announced for 24 December, at which 'the procedure to be adopted at the ensuing Congress will be considered'.[5] Such organisation of a group within the Congress was something new; and whether or not it convinced a majority of delegates, its coherence and single-mindedness were bound to upset the proceedings.

The time for the Congress approached. 'Surat is *en fête*', cabled Reuter's correspondent to London.

> The streets are daily decorated with bunting, and scrolls bearing appropriate mottoes are seen everywhere. Numerous triumphal arches have been erected. The approaches to the railway station are thronged by crowds who cheer the delegates as they arrive. The Congress will meet in a specially erected pavilion in the grounds known as the French Gardens, situated on the banks of the river Tapti. A hundred marquees have been provided for accommodating the delegates, who will, it is expected, number 1500. The scene in the vicinity of the camp is most animated. A miscellaneous stream of automobiles, bullock carts, and sight-seers is continually passing and re-passing.[6]

But beneath the bunting rumbled discontent. Tilak opened

[1] Council minutes, 6 December 1907, Bombay Presidency Association Papers.
[2] Weekly Report DCI, 21 December 1907. Home Political B, January 1908, 26, NAI.
[3] Chintamani to Krishnaswami Iyer, 9 December 1907, Servants of India Society (Madras) Papers, File C.
[4] Khaparde, Diary, 17 December 1907, Khaparde Papers, NAI; Mudholkar to Gokhale, 17 December 1907, Gokhale Papers, Reel 8, NAI.
[5] Weekly Report DCI, 21 December 1907, Home Political B, January 1908, 26, NAI.
[6] *India*, 3 January 1908.

his campaign on the evening of 23 December. He told a very large crowd that the Congress was going to go back on the Calcutta resolutions about swadeshi, swaraj, boycott and national education; and that this must be prevented at all costs.[1] The next day the National Conference met. About 600 delegates attended, almost all of them of Maharashtra.[2] N. C. Kelkar, Tilak's right-hand man in Poona, was appointed Secretary. Aurobindo Ghose was elected President.[3] The Conference authorised Kelkar to write to the Chairman of the Reception Committee about the composition of the Subjects Committee. The Calcutta Congress had laid down clear provincial proportions for this all-important body but not the exact method of electing members. The extremists stated that, unlike in previous years, there were likely to be fiercely contested elections for the committee and so far as they knew there was no procedure for holding them. Kelkar wrote 'The Reception Committee has probably given its thought to this matter and proposed some *modus operandi*', but he stressed that all parties should agree on procedure beforehand 'so that there should be no confusion and no occasion for disagreement of views or deadlock at the eleventh hour'.[4]

Sir Pherozeshah Mehta, however, had already made attempts to fill the twenty-five Bombay seats on the Subjects Committee. A printed form was circulated to the Bombay delegates beginning 'I, the undersigned, record my vote in favour of the undermentioned gentlemen being elected Members of the Subjects Committee for the Bombay Presidency.' The list, although it included Tilak and his friends R. P. Karandikar, V. R. Natu, C. V. Vaidya, and S. R. Gokhale, consisted overwhelmingly of men from Gujarat and Bombay city. Moreover, Mehta himself, Wacha, Ambaral Shankar Desai, Gokhale, and the Chairmen and Secretaries of the Surat Congress were not included on it, since they were ex-officio members of the Subjects Committee. As a disappointed Nationalist commented to the *Hindu* 'Here is Sir Mehta's Caucus. Evidently he has proved

[1] Khaparde, Diary, 23 December 1907, Khaparde Papers, NAI.
[2] Khaparde, Diary, 24 December 1907, *ibid.*
[3] Note on the Nationalist Conference, 24 December 1907, Gokhale Papers, Reel 4, NAI.
[4] Secretary Nationalist Conference to Chairman Congress Reception Committee, 24 December 1907, Gokhale Papers, Reel 4, NAI.

an apt pupil of Mr Harrison of the Bombay Caucus fame.'[1] Thus, Tilak was outnumbered in the Bombay delegation on the Committee, and he could see that the delegates from far-away provinces, with the exception of the Central Provinces and Berar, were also likely to be against him. For all his legalistic talk, Tilak must have realised he could not get his way by manipulating the existing constitution. What they lacked in numbers, extremists would have to make up for in force.

The Congress met for the first time on 26 December. The delegates heard an address of welcome, and listened to a speech proposing that Rash Behari Ghosh, 'a large spectacled man of sixty-two, with a strongly marked face and the brave look and bearing of a European judge', be elected president.[2] Surendranath Banerjea rose to second the motion but was interrupted by cries of 'Remember Nagpur' and 'Remember Midnapore' and was unable to finish his speech.[3] The session was suspended. It re-assembled the following day after a night of fruitless negotiation, and Surendranath was heard out. The extremists resolved to oppose the election of the President, and Tilak rose to address the meeting as soon as Surendranath sat down. He was ruled out of order by both the President-elect and the Chairman of the Reception Committee. He refused to sit down; uproar ensued and a shoe 'a Mahratta shoe! – reddish leather, pointed toe, sole studded with lead' flew through the air.

It struck Surendra Nath Banerjea on the cheek; it cannoned off upon Sir Pherozeshah Mehta. It flew, it fell, and, as at a given signal, white waves of turbaned men surged up the escarpment of the platform. Leaping, climbing, hissing the breath of fury, brandishing long sticks, they came, striking at any head that looked to them Moderate, and in another moment, between brown legs, standing upon the green-baize table, I caught glimpses of the Indian National Congress dissolving in chaos.[4]

[1] *The Hindu*, 7 February 1908. Early in 1907 a caucus was formed by Mr Harrison, the Accountant-General of Bombay, and others, to prevent Sir Pherozeshah Mehta from being elected by the Justices of the Peace to the Municipal Corporation. See H. Modi, *Sir Pherozeshah Mehta: a political biography* (Bombay, 1963), pp. 284–94.
[2] H. W. Nevinson, *The new spirit in India* (London, 1908), pp. 234–5.
[3] *Ibid.* p. 248. The allusion to Midnapore referred to the recent Bengal Provincial Conference when Surendranath Banerjea had sat on the platform next to the District-Superintendent of Police, who had been summoned to keep order.
[4] *Ibid.* pp. 257–8; see also Weekly Report DCI, 11 January 1908, Home Political B, January 1908, 113, NAI; Khaparde, Diary, 27 December 1907, Khaparde Papers, NAI.

In the bitter recriminations which followed, Tilak rushed first to print. At Calcutta, he argued, the Congress had

unanimously resolved to have for its goal Swaraj or Self-Government on the lines of the self-governing Colonies, and passed certain resolutions on Swadeshi, Boycott and National Education. The Bombay Moderates, headed by Sir Pherozeshah Mehta, did not, at the time, raise any dissentient voice, but they seem to have felt that their position was somewhat compromised by the resolutions; and they had, since then, been looking for an opportunity when they might return to their old position regarding ideals and methods of political progress in India.[1]

At the Bombay Provincial Conference, held at Surat in April, Mehta had managed to exclude from the agenda the resolutions about boycott and national education. The Surat Congress Committee was packed with Mehta's friends; Gokhale had cleverly engineered the nomination of Rash Behari Ghosh for president, 'brushing aside the proposal for the nomination of Lala Lajpat Rai, then happily released, on the grounds that "we cannot afford to flout Government at this stage, the authorities would throttle our movement in no time" '.[2] Gokhale had also drafted the resolutions, but had refused to make them available to delegates until the afternoon of the opening session. All this had confirmed Tilak in his opinion that the Bombay leaders were bent on retreating from the Calcutta resolutions. When he arrived at Surat, Tilak 'denounced such retrogression as suicidal in the interests of the country, more especially at the present juncture, at a large mass meeting . . . and appealed to the Surat public to help the Nationalists in their endeavours to maintain at least the *status quo* in these matters'.[3] All the rest followed naturally. The draft resolutions were reactionary; Tilak's willingness to negotiate was spurned; he was left with no alternative but to block the Bombay cabal by opposing the election of the president in the Congress session. Finally, his followers had not started the violence: indeed the moderates had provoked it by arming volunteers and Muslims in the pandal with sticks.[4]

The Congress version of the Surat débâcle was prepared by Gokhale and published in the form of a letter to the press on 8 January 1908. Gokhale met some of Tilak's points with flat

[1] B. G. Tilak et al. *The 23rd Indian National Congress, Surat*, p. 1.   [2] Ibid.
[3] Ibid. p. 2.   [4] Ibid.

denials: he had not nominated Rash Behari Ghosh for president; that had been the work of the Surat Reception Committee. He had not said that if the Congress had elected Lajpat Rai the government would 'throttle' the movement. The reason why Rajpat Rai had not been elected was that Congress wanted to have the greatest possible freedom to discuss the injustice of Lajpat Rai's deportation the previous May. Gokhale admitted that he had drafted the resolutions, but the delay in publishing them was the fault of the printer. Besides, there were plenty of precedents for the draft not being published until the first session, and never before in Congress history had it been axiomatic that the draft resolutions – which bound no one, and were merely material laid before the Subjects Committee for discussion – should be a copy of those of the previous year. As to the wording of the draft, as soon as Gokhale had heard that Tilak took exception to the resolution about self-government, he had altered it to match the Calcutta version. The alterations in the other resolution were trivial, and solely intended to clarify their meaning. The Surat Reception Committee 'had not departed in a single particular from the established practice of of the last twenty-two years'.[1]

All the innovations had been Tilak's. He had set up his own camp.

> He harangued them daily about the supposed intentions of the Reception Committee and the high-handedness of imaginary bureaucracy in the Congress. He made ... wild and reckless statements, some of which it is difficult to characterise properly in terms of due restraint. He created a pledge-bound party to vote with him like a machine, whatever the views of the individual delegates might be ... On the first day, by sheer rowdyism, [he] compelled the sitting to be suspended. On the second ... there was no expression of regret forthcoming for the discreditable occurrence of the previous day and though one day out of three had been lost, Mr. Tilak himself came forward to interrupt the proceedings again.[2]

In fact, throughout the summer Tilak had been working for control of Congress, or, failing that, its destruction. He had grossly misrepresented the reasons for the move to Surat, although he had attended the meeting in Bombay when the decision had been taken. He had conducted an agitation against Rash Behari Ghosh before coming to Surat, and he must be

[1] Gokhale to Editors of Newspapers, 8 January 1908, Gokhale Papers, Reel 5, NAI.
[2] *Ibid.*

held responsible for the violence that occurred in the pandal.[1] Tilak's bid for leadership at Surat was a failure. Although he alleged that Mehta and Gokhale sought to pervert the Congress from a 'national into a sectional movement'[2] it was his party that was in the minority.[3] The invitation to a Moderate Convention, called for the day after the split, was signed by leading Congressmen from the provinces. Lajpat Rai and Aswimi Kumar Dutt, either of whom would have made excellent presidents from Tilak's point of view, both joined the Convention.[4] At a meeting called by Tilak after the split 'the only persons accommodated with chairs were the journalist Nevinson and the chairman Aravindo Ghose who took the chair on the motion of Khaparde'.[5] The only other personality of note present was Ajit Singh, to whom the extremists presented a cap embroidered with gold as a tribute to his suffering in exile.[6] When the division became clear – and there remained some anomalies: R. P. Karandikar was signatory to the Moderate Convention and member of the Extremist Committee[7] – the extremists comprised Tilak, his lieutenants Khaparde and Kelkar, and his Maharashtrian following. During the years preceding the split, Tilak had thrown out feelers for support to politicians in other provinces. He had been successful in winning Bipin Chandra Pal (who was in prison for contempt of court during the Surat Congress) and Aurobindo Ghose in Bengal, but they had not brought a large following to Surat. He had won virtually no one from Madras and, in the end, only Ajit Singh from the Punjab. Most Congressmen, however much they might have sympathised with Tilak's ideas, saw that the Congress was not the appropriate place for them. They believed

---

[1] *Ibid.*   [2] Tilak, *The 23rd Indian National Congress*, p. 8.
[3] Tilak estimated his following to be about 600. Tilak to Krishnavarma, 14 February 1908. Tilak Papers, *Kesari* Office, Poona. Nevinson, who was biased in Tilak's favour, estimated attendance at the Congress as 'perhaps sixteen hundred, of whom five hundred might be called Extremists of one kind or another'. Nevinson, *The New Spirit in India*, p. 244.
[4] Weekly Report, DCI, 4 January 1908, Home Political B, January 1908, II, NAI.
[5] Para. 13 (f) (SB Bombay, 11 January 1908), Bombay Police Abstracts, vol. XXI, 1908 Bombay HFM; *ibid.*
[6] Khaparde, Diary, 29 December 1907, Khaparde Papers, NAI. Ajit Singh had been deported with Lajpat Rai following the Punjab disturbances in 1907.
[7] 'So am on both Committees. But what is possible then? Mr. Tilak says in the event of a compromise connecting links are needed.' Karandikar, Diary, 28 December 1907, Karandikar Papers, Poona.

that it was folly to jeopardise the imminent prospect of substantial reforms in government. The Congress should restrict its activities to ensuring that these reforms were as generous as possible. Just as the Congress leaders had sacrificed the Social Conference for the sake of the Congress in 1895, so they sacrificed Tilak for the Congress in 1907.

The creation of the 'new party' and the 'new nationalism' did credit to Tilak's polemical skill, but the Nationalists were weaker than the moderate alliance. *The Indian Social Reformer* reported that Tilak

> looked dazed at the chorus of 'Shame', 'Shame', which was hurled at him and it was only the fear that to step down would mean the irretrievable loss of his prestige with his followers that kept him glued to the platform ... Whatever the reason, his obstinacy in standing on the platform against the ruling of the President was the crowning mistake of his life and it has cost him his political career ... Only a deportation or a prosecution can reconstruct his lost popularity. He has traded for ten long years on the prosecution that a blundering administration launched against him. He has now shown of what stuff he is made. He has wrecked the Congress.[1]

Over confident that his popularity in Maharashtra could be transported anywhere, Tilak had hoped that it could be used to wrest the Congress from the hands of the Bombay city leaders and Gokhale. Yet Tilak, by attacking Mehta and Gokhale, and by formulating a convincing extremist programme, had put the Congress itself in jeopardy. In 1907 the Congress hoped to win substantial reforms from the government. In this context, Tilak's personal attacks, his inflammatory journalism, and the activities of his henchmen on tour in India came too close to destroying the whole purpose of the Congress to be allowed to pass unnoticed. In the eyes of his enemies he had exhibited 'not only want of statesmanship but utter absence of foresight and appreciation of existing facts and forces'.[2] However much he may have been admired, and however important his ability to raise popular support in Maharashtra, in the early Congress he was a liability. Having failed to capture the Congress at Surat, he was to be excluded from it in future.

Although the recriminations that followed the Surat Congress re-echoed for the next decade, almost immediately the

[1] Mudholkar to Gokhale, 15 October 1906, Gokhale Papers, Reel 8, NAI.
[2] *Indian Social Reformer*, 29 December 1907, RNP (Bombay), 1908, pp. 19–20.

politicians realised that this open division would inflict permanent injury on the Congress unless a compromise was found or the Congress itself was reorganised on a new basis. A majority of the Congress politicians at Surat supported the Congress Convention Committee set up by Gokhale and Mehta to consider what should be done following the disruption of the Congress session on 27 December. Tilak's followers matched this body with a Congress Continuation Committee. Both committees claimed to be the legitimate successors of the Congress, and both were anxious to show that they were in the right; but the debate almost immediately deteriorated into a discussion of technical niceties and constitutional points of order. Gone were all the radical differences in aim of the parties; in their place came discussion of legal trivia in an attempt to find a face-saving formula for re-uniting the Congress. As the *Mahratta* later remarked 'In fact the break up of the Congress and the desire for reunion were almost simultaneous.'[1] However, the desire for reconciliation was at first stronger amongst the extremists than amongst the Congress leadership. Clearly in a minority at Surat, Tilak and his party stood in danger of being isolated in Indian politics. The Bombay leaders, warmly supported by politicians from the United Provinces, and having gained a temporary moral ascendancy over Tilak, now decided to prevent any compromise that would allow him and his following to come back to the Congress.

While the Congress session was adjourned, the provincial leaders began to arrange conferences to paper over the split. Curiously enough, it was Bengal that first managed, in February 1908, to hold a provincial conference at which both parties participated and erstwhile enemies embraced each other in public.[2] This rapprochement 'gave the keenest satisfaction to Indians all over India, and it demonstrated beyond doubt that the chasm that is reported to divide one class of Indians from another is not so unbridgeable as is seriously imagined in some quarters'.[3] Indeed, the Bengal conference was followed by one in the United Provinces which also augured well for the future

[1] *Mahratta*, 23 February 1908.
[2] *Hindu*, 13 and 17 February 1908; Govt. East Bengal and Assam to Govt. India, 26 February 1908, Home Political A, 26 February 1908, 45; Weekly Report DCI, 15 February 1908, Home Political B, February 1908, 109, NAI.
[3] *Hindu*, 17 February 1908.

of Congress. At Lucknow, early in March 1908, Madan Mohan Malaviya presided over the second United Provinces Provincial Conference where the split was totally ignored. Although some were disposed to think that this reinforced the new spirit of harmony within the Congress,[1] more alert observers realised that the extremist cause was dead in the United Provinces and that the unanimity there reflected the strength of the local moderates. This being so, it is not surprising that the Convention Committee decided to play their next move in northern India.

The leading Conventionists, especially the Bombay city and United Provinces men, were convinced that no good purpose would be served by merely resuming the adjourned Surat session. In their view, Tilak and his followers had to be excluded from the Congress once and for all. Their strategy was to devise rules for the Congress based on their published declaration of 31 December 1907. This would define the objects of Congress in a way Tilak would find difficult to accept. Moreover, the leaders decided that the time had come to require a more formal election of delegates to Congress. Once a constitution had been framed, the Congress would meet again under its provisions. The Convention Committee announced its intention of holding this important constitution-making meeting at Allahabad on 18 and 19 April 1908.

Advice poured in from all sides urging restraint and compromise. The Bengali leaders, continuing to display an unwonted unity in the face of the all-India split, were all for conciliation, seeing in it the chance of splicing their own Bengali demands into the all-India programme and of reconciling the difficulties of having to be extremists in their own province and moderates in the Congress pandal. Moreover, if they could bring about a compromise it would strengthen their position within the all-India leadership. They suggested that both parties should accept the four resolutions on swadeshi, boycott, swaraj and national education passed at Calcutta in December 1906 and agree to Dr Rash Behari Ghosh re-convening the adjourned session of the Congress. They were particularly anxious that the Convention Committee should not take any steps that would prevent any politician from attending

[1] *Ibid.* 13 March 1908.

Tilak, Gokhale and the Indian National Congress, 1907 to 1915

a new Congress meeting.[1] Sensing that this solution had much to commend it, the extremists in all provinces accepted the Bengali proposals.[2] The Bombay and United Provinces' leaders, however, did not.

The Convention, held in Mayo Hall, Allahabad, was attended by sixteen delegates from Bombay, a very strong local contingent, fifteen men from Bengal, about five from the Punjab and one each from Madras and Berar.[3] After some heated debate, and one sharp division, a constitution for Congress was approved to take effect immediately. The constitution defined the object of Congress as 'the attainment by the people of India of a system of government similar to that enjoyed by the self-governing Members of the British Empire'. This end was to be achieved by 'constitutional means' and 'by promising national unity, fostering public spirit, and developing ... the intellectual, moral, economic and industrial resources of the country'.[4]

Members of the Congress were required to sign a declaration supporting this programme and to abide by all the other provisions of the constitution. The most important of these vested the right of electing delegates to the annual session of the Congress in Provincial Committees, District Committees established by them, and political associations affiliated to them. Over the Provincial Committees ruled an All-India Congress Committee which was ultimately responsible for Congress activity.[5]

Thus the constitution not only laid down a creed which, however general and platitudinous, offended most extremists, but it also imposed conditions and restrictions on membership of the nationalist movement. It proved the first step towards turning the Congress from a loose association into a more effectively organised body directed by a central committee.

The main controversy at Allahabad was about including any definite creed in the constitution. The Bengal delegates, led by Surendranath Banerjea, together with the Punjabis present, fought vigorously against having a defined creed; but they only

[1] *Hindu*, 11 April 1908.
[2] See the open letter from G. Subramania Iyer to Gokhale, *Hindu*, 17 April 1908.
[3] *Hindu*, 20 April 1908.
[4] *Constitution of the Indian National Congress Organisation (Adopted at the Meeting of the Convention Committee held at Allahabad on the 18th and 19th of April 1908)* (Allahabad, 1908), Article 1.
[5] *Ibid.* Articles 2, 4, 6, 7, 13, 20.

managed to get the words 'aims and objects' substituted for 'creed' in the offending clause. Bengal and Punjab again resisted the requirement that delegates to the Congress should sign a statement accepting the aims of the movement. Here 'the discussion became very heated . . . Mr. Wacha got so awfully irate that he threatened to wash his hands clean of this business if he was not allowed to foist the creed. The utmost confusion then prevailed. Mr. Khare's emotion almost choked his articulation and he panted hard for breath.'[1] But again the votes of Bombay and the United Provinces carried the proposal.

The final division came over the crucial question whether the adjourned session of Congress should be re-convened and given an opportunity to endorse the new constitution or whether a new session should be called under the new rules. Asutosh Chaudhuri, on behalf of the Bengal delegates, moved that the President be invited to summon the adjourned Congress in December. He was seconded by Lajpat Rai. Khare, from Bombay, then moved an amendment that the President arrange for a meeting of the Congress under the Allahabad constitution in December. The difference between the two proposals was considerable. The Bengalis to a man supported the original resolution but, after three hours of discussion, Khare's amendment, giving Congress leaders a free hand to implement the new constitution immediately, was carried.[2] Having refused to accept the Bengali suggestions on all the really important points, nearly all the rest of the Bengal delegates' detailed draft constitution was then accepted without further debate.[3]

In effect, what happened at Allahabad was that a meeting of between fifty and sixty men of the Convention Committee (in which those from Bombay city and the United Provinces predominated) had devised a constitution for the Congress which gave them power to select delegates through definite procedures, which accepted the necessity of holding the next session of the Congress under the new rules, and which under one provision or another excluded Tilak and his party from the Congress. Bengali and Punjabi Congressmen had been reluctant to go so far, but they had been outvoted. As Motilal Nehru was able to report to his son, then studying at Cambridge,

[1] *Hindu*, 20 April 1908. [2] *Ibid.*, 21 April 1908. [3] *Ibid.*

Tilak, Gokhale and the Indian National Congress, 1907 to 1915

I am glad the members or at least an overwhelming majority of them were at one with me that no compromise of any kind was admissible with the extreme party. We have laid down our principles in no uncertain terms and will exclude everyone who does not sign the 'creed'. This is the only condition under which a joint Congress can be held. If the other side persist in their wild propaganda they will soon discover to their cost that their very existence was only possible under the protection of the more sober, thoughtful section represented by those who either took part in the convention or sympathised with it. However it is a question of time. The next Congress will decide the fate of both parties.[1]

Meanwhile, in western India, Tilak had been pursuing the twin policies of trying to arrange a compromise with the moderates and of trying to undermine them locally. As early as 3 January preliminary soundings were made for the holding of the 1908 Bombay Provincial Conference. The delegates who had attended the provincial conference at Surat in April 1907 had accepted an invitation to go the next year to Dhulia, in the heart of Tilak country, to conduct their deliberations. A meeting of the working committee of the 1908 conference, composed of moderate and extremist Maharashtrians alike, drew up an agenda and invited nominations from all over the Presidency for places on the Reception Committee.[2] The suggested programme omitted any boycott resolution, urged that the resolutions on swadeshi, swaraj, and national education follow the lines of the Calcutta resolutions on those topics, and proposed that a committee composed of Wacha, Gokhale, Tilak and M. G. Deshmukh, work for reunion in the Presidency.[3]

It was clear that Maharashtrians of all shades of opinion were uneasy about the split. Many of the moderate or non-aligned men in Poona were convinced that, for all his faults, Tilak should not be ignored, while N. C. Kelkar, in the heart of the extremist camp, had all along been dubious of his leader's vendetta with the moderates.[4] Tilak himself appealed to R. C.

[1] Motilal Nehru to Jawaharlal Nehru, 25 April 1908, Nehru Papers, NMM.
[2] M. K. Apte and others to Gokhale and others, 11 January 1908, Gokhale Papers, Reel 1, NAI.
[3] *Ibid.*
[4] Late in 1907, Kelkar came close to resigning as editor of *Mahratta* because he felt unable to press so vigorously the opinions Tilak was expressing in *Kesari*. It seems that a situation very similar to that of the mid-1880s had developed again. Tilak refused to accept Kelkar's resignation, although it was handed in again in January. In the event, Kelkar stayed. See the correspondence between the two men in M.D. Vidwans (ed.), *Letters of Lokamanya Tilak* (Poona, 1966), pp. 256–61.

Dutt, a neutral outsider to the Bombay quarrels, to intercede on his behalf with the Bombay leaders, but, as Dutt told Gokhale, 'All that he got from me was my firm declaration that if the Moderates recede now from their published "creed", they will be committing *political suicide*.'[1] Nevertheless, *Mahratta* continued its conciliatory tone and made light of the differences between the parties.[2]

On 23 March a Poona district conference was held under the chairmanship of G. V. Joshi, which was attended by nearly three hundred people 'including Messrs Tilak, Kelkar, Dr Patvardhan, Paranjpe of *Kal*, editors of moderate papers, members of the Servants of India Society, Deccan Sabha, Professors of the Fergusson College, several distinguished pensioners, and almost all the leading Moderates and Nationalists excepting the Honourable Mr Gokhale who is in Calcutta'.[3] Joshi, a well-known figure from the 1870s and 1880s,[4] appealed to 'Maharashtra to rise equal to the occasion and guide the nation along the right path by combined political effort'.[5] Again, stress was placed on the need to heal the breach in the Congress. A resolution, proposed from the chair and carried unanimously stated that 'it was imperative that the leaders of different parties in the Congress should settle differences by taking counsel together, and so arrange matters as to have a united Congress this year'.[6]

The Bombay Presidency Association, however, was not to be deceived. The approaches made from Poona and Dhulia were

[1] Dutt to Gokhale, 11 March 1908, Gokhale Papers, Reel 4, NAI. The words italicised are underlined in the original.
[2] 'Differences have no doubt arisen of late in the Councils of the Congress relating to the principles as well as the methods of political work in the country. But the differences are not yet too radical or irreconcilable to make reunion impossible. An independent test is afforded in this matter by the fact that had not the Congress broken up in the fashion in which it actually did, it is conceivable, nay, almost certain that no one would have talked of secession. But the breaking up of the Congress in that fashion was nothing more than an accident, and there is no necessary logical connection between such a break-up and a permanent split.' *Mahratta*, 12 April 1908.
[3] *Hindu*, 24 March 1908.
[4] He was one of the founding fathers of the Poona Sarvajanik Sabha and although he spent his life as a school-teacher, he was famed for his writings on economics and also served on the Bombay legislative council. See *Writings and speeches of Hon. Rao Bahadur G. V. Joshi, B.A.* (Poona, 1912).
[5] *Hindu*, 24 March 1908. [6] *Ibid.*

abruptly snubbed.¹ The men working in the mofussil refused to be deterred by Bombay's intransigence and continued their preparations for the conference. On 31 March the council of the Presidency Association met and, functioning as the Bombay Provincial Congress Committee, resolved 'that having regard to the events that took place at Surat last December... no Provincial Conference be held this year'.² The secretaries at Dhulia were informed that their activities were unconstitutional and that their meeting would not be recognised as an official provincial conference.³

Although Tilak wanted to see the Congress put together again, he saw no reason why he should submit to impossible terms. He had written to Krishnavarma in February that the 'scuffle' at Surat had 'increased the responsibility of our party and I do not know, as yet, whether we may not have to devote ourselves to the organisation of our party throughout India for the whole of 1908'.⁴ Meeting expert intransigence from Mehta and his friends, Tilak decided to undermine the Bombay Presidency Association. He was determined to hold the provincial conference, and it obviously stood no chance of being accepted as such unless delegates attended it from the capital city. So, on 17 April, a meeting was held in Bombay under the presidency of C. V. Vaidya. He

explained that the Presidency Association used to return delegates to the Provincial Conference every year to represent Bombay City but as that body [had] made no arrangements to return delegates to the Conference to be held at Dhulia on the 27th instant, it was considered necessary to convene a meeting of citizens to elect delegates. About sixty names of persons of the moderate party as also other names representing the nationalists were read out as delegates elected for the conference and were approved. It was further resolved that the meeting was of opinion that the adjourned meeting of the 23rd Congress be held in any suitable town in December next.⁵

¹ Minutes of council meeting, 31 March 1908, Bombay Presidency Association Papers. See also Apte to Gokhale, 1 March 1908, Gokhale Papers, Reel 1, NAI.
² *Ibid.*
³ Minutes of council meeting, 24 April 1908, Bombay Presidency Association Papers.
⁴ Tilak to Krishnavarma, 14 February 1908, Tilak Papers, *Kesari* Office, Poona.
⁵ *Hindu*, 20 April 1908. This move was not calculated to reassure the moderates. A week earlier, Mudholkar, seeing the way Tilak's campaign was building up, had written to Gokhale: 'it is every day becoming more and more plain that there can be no true union between the Tilak–Pal–Ghose faction and the old Congress workers. I thought at one time that Tilak was returning to sanity and

179

Tilak, Gokhale and the Indian National Congress, 1907 to 1915

The Allahabad Convention seemed to have ended all hope of an immediate rapprochement. *Mahratta* became more critical of the moderates. Commenting on the Allahabad meeting it attacked the moderates for their 'determined opposition' to any proposals for compromise. The 'resolution about the signing has, we fear, spoilt the whole thing', since extremists would either not sign, or would sign falsely, and the uproar at Surat would be repeated.

If the Moderates be inclined to complacently congratulate themselves upon having forced the parting of the ways in this fashion, the feeling is bound to be only temporary. For, the responsibility will be entirely theirs and there will be time enough for the reckoning. We do not think it is statesmanship, but the reverse of it that is evidenced by the resolution of the Allahabad meeting.[1]

Given the way in which Tilak had been outmanoeuvred, his performance at the conference held at Dhulia between 27 April and 1 May was remarkable. Under the presidency of G. V. Joshi,[2] the usual set of resolutions was debated and passed. Everyone, however, was aware that the only serious matter was how to ensure that the extremists were not left outside the Congress for long. The conference passed a resolution arguing that 'it is necessary to make a united effort to arrange for the holding of the Indian National Congress, as before, in December next, and that this Conference appoints a committee ... to place themselves in communication with the leaders of all parties throughout the country including the Convention Committee and the Congress-Continuation committee with a view to that end'.[3]

Tilak made the main speech. Waiting to move the motion until 'the cool breeze' of evening had set in, he began by saying 'I do not think that the difficulties [of reaching a compromise]

---

sobriety. But inordinate vanity and the inebriation of the applause of the mob – literate and illiterate – have rendered him incapable of straight forward or wise action.' Mudholkar to Gokhale, 11 April 1908, Gokhale Papers, Reel 8, NAI.
[1] *Mahratta*, 26 April 1908.
[2] D. A. Khare had originally been elected president, but he decided to go with the moderates to Allahabad rather than to Dhulia. See Apte and others to Gokhale and others, 11 January 1908, Gokhale Papers, Reel 1, NAI, and *Hindu*, 18 March 1908.
[3] *Report of the proceedings of the fifteenth provincial conference held at Dhulia in a specially erected pandal on 27th, 28th, 29th, 30th April, and 1 May 1908* (? Poona, 1908), p. 28.

are insurmountable or that the schism is irreparable',[1] and went on to give an astute account of the duty and the function of the Congress. His speech is worth quoting extensively because it shows how even the most extreme of the extremists was aware of the kind of organisation the Congress had to be. The clichés and the anodyne phrases of Tilak's speech clothed the argument that, if the national movement was to embrace every caste, class and religion – which it must – then its leaders had to make compromises with each other, they had to realise that the Congress existed for specific political purposes, and that no good would come of straying from them.

Tilak recounted the early success of the Congress:

> We have been accustomed to be united for the last 22 years, but unfortunately within this particular year, 5 or 6 months ago ... differences of opinion gave rise to a controversy among the members of the Congress, and that controversy culminated in a split in the Congress Camp. The Congress is for national purposes and for all the people of India; people of all shades of opinion. India is not a nation monopolised by the nationalists, nor is it a nation of members of one caste, one religion or one creed. It includes men of all shades of opinion, and according to their opinion the country is to be served. To render service to the country is not the monopoly of Mussalmans, Hindus, Parsis or Jains, but all the Indian people. Each has to serve his country according to his view. But all of them have to meet on a common platform. We know there are two parties in India, one representing the view that India should have absolute independence and the other requiring that India should have limited independence. The cause of the split is that people of different views did not like to agree on the general question. That was the real difficulty. Men of opposite views would not condescend to work with one another. In order that opposite sections may be induced to work shoulder to shoulder in the common cause for the benefit of the country we must try to remove from their minds any doubts or grudges that may be existing there. Then only is it possible to bring about real unity among our people.[2]

Tilak then pointed to the case of Parliament: there people of different classes and religions, and people of widely differing political opinions, worked together, accepting the rule of the majority, for the good of British society as a whole. No one group had the right to drive another out of Parliament, and

---

[1] Tilak's speech is reported *ibid.* pp. 28–31. Only five ultra-moderates voted against it. *Ibid.* p. 31. The English translation quoted here is to be found in para. 400 (SB Bombay, 23 May) Bombay Police Abstracts, vol. XXI, 1908, Bombay HFM.
[2] Para. 400 (SB Bombay, 23 May) Bombay Police Abstracts, vol. XXI, 1908, Bombay HFM.

all, even the most radical, accepted the Parliamentary framework. This lesson 'we have not yet learnt as thoroughly as we ought to' he continued. 'In the case of institutions of castes, you may say "I don't like a Mahomedan to enter my house" but that principle you cannot adopt in reference to a public institution like the Congress. You cannot say "I won't allow a Mahomedan in the Congress."' Similarly, the Congress was a place for all parties, for those 'who want full independence, those who want half independence and those who want no independence at all'. The Allahabad Conventionists had decided to drive the extremists out of the Congress. But they were wrong to do so for

You have to bring all the sections together and make them behave like so many brothers. If there is any place where we can afford to live as brothers it is in connection with the Congress itself. The Congress is the only place where this can be accomplished. It is the National Temple of Independence where there is no prohibition [on] anyone to enter. It is not a Hindu temple, or a Mahomedan masjid, or a Jain mandir or anyone's jahagirdari. It is the house of all people.[1]

Whether or not there could have been a reconciliation later in the year is, however, a matter for idle speculation. For, in the weeks following Tilak's speech, several things happened that changed the political situation utterly. The summer of 1908 saw the disintegration of the extremist leadership. Bipin Chandra Pal, who was released from jail in April, left almost immediately for London, believing that the best hope for advancing India's cause lay in agitation in England.[2] The severest reversal in fortune rapidly followed: Tilak was arrested on 25 June and charged with seditious writing for an article which had appeared in *Kesari* on 12 May. The article, which was a leader on the Muzzaffarpur murders,[3] was alleged to justify terrorism, and on 23 July he was sentenced to six years' imprisonment and deported to Mandalay.[4] The effect on Indian

[1] *Ibid.*
[2] H. & U. Mukherjee, *Bipin Chandra Pal and India's struggle for Swaraj* (Calcutta, 1958), p. 110.
[3] Khudiram Bose, a young Bengali, intending to assassinate an unpopular British judge in Muzzaffarpur, killed instead two English women who had been lent the judge's carriage for the afternoon. Ironically they were the wife and daughter of Pringle Kennedy, an English barrister who was noted for his sympathy towards Indian political aspirations.
[4] Home Political A, October 1908, 61–103, NAI; N. C. Kelkar, *Full and authentic report of the Tilak trial (1908)* (Poona, 1908).

politics was immediate. His followers everywhere became noticeably less voluble, and his lieutenants stopped political work.[1] Khaparde, whose arrest the Central Provinces' government was refused,[2] was subjected to continual police surveillance and petty harassment. Government officials were forbidden to visit him, and, while he was in London conducting Tilak's appeal before the Privy Council, the government deprived him of his seats on the municipality and district board in Amraoti on technical trivialities.[3] Aurobindo Ghose also left politics and, escaping arrest by seeking refuge in French Pondicherry, decided to devote the rest of his life to religion.

Tilak's arrest not only damped extremist political activity; it also affected that of the moderates. Gokhale, who was shocked at the severity of Tilak's sentence, recognised that politically it 'will really be a great blow to our party, for part of the resentment against the government is likely to be directed also against us'.[4] Indeed, some Marathi papers went so far as to suggest that Gokhale had instigated Tilak's arrest, and melas at the 1909 Ganpati festival sang of Gokhale as Tilak's murderer.[5] Further, government policy did little to suggest that much was to be gained from closer association with the regime. The Congress leaders accepted the expedient of separate electorates for Hindus and Muslims in the Morley-Minto reforms, thus losing the approval of some of their Hindu following; and the reforms were followed by a Press Act in 1910 which was more severe in its provisions than any of its predecessors. Gokhale was a member of the Imperial Council when the Act was passed, and although he did not approve of it, he was persuaded not to vote against it.[6] The years following Surat saw no immediate prospect of the division in the Congress being healed, although regular meetings continued to be held: at Madras in 1908,

[1] Sydenham of Combe, *My working life* (London, 1927), pp. 223-6.
[2] Stuart to Craddock, 17 May 1909, Notes, Home Political Deposit, June 1909, 3, NAI.
[3] Khaparde, Diary, 14 January 1911, 1 April 1912, Khaparde Papers, NAI.
[4] Gokhale to Patvardhan, 23 July 1908. Quoted in Wolpert, *Tilak and Gokhale*, p. 229.
[5] *Ibid.* pp. 229-30; Gokhale prosecuted the editor of *Hindu Punch* and took out a court injunction to prevent the circulation at the Ganpati Festival of pamphlets alleging his complicity in Tilak's arrest. Servants of India Society Letter Book, 21 October 1909, Servants of India Society Papers, Poona.
[6] Wolpert, *Tilak and Gokhale*, pp. 241-3.

Lahore in 1909, and Allahabad in 1910. There had also been an extension of the government's arbitrary powers, compensated for only in part by the legislative councils reform. Congress was thus weakened on two fronts, and apathy about it settled on Indian politicians.

Now it was the moderates' turn to initiate schemes for reunion. When Sir William Wedderburn came to preside over the Allahabad Congress in 1910, it had become 'quite obvious that the scheme of the constitution as a means of pushing on the Congress organisation throughout the country had totally failed and that its only utility – real at the beginning, doubtful later on – was to keep those who had seceded from the Congress in 1907 out of that body'.[1] Gokhale got the impression, from dealing with Wedderburn's correspondence, that the time was ripe for a move towards uniting the Congress. Among extremists in the Deccan, Berar and the Central Provinces, he detected 'a general desire on the part of the seceders to rejoin the Congress [but] their self-respect prevented them from asking their opponents to enroll them as members of the existing Committees or to seek affiliation for their own organisations by the Provincial Committees'.[2] To facilitate their return to Congress, Gokhale, seconded by Malaviya, suggested that article XX of the constitution be amended to allow election of delegates to Congress by public bodies, or by public meetings held under the auspices of those bodies, which accepted article I 'as a basic principle of their activity' but which were not necessarily affiliated to the Provincial Congress Committees.[3] The resolution was carried in the Subjects Committee of the Congress, but was accompanied by 'quite a scene. Wacha walks out "I wash my hands of the Congress". Bhupendranath Basu "I have nothing to do with Congress". Gokhale sits down in disgust.'[4] Rather than risk splitting the Congress again, the resolution was shelved.[5] The following year Gokhale was unable to attend the Congress session and his resolution was put again but 'in a mutilated form, namely, by bestowing the right of election on public meetings held under the auspices of the

[1] Gokhale to Besant, 21 November 1914, Besant Papers, Adya.
[2] Ibid.   [3] Ibid.
[4] Karandikar, Diary, 27 December 1911, Karandikar Papers, Poona.
[5] Gokhale to Besant, 21 November 1914, Besant Papers, Adya.

Congress Committee only. This, of course, was not calculated to satisfy and did not satisfy the seceders.'[1]

Preparatory to Tilak's release in 1914, some Maharashtrians, chief among them R. P. Karandikar, who, as instructed by Tilak at Surat, had retained his links with the Congress, decided to re-start the Bombay Provincial Conference. No attempt had been made to hold any meetings since that organised by Tilak's party in 1908. Fifty-six gentlemen from Satara advertised the holding of a provincial conference in that town in April 1914. They hoped that both extremists and moderates would attend the meeting. As an inducement to the moderates the convenors specified that only those persons 'who accept the attainment by constitutional means of Self-Government within the Empire, as laid down by Article I of the Congress Constitution' would be eligible as delegates, or as electors of delegates, to the Conference; but as a concession to extremists it was agreed that 'the intending delegates need not express in writing their acceptance of this object'.[2] The Bombay Presidency Association and the Deccan Sabha declared that the proposed conference was a violation of the Congress constitution,[3] but it was nonetheless held at the end of April.[4] One of the Maharashtrian moderates, G. K. Chitale, attended, and the most important resolution passed was one urging the reunion of Congress.[5] Significantly it was 'practically a Maharashtra Conference, for hardly any one from other parts of the Bombay Presidency attended it'.[6] The network of support Tilak had drummed up in the 1890s was beginning to get organised again.

Tilak himself was released in Poona in the early hours of 17 June 1914.[7] His first political utterance boded well for

[1] *Ibid.* The words italicised are underlined in the original.
[2] Circular about proposed Provincial Conference, 6 March 1914, Deccan Sabha Papers, Poona.
[3] Meeting of the Deccan Sabha, 29 March 1914, *ibid.* See also *Indu Prakash*, 27 March 1914, RNP (Bombay), 1914, 13, pp. 21–2.
[4] *The sixteenth provincial conference held at Satara on 26th, 27th, and 28th April 1914* (Satara, 1914).
[5] *Mahratta*, 3 May 1914.
[6] *Praja Bandhu*, 3 May 1914. RNP (Bombay) 1914, 19, p. 23.
[7] G. P. Pradhan & A. K. Bhagwat, *Lokamanya Tilak: a biography* (Bombay 1958), p. 248. He was, however, kept under very close police surveillance. See para. 1228 (L) (SB Bombay, 4 July), Bombay Police Abstracts, vol. xxvii, 1914, Bombay HFM.

unification of the factions in the Congress. Surveying the six years he had been in exile he wrote that

> in spite of certain measures like the Press Act... I for one do not give up the hope of a country steadily making further progress in the realization of its cherished goal. The reforms introduced during Lord Morley's and Lord Minto's administration will show that Government is fully alive to the necessity of progressive change and desire to associate the people more and more in the work of Government... this indicates a marked increase of confidence between the Rulers and the Ruled, and a sustained endeavour to remove popular grievances.[1]

It seemed possible that Tilak might be prepared to work within the limits imposed by the Congress constitution. Gokhale was encouraged, and determined that 'every effort must now be made to close the unfortunate divisions of 1907'.[2]

Gokhale suggested negotiations on the basis of his resolution put before the 1910 subjects committee. By releasing public bodies and political associations which declared their acceptance of article I of the Congress constitution from the necessity of obtaining affiliation to the Provincial Congress Committees, Gokhale believed that Tilak and his followers could be persuaded to rejoin the Congress, since they could be elected delegates to it by their own meetings. Gokhale wrote to Annie Besant, who was emerging as a prominent spokesman for Madras,

> I understand from Mr. Kelkar that while he personally accepts the reasonableness of this solution Mr. Tilak is not inclined at present to accept it. But that is Mr. Tilak's way, and this need not discourage us. But even if Mr. Tilak, in the end, accepts this solution – and knowing him as I do I feel almost certain that he will accept it – it will be necessary to secure the assent of the Bombay Party represented by Sir Pherozeshah Mehta and Mr. Wacha, to the change.[3]

It was arranged that N. Subba Rao, as Secretary of the forthcoming Congress in Madras, who was discussing the matter with Tilak, should also visit Bombay, while Gokhale persuaded the Bengali leaders, Surendranath Banerjea and Bhupendranath Basu, to accept the proposals.[4]

All seemed set for a compromise until Subba Rao reported his discussions with Tilak. The latter, sensing that he had more

---

[1] *Mahratta*, 30 August 1914.
[2] Gokhale to Besant, 18 November 1914, Besant Papers, Adya.
[3] Gokhale to Besant, 21 November 1914, *ibid*.
[4] *Ibid*.

to gain by holding off from the Congress for the time being, laid down his terms for re-entry in such a way that Gokhale found them unacceptable. In a statement drawn up with Subba Rao and N. C. Kelkar, Tilak argued

> The Extremists or Nationalists form the advance wing of the Congress. Their attitude is generally one of constitutional opposition to the Government, while that of the Moderates or Constitutionalists is generally one of co-operation with Government. Though the ideal of both is the same, namely self-government within the Empire, the difference between them lies in the methods adopted for reaching that goal.
>
> The Nationalists are, and have been, willing to join the Congress, but they feel that they are humiliated by the way in which the Congress constitution was framed especially with reference to the election of delegates. They do not want to come into the Congress through the present Congress Committees, and object to personal inquisitions not regulated by rules . . . and hence they do not desire to apply for the affiliation of their associations to the present Provincial Congress Committees. They wish to join the Congress only if separate and independent constituencies, of course accepting Article I of the Constitution, are created which should automatically have the right to elect delegates, either at meetings of such bodies or at public meetings convened under their auspices.
>
> If this is done it is their intention to take steps to widen the door of election as before to all public meetings if necessary, and get recognition of their methods by educating public opinion and working for, and securing a majority in the Congress, if possible. They are and have been willing to take the decision of the majority as binding on them and in cases where such a decision is against them, they would wait till opinion is created in their favour and not leave the Congress by quarrelling . . .
>
> If such constituencies were not created, they would have to organise a National League [for] their work independently of Congress.[1]

On receiving this note, Gokhale, who had previously been 'whole heartedly in favour of bringing back into Congress fold seceders accepting first article' provided they came in through existing Congress organisations,[2] now became implacably hostile to accommodating Tilak. The latter's stand seemed to Gokhale to be unchanged from his position in 1907; and Gokhale saw no reason why all the trials of that period should have to be endured again. As he explained to Bhupendranath Basu, the President-elect of the forthcoming Congress,

[1] N. Subba Rao, 'Mr. Tilak's views reduced to writing by me and revised by him and Mr. Kelkar', 9 December 1914, Subba Rao File, Bhupendranath Basu Papers, NMM.
[2] Gokhale to Basu, 25 November 1914, Telegram, Gokhale File, *ibid.*

Tilak, Gokhale and the Indian National Congress, 1907 to 1915

> My hope was that if we enabled the seceders . . . to come in, they would, having seen the impossibility of political action on any other lines, cooperate with us in furthering the programme of the Congress by present methods. That hope, however, has now been shattered. Mr. Tilak has told Subba Rao frankly and in unequivocal terms that though he accepts the position laid down in what is known as the Congress creed, viz. that the aim of the Congress is the attainment by India of self-government within the Empire by constitutional means, he does not believe in the present methods of Congress, which rest on association with the Government, where possible and opposition to it, where necessary. In place of these he wants to substitute the method of opposition to Government, pure and simple, within constitutional limits – in other words, a policy of Irish obstruction.[1]

Subba Rao also reported to Bhupendranath Basu that his negotiations in western India had come to a dead halt because 'Some of our friends in Bombay apprehend that Mr. Tilak's presence with his party will not strengthen the Congress but will lead to a repetition of the scenes at Surat.'[2]

Annie Besant, who had been campaigning for reunion since the early summer of 1914,[3] was disappointed to find her hopes dashed. Although she had to admit the reasonableness of the moderates' stand,[4] she still continued to seek ways of securing the extremists' attendance.[5] In view of her activities Gokhale instructed Srinivasa Sastri, a Madras member of his Servants of India Society, to oppose Mrs Besant in public if she continued to devise means whereby Tilak could attend the Congress.[6] Furthermore, Gokhale sent Besant a copy of the letter he had written to Bhupendranath Basu on 14 December explaining why he had changed his mind about re-admitting Tilak and his friends to the Congress. Needless to say this letter, or parts of it, became common knowledge to those attending the Madras Congress. Motilal Ghose, who had been persuaded to go to Madras by Bhupendranath Basu, published in the *Amrita Bazar*

---

[1] Gokhale to Basu, 14 December 1914, *ibid.*; copy, Gokhale Papers, Reel 3, NAI.
[2] Subba Rao to Basu, 18 December 1914, Subba Rao File, Bhupendranath Basu Papers, NMM.
[3] Besant to Basu, 24 November 1914, Besant File, *ibid.*; Wacha to Basu, 27 November 1914, Wacha File, *ibid.*
[4] 'I find the Poona party – whom I met with Mr. N. Subba Rao . . . unwilling to come into Congress unless Congress admits them against its Rules. This no organised body can do.' Besant to Basu, 9 December 1914, Besant File, *ibid.*
[5] For example, by trying to persuade Tilak to have the Poona Sarvajanik Sabha affiliated to the Bombay Provincial Congress Committee. Besant to Basu, 15 December 1914, *ibid.*
[6] Gokhale to Sastri, 25 December 1914, Gokhale Papers, Reel 3, NAI.

Patrika, on 12 January 1915, a highly condemnatory account of the Bombay and Madras leaders' handling of the affair, and his story was taken up by other leading newspapers.[1] Tilak was able to don the mantle of injured innocence and demanded explanations from Gokhale.[2]

Although Besant had tried to bring the two sides together she had not reckoned with the bitterness of the Poona quarrels. The more she tried to formulate a compromise, the more adamant Gokhale became in his opposition to her proposals. She argued that Tilak, if he could be persuaded to return, could be adequately controlled by the constitutional safeguards in the Congress. Gokhale replied tartly

> You have no experience of what we had to go through in 1906 and 1907. And you cannot ask us and you have no right to ask us to begin that struggle again. You say if Tilak tries to give trouble again we should fight and put him down. But it is not an easy fight – certainly not to be lightly entered on again. The parties are not evenly matched. There is naturally a great volume of anti-foreign feeling expressed and unexpressed in the country and it loads the scales heavily on Tilak's side. We have to ask our countrymen to be reconciled to foreign domination – even though it is a transitional arrangement – and our propaganda has to rest on one of its sides on some measure of faith in the sense of justice of British Democracy. Tilak has no difficulty in ridiculing the latter as 'mendicancy' and denouncing the former as pusillanimous and unpatriotic cringing to the authorities. The number of men who can form a sound political judgement in the country is not large. But you can find any number of unthinking men, filled with honest but vague longing for the emancipation of the country, ready to follow any plausible leader whom in their hearts they believe to be wholly 'against the foreigner'. It was with the likes of such a following that Tilak captured the Poona Sarvajanik Sabha – the work of Ranade's hands – and destroyed its usefulness in twelve months ... It was with the help of such a following that he nearly wrecked the Congress at Poona in 1895. And finally it was with the help of such a following that he actually wrecked the Congress at Surat in 1907. I was one of the principal antagonists in all these three contests. And I know what he can do with his following and what he cannot.[3]

In a rather gentler vein a week later, Gokhale told Besant 'You thought that the best way to deal with Tilak was to deal with

[1] He seems to have done this purely out of spite for being ignored at the Madras Congress. See Ghose to Basu, undated, January 1915, and Basu to Ghose, 15 January 1915, draft, Ghose File, Bhupendranath Basu Papers, NMM. See also Gokhale to Basu, 21 January 1915, Gokhale File, *ibid*.
[2] Tilak to Gokhale, 21 January 1915; Gokhale to Tilak, 21 January 1915, copies, *ibid*.
[3] Gokhale to Besant, 5 January 1915, Gokhale Papers, Reel 3, NAI.

him generously. Had you known him better you would have put caution before generosity.'[1]

As a result of Gokhale's directions from Poona, the Madras Congress abandoned its attempt to amend the Allahabad constitution. *Kesari* complained that only Bombay's leaders had prevented reunification of Congress, since extremist delegates had been elected from Bengal, but in the end did not attend because Tilak was kept out. It pointed to the very high proportion of Madras delegates at the Congress as evidence that the other provinces also disapproved of Bombay's stand. 'To be plain, Sir P. M. Mehta, Mr. Wacha and Mr. Gokhale do not want the Nationalists in the Congress. And so long as other Moderates are afraid of this dislike of these leaders, compromise is not possible.' The article went on to argue 'This question should be solved by provinces other than Bombay. And it is not possible to do so in 1915. Sir Vithaldas Thackersey invited the next Congress on behalf of the City of Bombay.'[2] It seemed as though once again Tilak had been outmanoeuvred.

During the course of 1915, however, several changes occurred in Indian politics which rapidly brought an end to the Maharashtrian quarrelling. Gokhale, Tilak's most intrepid and accomplished opponent, died in Poona on 19 February 1915. Pherozeshah Mehta, the most obdurate of the Bombay men, died in November of the same year. The deaths of these two leaders greatly weakened the opposition to Tilak in the Congress. The hostility towards him on the Bombay committees, however, was strong enough for him to agree not to try to attend the session to be held in that city in December 1915. But, in his absence, the politicians agreed that the wrangling had gone on long enough: the Congress decided to amend its constitution so that the old extremists would be free to attend the next assembly.[3] And so, at Lucknow, in December 1916, Tilak sat on the Congress platform for the first time since the ill-fated meeting at Surat in 1907.

[1] Gokhale to Besant, 10 January 1915, Besant Papers, Adya.
[2] *Kesari*, 5 January 1915, RNP (Bombay) 1915, 2, p. 22.
[3] 'The amendment to the Constitution giving automatic affiliation to political bodies in existence for two years on 31 December 1915, fixing the maximum number of their delegates at 15, was carried at the meeting of the All-India Congress Committee on the strength of the majority of the other provinces over Bombay. They insisted that some compromise must be made. It now remains to

Tilak, Gokhale and the Indian National Congress, 1907 to 1915

The reconciliation between Tilak and the Congress, however, went almost unnoticed, for there were more important things to consider at Lucknow than the return of the Maharashtrian leader. The changes being forced on the Indian administration by the war, the future political uncertainty, and the prospect of further and fundamental constitutional reforms, made it necessary for the Congress to forget old battles and to prepare itself for a new struggle. As had happened in the late 1880s, and again between 1904 and 1908, politicians from all over India looked to the Congress as a means of political mobilisation and as an arena for alliance, compromise and agitation.

Tilak played an important part in the confused national politics of the years 1917 to 1920. During the last years of his life he achieved more as a Congress politician than he had been able to do in the decades before. With his Maharashtrian support, organised in the Home Rule League, Tilak campaigned both in India and in England for constitutional reforms, and he left to his successors embryonic electoral machinery with which to win seats on the new legislative bodies. Yet Tilak's political outlook remained remarkably similar to his earlier programmes. He was as astringent and as uncompromising as ever, and to the end the basic principle of his policy was to obstruct the imperial government to the constitutional limit. In 1920 he still stood by many of the old extremist tenets of 1906 and 1907. But the political reforms offered by Chelmsford and Montagu gave so much more power to Indians, both in the legislative councils and in the government itself, that Tilak was not prepared to dismiss them out of hand. He was prepared to present his case through the regular constitutional channels, and in 1917 he set out on the well-worn track to Westminster. However, other Indian politicians had not remained the same. From the Congress at Lucknow through to the summer of 1920, Tilak found himself occupying a middle position in the range of nationalist opinion. Ironically, Bombay city (although this time with Gujarati and not Maharashtrian connections) still in alliance with the United

be seen if the Sarvajanik Sabha will accept the creed and demand affiliation. The Bombay Moderates strongly opposed the amendment, but their wishes were overruled.' Para. 39 (j) (Bombay, 6 January 1916), Bombay Police Abstracts, vol xxix, 1916, Bombay HFM.

Provinces, provided the radical alternatives to official Congress policy. As before, none could for long withstand this particular combination.

Tilak did not live to see the Gandhian capture of the Congress, and his death put to his lieutenants the difficult problem whether the old Maharashtrian extremists would work the reforms or sail with the non-cooperators. Gradually also the Poona politicians began to mend their quarrels. Faced with serious threats to their leadership, not only within the Presidency but even within the Poona-dominated districts of it, an uneasy truce settled on the embittered Brahmin parties. Moreover, it soon became clear that, in terms of exercising a preponderant influence in the national councils of the Congress, the Maharashtrian golden hour had passed. But Tilak's name continued to be conjured with. From the grave he provided a symbol of implacable resistance to imperial rule that was burnished bright by the new managers of the Congress. It was some reward for the years of exile and failure.

A PERSPECTIVE

This study has tried to establish the most important historical facts about the Indian National Congress and the politicians who led it between 1885 and 1915. The main thrust of the argument has been that, from the later nineteenth century, a new kind of political activity emerged in India which can properly be designated national in scope. This development was driven on by alterations in the ways in which India was governed, and it reflected changes both within India and within the larger empire of which India was a part. The Indian National Congress was formed to present Indian demands at the centres of policy-making within the imperial government. It worked within the political framework of the raj; its activities were appropriate for only certain types of politics; it had an open, flexible and pragmatic organisation; and its successful assumption of the role of national spokesman gave it an authority of its own and allowed it to exert an independent influence on the course of political change in modern India.

Although all-India politics grew stronger as the nineteenth century gave way to the twentieth, they did not constantly dominate the minds of Indian politicians. Policy-makers and national leaders were not directly concerned with the day-to-day administration of the government, or with the detailed distribution of power and patronage in the localities. They were more concerned with the main structure of the political system itself, which came under discussion only occasionally. National politics dominated Indian affairs when either constitutional or administrative reform was being conceived by or forced on the government, or when the powers of the government were being enlarged to include more social and economic activities. During such periods Indian politicians found it necessary to make themselves heard in the national arena because decisions taken in principle then might eventually affect the patronage, working and control of the government and its agencies in the towns and villages. There is no simple chronological growth of nationalism in India: nationalist activity booms and slumps in phase with the national activity of the government.[1]

[1] For example, truly national issues came forward in only nine or ten of the thirty

A perspective

A strong case can be made for the separate study of all-India politics, but in the process of our narrative we have seen the intricate connections that existed within the nationalist movement between parochial, provincial and national politics. The Indian National Congress was always linked to a great variety of other political and social organisations in the localities. Through them the Congress built up its wide and heterogeneous support, and by coming into contact with regional, cultural and economic associations it became known to the peasant as well as to the zemindar, the artisan as well as the banker, the priest as well as the lawyer. Just as the Congress grew by leaps and bounds rather than by maintaining a steady pace, so too the extent and depth of its support varied from year to year and from situation to situation. Far from making a steady progress from being an elite body to becoming a mass movement, the Congress, from its infancy, was able to transform itself into a party of the most general support.

However, too tight a bond between the Congress and a strong local or regional movement could threaten its continued viability as a national organisation. The rumpus in Poona in 1896 and the agitation in Bengal in 1906 both threatened to push the Congress into positions that were inexpedient for it to maintain. It was not in the general interest to become involved in the controversies about social reform, which in any case lay beyond the scope of the Congress; nor did it make national sense to place as much emphasis on the undoing of the partition of Bengal as the Calcutta leaders felt it necessary for the Congress to do. Similarly, it was better to keep informal and equivocal the relationship between the Congress and cultural or religious revivalist movements: pride in Maharashtrian traditions made for success in the Deccan, but it would be irrelevant or even counter-productive elsewhere; too close a connection between Congress politicians and the apostles of Hindu revivalism would make it difficult for non-Hindus to support the movement.

As the Congress became established, men with powerful grievances gravitated to it. Such an alliance might impart energy and vigour to the national campaign, as it did during years we have been examining, and it is this which accounts for the rise and fall of interest in the Congress during those years.

A perspective

the swadeshi-boycott agitation, but there were difficulties in handling support of this kind. A troublesome district might be pacified by a sudden turn of events and the Congress would be deprived overnight of its following: much of the rural support for the Congress in the Punjab in 1907 collapsed when the government reversed its policies on revenue collection and the payment of canal dues. Just as likely, however, a local grievance would be managed by entrenched local leaders who would seek to gain as much as possible from their connection with the Congress but who would refuse to be ruled by it. Many promising rent-strikes or revenue disputes would later give the Congress a convincing rural base, many a student or communal agitation would bring people out into the streets in support of the movement, but they were liable to continue when national circumstances required them to cease, and their persistence would embarrass rather than aid the national leadership. The agitation against partition organised in the eastern districts of Bengal was not ultimately controlled by Bengali Congress leaders. It was a self-contained agitation and had features similar to those found later in the Khilafat campaign, the kisan sabhas, and the peasant movements in the Andhra deltas and Midnapore. Sometimes the national Congress was able to make use of such local disturbance, but at other times it was better to be dissociated from it.

Any national movement in India would be difficult to control. As the Congress became involved with more of Indian society so there was an increased need to give some shape to the party and to establish some kind of machinery for maintaining control over its supporters. The Congress needed to state quite clearly what its aims and intentions were, and it needed to be able to transmit this information from its centre through to the district support. The most significant development during the period we have been studying has been the constant attempts to clarify the purpose of the Congress. From the earliest sessions the Congress leaders tried to define the kind of political issue that it would be appropriate for a national body to take up. This meant, with some important exceptions, excluding most regional, communal or local issues[1] and it meant confining its attention to the national business of the govern-

[1] Of course a local issue could assume national importance: the partition of Bengal

ment of India as published in its official reports, its laws and in the Parliamentary Papers.

The Congress had also to set up a chain of command to ensure that it could function effectively at an all-India level. We have seen several attempts to give the Congress a constitution, and we have recognised the difficulties that lay in the way of the Indian leaders in devising a satisfactory one. At Allahabad in 1908, however, the Congress leadership made a notable advance. Faced with the need to control Tilak and his party within the Congress, the national leadership steeled itself to accept the principle of expelling men from the Congress who wanted to be in it and who, indeed, considered themselves to be essentially part of it. In order to achieve this end a hierarchy of committees and a method of approving membership of the Congress were drawn up which were more elaborate than any scheme previously attempted. Moreover, they were effective: Maharashtrian and Bengali extremists were temporarily excluded from the Congress as a result of the operation of the Allahabad constitution. Although the criteria by which people would be judged for Congress membership would change over time, the principle of rejecting the recalcitrant was one to which, after 1908, the Congress high command had increasing resort.

The evidence we have presented suggests that, although the same people and the same interests were often involved, Indian politics were different in character from those in the provinces and the towns. National affairs were governed by their own special rules. The most important quality of the Congress was that it attracted a wide variety of followers and that it saw as its main function the arrangement of political bargains between them. This gave the Congress its facility for absorbing new social and political elements and its capacity for changing its shape as occasion demanded. Throughout its history the Congress maintained a broad political platform. Consequently, it held to no particularly coherent ideological position for long. This is not to say that Indian nationalists never produced well-conceived or dearly held political theories, but the Congress refused to be tied to any one of them. It functioned by tolerating and by making compromises between many opinions. As a

and the Punjab wrong would be two classic examples. But it was only when an issue could be deployed nationally that it would be taken up by the Congress.

A perspective

result the importance of ideology in all-India politics was tactical rather than strategic: political theorists provided the rallying cries of the Congress leadership, but they did not dictate the direction in which the Congress should move.

Politicians in India were many, but the Congress was dominated by a relatively small number of men. They had helped to draw up the rules of nationalism and they had a proper understanding of the boundaries of all-India politics. In effect these politicians had taken the nation for their parish and they sought to influence its development as a powerful man would control his locality. The expertise and relative permanence of the all-India leadership gave the Congress much of its stability and resilience. It also protected the Congress from the undue impact of sudden but perhaps transient political forces. Increasingly, politicians from outside came to prominence within the Congress only by accepting the conventions which guided it and by scoring their victories within its institutional framework. Of course the definition of what was acceptable behaviour in a Congressman would be subject to change, but the weight of vested interests within the Congress, and the devices which they could employ against their critics, acted as a powerful restraint on too sudden a shift of course. Even important new political forces in India were at first brought to bear indirectly upon the Congress, and only gradually did they intrude upon its leadership. Although occasionally, as between 1915 and 1922, there would be periods of uncertainty and of radical reshuffling within the leadership, the Congress high command was remarkable for the continuity and exclusiveness of its membership.

The restricted and specialised nature of Congress leadership also meant, however, that manoeuvre within it was almost the only way by which decisions were reached, and this provided ample opportunity for disputes. Congressmen knew that to be an effective force they had to appear united: but this did not prevent hard bargaining beforehand. Because the Congress consisted of skilled representatives of a host of interests, and because too unbridled debate of the differences between them would destroy the whole purpose of coming together, the road to compromise was marked by restricted factionalism fought out among the leaders themselves. The restraints imposed upon

A perspective

any form of national politics usually kept quarrels within the Congress in check; but a time of political change could provide a Congress leader with an opportunity to shift the balance within the established order. The combination of crises and reforms between 1904 and 1908 persuaded Tilak that the time was ripe for an attempt to capture the Congress from his opponents. The struggle between the extremists and the moderates was a fight for precedence conducted between near-equals within the leadership of the Congress itself. But it was more than the culmination of a personal vendetta, for the leaders on each side were also bound by the hopes and fears of the constituencies and interests which they represented.

The split at Surat was the first of many fierce struggles within the Congress hierarchy. Quarrels of the type which we have considered in such detail characterise the entire history of the Congress. Yet such factionalism is not necessarily unprincipled or without reason. By channelling discontents into definable party contests within small and recognisable political arenas, the nationalist movement was protected from the worst repercussions of the most violent disaffection. The disruption of the Congress at Surat posed the problem of disorder in its most acute form; the constitutional arrangement that followed proposed a partial but pragmatic solution to the crisis. The victors' triumph was to prove short-lived; the losers were not for ever defeated. The protagonists learnt valuable lessons from their experience which became embodied in Congress lore. The episode showed that what was broken could also be mended. The later generations of Congressmen benefited not only from the positive achievements of the founding fathers but also from their years of strife.

NOTE ON SOURCES

This book has been written almost entirely from unpublished source material. It can be divided into three groups: the correspondence and private papers of Indian politicians, the manuscript records of political associations, and the records of the government.

CORRESPONDENCE AND PRIVATE PAPERS OF INDIAN POLITICIANS

Agarkar Papers: a collection of about fifty letters belonging to the period 1882–95. The collection is in the possession of the Servants of India Society, Poona.

Basu Papers: letters sent to Bhupendranath Basu. The most important relate to a possible compromise between the moderates and the extremists at the Madras Congress in 1914. The collection is deposited in the Nehru Memorial Museum, New Delhi.

Besant Papers: the private correspondence of Annie Besant. Those relating to Congress affairs during 1914–15 have been used for this study. The papers are kept at the Theosophical Society, Adya, Madras.

Chitnavis Papers: this is a very large collection containing virtually all the correspondence received by Sir G. M. Chitnavis from the 1890s to 1929, with copies of some letters sent by him. The papers belong to the family in Nagpur, and some of them may now be consulted in the Nehru Memorial Museum.

Gokhale Papers: this collection of letters belongs to the Servants of India Society, Poona, and has been deposited in the National Archives of India, New Delhi. It includes letters from the 1890s to 1915 and is the single most important collection used in this study.

Khaparde Papers: this collection is now deposited in the National Archives of India. The most important item is G. S. Khaparde's Diary, which is very informative and often very amusing. The diary was kept from the 1870s to 1936. Some of the earlier years are missing, but it is complete from 1894. Khaparde wrote almost a full side of foolscap each day. This valuable source serves as an excellent foil to the Gokhale collection.

Mehta Papers: this is a small collection of papers of which a microfilm copy is available in the National Archives of India.

Naoroji Papers: an enormous collection of letters written to Dadabhai Naoroji. It belongs to the Dadabhai Naoroji Memorial Trust in Bombay, who plan to bring out an edition of these letters. The great bulk consists of letters written by D. E. Wacha to Dadabhai Naoroji. For all the time when Naoroji was in England, Wacha sent a fortnightly report on the state of politics in India. The Wacha–Naoroji correspondence covers a period of about twenty years, from the mid-1880s to 1906. The other part of the collection contains letters from almost all active Indian

Note on sources

politicians, and dates back to the 1870s. The correspondence is most useful for the history of the Congress up to 1906.

Tilak Papers: unfortunately many of Tilak's letters have been lost, and many others were irreparably damaged by flood. The collection does, however, contain letters of importance for the 1890s, and for the period 1916–20. The Kesari–Mahratta Trust, who own the correspondence, have also managed to preserve originals and some copies of Tilak's correspondence with Shyamji Krishnavarma. Some of these letters were published in the *Mahratta* in 1936 and again in 1941. Tilak's papers may now also be consulted at the Nehru Memorial Museum in Delhi. The cream of the collection has been published in M. D. Vidwans (ed.), *Letters of Lokamanya Tilak* (Poona, 1966).

In addition to these collections, use has also been made in this study of the following: Curzon Papers (India Office Library, London), R. P. Karandikar Papers (held by V. R. Karandikar, Poona), Lansdowne Papers (British Museum), and the Motilal Nehru Papers (Nehru Memorial Museum).

MANUSCRIPT RECORDS OF POLITICAL ASSOCIATIONS

Bombay Presidency Association Papers: this collection consists of manuscript minute books of the association dating from 1885 to 1915, some account books, and some miscellaneous records.

Deccan Education Society records: these include the original manuscript of Tilak's resignation from the society (covering ninety-one sides of foolscap) various minutes written by Agarkar, manuscript minute books for the period 1884–1911, and some miscellaneous correspondence.

Servants of India Society records: the manuscript letter books of the Society exist for 1905–11; the Society also holds a correspondence file of the Deccan Sabha; and at its Madras branch, some miscellaneous letters from and to Gokhale not included in the main collection. The Madras branch also has copies of some of Gokhale's and Srinivas Sastri's papers, together with some original Sastri and Krishnaswami Iyer letters.

GOVERNMENT RECORDS

The National Archives in New Delhi house a wealth of government of India records. Almost a thousand files of Home Department documents have been consulted in the course of research for this book. The Home Department sub-divided its records into various branches – Public, Political, Educational, Establishments, Judicial, Municipalities, etc. Each file contains anything from one to over a hundred 'Proceedings' and may be anything from one paragraph to several volumes in length. The Proceedings were classified A, B, or Deposit, in descending order of immediate importance; but the B and Deposit classifications often contain the most detailed information. The references in this volume give first the nature of the document, then the branch of the Home Department in which it was filed, and then

Note on sources

the date and number of the Proceeding. The records in India are occasionally prefaced by Notes written in the Department and by members of the Council when the files were circulated for comment. These Notes often contain more valuable information than the files themselves. Copies of the most important government Proceedings were sent to London, but without the Notes. The records are filed according to a different system in the India Office Library.

The second important collection of government records consulted has been that containing the volumes of Police Intelligence for Bombay. These 'Secret Bombay Presidency Police Abstracts of Intelligence' were begun in 1888, and they have been consulted in the Offices of the Maharashtra State Committee for the History of the Freedom Movement in India. The volumes contain information of very variable value. Some of the reports are genuinely confidential notes by district magistrates or district superintendents of police about political, and straight-forward criminal, affairs under their jurisdiction. A great deal of the information, however, has been collected from newspapers, or gathered by specially employed reporters. The information is, therefore, not so important as its original 'Secret' classification might lead one to expect, and it has all the defects of other journalistic sources. The Abstracts, were, however, intended to keep the government's officers informed of what was happening in their province, and, provided the difficulties of using the material are borne in mind, the volumes are invaluable compilations of facts and opinions. For 1888 the Abstracts were numbered consecutively within each week, but from the following year they were arranged by paragraph and numbered consecutively throughout the year. Apart from references to 1888, therefore, this source has been referred to in the footnotes as follows: first, the number of the paragraph, then the place and date of the origin of the report, followed by the volume number and the year.

Some of the volumes of Proceedings of the Bombay Government have also been consulted in the India Office Library.

One further government source needs mention: the compilations of clippings and translations from the Indian press. *The Reports on the Native Press* for Bombay for this period are in the India Office Library. Apart from useful translations from the vernacular newspapers, this source has preserved many extracts from newspapers that have long since disappeared.

PUBLISHED SOURCE MATERIAL

The most important published source material used for this book consists of the official publications of the government of India, Parliamentary Papers, reports of the Indian National Congress, newspapers and pamphlets. These source materials are already well known and call for no special comment. Full references are given in the footnotes.

SECONDARY WORKS

There are several adequate bibliographies covering the period and topics

Note on sources

dealt with in this book and so it has not been thought necessary to make a new one here. The most useful general bibliography is M. L. P. Patterson and R. B. Inden, *South Asia: an introductory bibliography* (Chicago, new edition forthcoming). There is an excellent general bibliography that includes many of the contemporary pamphlets and books: Patrick Wilson, *Government and politics in India and Pakistan 1885-1955* (Berkeley, 1956). Almost all the worthwhile secondary authorities, and an indication of the wide range of government material available, are listed in A. Seal, *The emergence of Indian nationalism: competition and collaboration in the later nineteenth century* (Cambridge, 1968). A full list of publications dealing with Bombay city is given in Christine Dobbin, *Urban leadership in western India: politics and communities in Bombay city 1840-1885* (Oxford, 1972). Books about the Maharashtrian politicians are given in S. A. Wolpert, *Tilak and Gokhale: revolution and reform in the making of modern India* (Berkeley and Los Angeles, 1962). The most notable additions to Wolpert's bibliography would be: B. G. Khaparde, *Shri Dadasaheb Khaparde Yanchem Charita (Life of G. S. Khaparde)* (Poona, 1962), D. B. Mathur, *Gokhale: a political biography: a study of his services and political ideas* (Bombay, 1966), N. R. Phatak, *Adarsha Bharat Sevak: Gopal Krishna Gokhale Yanchem Charita (Life of G. K. Gokhale)* (Bombay, 1967), *Speeches and writings of Gopal Krishna Gokhale*, vol. I, *Economic* (edited by R. P. Patwardhan and D. V. Ambekar, Poona, 1962), vol. II, *Political* (edited by D. G. Karve and D. V. Ambekar, London, 1966), vol. III, *Educational* (edited by D. G. Karve and D. V. Ambekar, Poona, 1967), and M. D. Vidwans (ed.), *Letters of Lokamanya Tilak* (Poona, 1966).

Many of the arguments in this book have been tested against the unpublished work of other scholars. Particular mention must be made of C. A. Bayly, 'The political development of the Allahabad locality 1880-1920' (D.Phil. thesis, Oxford, 1970), F. C. R. Robinson, 'The politics of U.P. Muslims 1906-1922' (Ph.D. thesis, Cambridge, 1970), and D. A. Washbrook, 'Politics in the Madras Presidency 1880-1920' (Trinity College Fellowship dissertation, Cambridge, 1971).

INDEX

Agarkar, G. G. 68, 71; and social reform 69–70, 71–2; and Tilak 72–5
Age of Consent Bill 78–81, 84
Ali, Mahomed 133
Allahabad, Convention at 174–7, 180
Apte, V. S. 68, 74, 75
Arms Act 30

Baba Maharaj *see* Pandit, W. H.
Baidya 26
Baji Rao II 81
Bande Mataram 143
Banerjea, S. N. 19, 122, 123, 130, 133, 136, 137, 139, 140, 143, 168, 175
Basu, Bhupendranath 130, 139, 184, 187, 188
Bavda 102
Benares Hindu University 158
Bengal, and Congress 128–9, 130, 136–8, 141–2, 145, 147, 165, 173, 174; factionalism in 130; legislative council 18; partition of 45, 87, 129, 133, 141, 143, 159
Berar, and Congress 45, 155, 160; government of 23, 155
Besant, Mrs A. 186, 188, 189
bhadralok 63
Bhandarkar, R. G. 70, 79, 80, 100
Bhansali 113
Bhanu, C. G. 75
Bhat, Balaji Vishvanath 58
Bhatia 113
Bhora 113
Bombay Association 11
Bombay, city and Congress 39, 40, 118, 137, 141, 174, 190; development of 11–12; and India 113–14, 115, 116, 191–2; and national politics 115, 116, 191–2; social composition of 112–13; and the United Provinces 157–9, 191–2
Bombay, government of, and Kolhapur 102, 104; and Poona politics 96–7, 98; and Tilak 106–7, 108
Bombay Presidency, balance of power within 20–2, 53, 108, 110–11, 114, 116, 117, 121; and Congress 2–3, 39, 40, 43, 52, 118, 120, 126, 127, 141, 165, 190: legislative council 9, 18, 20–2, 109–10
Bombay Presidency Association 11, 20, 37, 43, 116, 118, 130, 157, 159, 178–9, 185
Bonnerjee, W. C. 14, 20
Bose, Bhupendranath 137
Bose, Bipin Krishna 156, 164
Bose, Satyananda 141
boycott 129–30, 138, 141–2, 143, 144–8, 149–50, 169, 174, 177
Bradlaugh, C. 16
Brahmin, Chitpavan 54, 55–66, 67, 97; Deshastha 55, 60; Mahratta 27; Tamil 28
British Indian Association 11, 37
British Indian Association of Oudh Talukdars 20

Calcutta 8, 10; Congress at 5, 136–8, 139–40, 141–9
Campbell Bannerman, Sir H. 148
Caste and politics 55, 63, 64–7, 101, 102–4, 107, 112–13
Central Provinces 27, 45; and Congress 151, 154–6, 159–64
Chand, Lal 47
Chandal 48
Chandavarkar, N. G. 30
Chandra, B. 31
Chapekar brothers 97
Charlu, Ananda 35, 144
Chaudhuri, Asutosh 147, 176
Chiplonkar, V. K. 67, 68, 72
Chitale, G. K. 185
Chitnavis, Sir G. M. 154, 156, 159, 161, 163
civil service 24–8, 59–60, 63, 64, 65, 67, 102
Colvin, Sir Auckland 30
Congress, purpose and achievement 2, 5, 33, 34–5, 44, 49, 51, 127, 172–2, 181–2, 193–8; constitution of 35, 36–7, 38–9, 41, 43, 44, 51–2, 138, 151–3, 175–7, 184–5, 187, 190, 196; central committee of 40, 41–2, 140,

203

Index

Congress (*cont.*)
152, 164, 175; district committee 41, 42, 152, 175; provincial committee 41, 42, 159, 160, 175, 184; reception committee 137, 140, 159, 160–1, 166; subjects committee 40, 41–2, 140, 152, 184; Convention committee 173, 174, 176, 180; relationship with government 6, 10, 11, 193; and reform of government 13–14, 30, 127, 133–6, 143, 148, 183, 191; and legislative councils 15–16, 19, 22–3; and civil service 24–6, 27–8, 121, 127; and judicial reform 29, 30, 127; and economic development 31–2; and social reform 35, 119–20, 121–3; regional and social bias of its political programme 32–3, 128; and agitation in England 13, 14, 33–4, 41, 125–6, 127, 130–1, 135–6; organisation of 33, 35–6, 37, 38–9, 40, 51, 118, 120, 151–3; leadership 8–10, 32–3, 49–50, 197; factionalism within the leadership 50, 51–2, 131–2, 133–4, 136–49, 155, 159–64, 165–72, 175–7, 178–9, 186–90, 197–8; support for 39, 44, 45, 46–7, 48–9, 124–5, 128; regional alignments within 138–9, 146–8, 157, 175–6; and regional rivalry 46–7, 117, 130, 137; and Aligarh 46; and Bengal 128–9, 130, 136–8, 141–2, 145, 147, 165, 173, 174; and Bombay 2–3, 5, 39, 40, 43, 52, 116, 118, 120, 126, 127, 137, 141, 165, 174, 190; at Calcutta 136–8, 139–40, 141–9; and the Central Provinces 151, 154–6, 159–64; and Deoband 46; and local issues 46, 119–24; at Nagpur 151, 154–6, 159–64; and political associations 12–13, 37–8, 40, 44, 108, 109; and Poona 118, 119–24; and provincial issues 45, 130, 132, 194; and Punjab 42, 45, 46, 47, 132, 154, and religious associations 48; at Surat 117, 164, 165–72, 198; and the United Provinces 157–9, 173–4
Congress Compromise 186–90
Continuation Committee 173, 180
Convention Committee 173, 174, 176, 180
Councils, legislative 9, 15–16, 17–22, 23, 129

Cross, Lord 29
Curzon, Lord 125, 129

Darbhanga, Maharaja of 20, 22, 143
Das, Seth Lachman 20
Deccan Education Society 68, 69, 70–1, 71–5, 78, 81, 104, 108, 109
Deccan Sabha 108–9, 185
Deccan Star 68
Deoband 46
Deodhar 137
Desai, A. S. 167
Deshmukh, M. G. 177
Dharap 75
Dhulia, Conference at 177, 178–9, 180–2
Digby, W. 33
Dinbandhu 67
drain, theory of 31–2
Dufferin, Lord 17
Dutt, Aswini Kumar 48, 171
Dutt, R. C. 31, 178

East India Company 6, 11
education, national 141, 142, 143, 148, 169, 177

Fergusson College 69, 74
Fuller, Sir J. B. 136, 146

Gandhi, M. K. 116
Ganpati 48
Ganpati festival 82–9, 92, 98, 99, 101, 105, 116, 183
Ghose, Aurobindo 130, 136, 143, 167, 171, 183
Ghose, Lal Mohan 19, 33
Ghose, Motilal 122, 134, 139, 143, 188
Ghosh, Rash Behari 165, 168, 169, 170, 174
Gokhale, Gopal Krishna 22, 31, 43, 52, 55, 55, 68, 71, 123, 137, 141, 146, 153, 163, 167, 177, 183; and Age of Consent Bill 79–80; and Bombay 116–17; and Congress 116–17, 126, 130–1, 132–3, 134, 135–6, 137–8, 139, 147–8, 149, 163–4, 166, 184; and the Congress Compromise 186–90; and England 117, 130–1, 135–6; and the legislative council 109–10, 117; political assets 108–9; and the Poona Sarvajanik Sabha 74–5, 93–4, 95; and Surat

Index

Gokhale (*cont.*)
169–70, 171, 172; and the United Provinces 157, 158–9; death of 190
Gokhale, S. R. 167
Gour, H. S. 162
government, and national politics 1, 6, 7, 8, 10, 11, 13, 16–17, 18, 23, 193; and religious matters 83–4, 85; and social reform 79

Harris, Lord 22
Hindu 28, 135, 167
Home Rule League 116, 191
Hume, A. O. 14, 38, 39, 43

Ichalkaranji 102
India 34, 119
Indian Association 11, 37, 38, 129
Indian National Congress *see* Congress
Indian Social Reformer 172
Indore, Maharaja of 72
Indu Prakash 116
Iyengar, Kasturi Ranga 135
Iyer, Sir K. Seshadri 28
Iyer, L. A. Govind Raghava 146

Jamkhandi 58
Joshi, G. V. 178, 180

Karandikar, R. P. 167, 171, 185
Kayasth 26, 46, 63
Kelkar, N. C. 167, 171, 177, 187
Kelkar, V. B. 70, 75
Kesari 68, 69, 70, 71, 75, 80, 86, 89, 98, 104, 121, 133, 182, 190
Khadilkar, K. P. 82
Khan, Sir Syed Ahmed 46
Khaparde, G. S. 106, 131, 132, 133, 134, 141, 144, 149, 150, 159, 160, 162, 166, 171, 183
Khare, D. A. 43, 152, 176
Khatri 26
Khilafat movement 116
Khoja 113
Kimberley, Lord 29
Kolhapur, Brahmins at 103, 104; and Poona politics 102, 103, 104–7
Kolhapur, Maharaja of 101, 102–7
Koshti 155
Krishnavarma, Shyamji 148, 159, 179
Kurundvad 58

Lansdowne, Lord 17, 19
Lohana 113

Madras 10, 11; and Congress 6; legislative council 18, 22
Madras Mahajana Sabha 11, 37, 38
Madras Mail 44
Mahmudabad, Raja of 46
Mahratta 68, 69, 70, 71, 75, 80, 121, 123, 134, 149, 173, 178, 180
Malabari, B. M. 78, 79
Malaviya, Madan Mohan 144, 147, 149, 157, 174, 184
mamlatdar 60
Marathi literature 60–2, 81–2
Mazumdar, A. C. 145, 146
Mehta, Sir Pherozeshah M. 13, 20, 22, 118, 121, 126, 127–8, 134, 135, 140, 149, 164, 165, 167, 169, 171, 172, 186, 190
mela movement 87–8
Memon 113
Minto, Lord 136
Miraj 58
Mitter, C. C. 20
moharram 85, 86
Moonje, B. S. 160, 161, 162, 163
Morley, J. 133, 135–6
Mudholkar, R. N. 41, 141, 156, 163
music rules 92–3

Nagpur Congress at 151, 154–6, 159–64
Nair, C. Sankaran 22
Namjoshi, M. B. 68, 74
Naoroji, D. N. 24, 31, 33, 125, 126, 127, 136, 139, 140, 144, 148
National Liberal Club 130
National Social Conference 78, 119–24
Natore, Maharaja of 20
Natu, B. R. 84, 98, 99, 101, 104, 105
Natu, H. R. 86, 98, 99, 101, 105
Natu, V. R. 167
Nehru, Motilal 176
Nevinson, H. W. 171
New English School 68, 72–3
non-Brahmin movements 66–7, 101, 102–5, 107
North-western provinces and Oudh *see* United Provinces

Pal, Bipin Chandra 130, 134, 136, 137, 138, 140, 142, 144, 145, 146, 147, 148, 159, 171, 182

205

Index

Pandit, Wassadeo Harihar 84, 105, 106, 107
Panjabee 154
Parsi 26, 113, 114
Patankar, P. N. 75
Patwardhan, V. R. 84
Patwardhans, jagirdars 57, 58
Peshwa 53, 58, 59, 83
Phadke, W. B. 55, 99
Phule, Jotirao 66
political associations 11–12, 12–13, 109
Poona 2, 11, 21, 53, 62, 91–2, 98; conference at 178; and Congress 118, 118–24; dissensions at 68, 71–5, 91, 93–5, 178, 192; and government 96–7, 98; and Kolhapur politics 102, 103, 104–7
Poona Sarvajanik Sabha 11, 37, 38, 74, 81, 91–2, 93; and Congress 118, 119–24; and famine operations 95–6; and government 96; and legislative council 21–2; and music rules 92–3; and Tilak 91, 93–5
Prabhu 26, 113
Public Service Commission 25, 60, 67
Punjab, and Congress 42, 45, 46, 47, 132, 154; disturbances in 159

Rai, Lajpat 42, 132, 134, 135, 139, 162, 165, 169, 170, 171, 176
Raigarh 89, 90
Rakhambai marriage case 70
Ramabai, Pandita 71
Ramdas 90
Ranade, M. G. 30, 68, 70, 78, 88, 90, 91, 93, 94, 95, 100, 119, 122, 123
Rand, W. C. 97
Rao, N. Subba 186, 187, 188
Rao, Raghunath 80
Ray, R. N. 140
riot 84–5, 86

Salisbury, Lord 24
Sangli 54
Sankeshwar, Shankaracharya of 57, 104, 105, 107
Sardars of the Deccan 20–1
Sastri, V. S. S. 188
Satara, conference at 185
Satya Shodhak Samaj 66
Sayani, R. M. 20
Scoble, Sir Andrew 79, 80
Servants of India Society 109, 188

Shahu Chhatrapati *see* Kolhapur, Maharaja of
Shivaji 48
Shivaji festival 82, 89–91, 98, 99, 101, 116
Singh, Ajit 171
Singh, Raja Rampal 20
social reform 78–9; and Congress 35, 119–20, 121–3; and Poona 69–70, 71, 72, 78, 100–1
Sudharak 71, 79, 89, 104
Surat, Congress at 117, 164, 165–72, 198
swadeshi 141–2, 143, 144–5, 148, 150, 169, 174, 177
swaraj 148, 149, 174, 177

Tai Maharaj 106
Telang, K. T. 15, 30, 79, 80
Temple, Sir Richard 54
Thakersey, Sir Vithaldas 190
Tilak, Bal Gangadhar 9, 22, 52, 55, 68, 163, 177, 185; arrest of 98–9, 182–3; and Baba Maharaj 105, 106–7; and Bengal 131, 133–4, 138, 141; and Bombay city 179; and Congress 119–24, 126–7, 131, 132, 135, 139, 142, 144–5, 148, 149–50, 153, 155, 159, 160, 161, 162, 163, 164, 165, 171–2, 174, 176, 181–2, 190–2; and Congress Compromise 186–90; and the Deccan Education Society 71–5; and the Dhulia conference 177, 179, 180–2; and Ganpati festivals 82, 86, 87, 88, 116, 183; and government 99–100, 106–7; and Kolhapur 104, 105–7; and legislative council 109–10; and orthodoxy 84, 100; political style 76–8, 95, 96, 99–100, 100–1, 107–8, 117, 123–4, 131–2, 149–50, 171–2, 191–2; and the Poona Sarvajanik Sabha 91, 93–5; release from jail 185; and Shivaji festivals 82, 89, 116; and social reform 69–70, 71, 78–81, 100–1; and Surat 166–9, 170–2; and 'Tenets of the New Party' 149–50, 157; and traditions 76–7, 81, 90–1, 95, 97–8; and the United Provinces 157, 159
Tribune 45
Turkachuramani, Pundit Sasadhur 80
Tyabji, B. 30

Index

United Provinces, and Bombay 157–9, 191–2; and Congress 157–9, 173–4; interests within 158; legislative council 16, 18

Vaidya, C. V. 167, 179

Vishalgad 102

Wacha, D. E. 27, 39, 43, 121, 126, 135, 139, 167, 176, 177, 186, 190
Wedderburn, Sir William 125, 134, 184